Social Psychology for Sociologists

SOCIAL PSYCHOLOGY FOR SOCIOLOGISTS

edited by

David Field

Department of Sociology
University of Leicester

NELSON

973,117

Thomas Nelson and Sons Ltd
36 Park Street London W1Y 4DE

Nelson (Africa) Ltd
PO Box 18123 Nairobi Kenya

Thomas Nelson (Australia) Ltd
597 Little Collins Street Melbourne 3000

Thomas Nelson and Sons (Canada) Ltd
81 Curlew Drive Don Mills Ontario

Thomas Nelson (Nigeria) Ltd
PO Box 336 Apapa Lagos

First published in Great Britain by Thomas Nelson and Sons Ltd 1974

0 17 711103 8 (Boards)
0 17 712103 3 (Paper)

Printed in Great Britain by Willmer Brothers Limited, Birkenhead

Contents

Acknowledgements

My first debt is to Gregory P. Stone for posing problems in a challenging and inescapable way. The idea of this book had its genesis in my talks with David Franks. That the idea became fact is due to the proddings of Ilya Neustadt, the enthusiasm of Andrew Schuller, and the encouragement and the hard work on my behalf by Michael Shaw. Mo Thompson and June Lee did the bulk of the boring clerical work.

My greatest debt is to the students of the Department of Sociology, University of Leicester, who sat through my attempts to 'put the pieces together' in my lectures and by their interest and questions provided me with support and stimulation.

To all these people: Thank you.

INTRODUCTION

This collection of readings is intended primarily for students specializing in the study of sociology. Its main aim is to focus on the elements involved in the ways in which individuals actively construct their behaviour within the limits imposed by the social contexts of that behaviour. The selections as a whole are intended to give weight and empirical substance to this view of man, although they are by no means intended to represent an exhaustive or definitive delineation of such a view. I believe that the selections, focusing as they do on the transactional nature of human conduct, will aid in directing attention to the individual *in* society, and society *as* individual conduct, and break down the more usual understanding and interpretation of 'individual and society' in terms of the usually unresolved dilemma of Society versus the Individual or the Individual versus Society.

*   *   *   *   *

One of the basic elements in any explanation of human behaviour is the 'model of man' which is used, for it is fundamental to the types of questions asked about human activity and to the explanations of it which are given. This collection of readings arises mainly from my discontent with the two dominant models of man used in sociology. I have roughly characterized these as the 'sociologistic' and 'symbolic' models. In the 'sociologistic' model the individual is regarded as essentially a passive respondent to the various pushes and pulls of social forces.[1] In the 'symbolic' model the individual is seen as actively creating his world through his mastery and use of symbols, in particular language.

The work of Durkheim exemplifies the 'sociologistic' approach very well. The emphasis on, and legitimation of, the focus by sociologists on social factors is clearly stated by him in his *Rules of Sociological Method:*

... there is in every society a certain group of phenomena ... ways of acting, thinking and feeling, external to the individual, and endowed with a power of coercion, by reason of which they control him.... (T)heir substratum can be no other than society, either ... as a whole or some one of the partial

---

[1] The psychological theories utilized by practitioners of this 'sociologistic' approach are invariably some version of Freudianism or Behaviourism. These approaches are also based on a 'passive' model of man, and as White (1959) has convincingly shown they are inconsistent with the available empirical evidence.

groups it includes . . . These ways of thinking and acting therefore constitute the proper domain of sociology. (Durkheim, 1950:1)

His study of suicide (Durkheim, 1952) has long been regarded as a model for sociological enquiry. In this study he takes as his data the rates of suicide, and demonstrates that these rates evidence certain regularities by social category over time. For example, he shows that religious affiliation correlates systematically with variations in suicide rates and explains this by reference to the differential patterning of religious systems of belief and action. Finally, he interprets his variety of findings by postulating two underlying social variables: integration, i.e. the extent to which individuals are integrated into the group, and regulation, i.e. the amount of control which the group exercises over the individual. Throughout his analysis of this seemingly highly individual and very personal act, Durkheim treats the individual suicide as peripheral to the explanation. The individual is, in a sense, 'dissolved' in the external and constraining 'social facts' which Durkheim sees as the main determinants of suicide rates. Although his key concepts of integration and regulation are summative of, and point directly to the different types of interaction between individuals in the social groups which Durheim analyses, these differences in interaction are never fully analysed.

The implications of this approach are clear : man is human because he is social. Indeed, man is nothing but social for if social constraints disappear serious problems arise. Durkheim's study of suicide clearly shows the advantages and limits to such a purely sociological approach to the understanding of human conduct. The advantages are that it demonstrates how social groups function. Certain recurrent patterns of social action can be located, and predictions as to their working and consequence can be made. However, this type of approach tends to focus too exclusively on extra-individual factors. The 'model of man' implied is that of a passive, inactive creature who responds to the various pulls and pushes of social factors in a mechanical and determinant way, a creature whom Dahrendorf called *Homo Sociologicus:*

that strange construction of man that emerges from modern sociological theory. He is a role-playing animal, an alienated man whose actions and thoughts have become calculable consequences of social norms and institutions. (Dahrendorf, 1961:203).

Inevitably (as in Durkheim's study) such an analysis leads one to ask how the individual actor *as an individual* fits into the picture.

The traditional 'sociologistic' approach has come in for heavy criticism from adherents of the 'symbolic' model (see Blumer, 1969, chapters 2 and 3). They argue that the major fault with the approach is that it ignores the active and symbolic nature of man, and that social structures become reified to the extent that there is no room for any meaningful individual choice or control over action. Rather, the world is many things to many people and can only be understood by an interpretative and interactive process. We do not passively learn about what the world *is*, but rather are active agents engaged in a joint venture of constructing our social world.

The implications of man's symbolic nature were subtly and systematically explored by G. H. Mead (1934). For Mead, the most important aspect of the human condition and the key to its understanding, is that man is a symbolic animal. His conviction that symbolic communication is the matrix of social life is best seen in his definition of society as a 'universe of discourse' and his focus on language as the key to the development of the individual and to the working of society. Society, for Mead, is based on the co-operative action of man. Language is the key mechanism in such action for it provides a common set of definitions thereby allowing communication between individuals and thus facilitating social action :

What language seems to carry is a set of symbols answering to a certain content which is measurably identical in the experience of the different individuals. If there is to be communication as such the symbol has to mean the same thing to all individuals involved. (Mead, 1934:54).

Because language allows individuals to see their behaviour in the same way as others it is a crucial element in social control. Social control is based, in this view, on voluntary conformity to shared meanings.

Each individual emerges as a social being by incorporating the set of common meanings available to him by language. This provides him with entry into the on-going conversation which is society and the means whereby he can 'stand outside of himself' and so treat himself as a 'social object' and look at his actions in terms of others' perspectives on such action. Without such self-objectification and self-reflexivity, it is claimed, the problems of co-operation and control and of consistency in action would become very problematic. It is because the ideas one has of oneself are derived from a common pool of meanings, and because they are shared by others that human society functions as 'smoothly' as it does. Thus, language provides the individual with the means to function in his setting, for, by virtue of its shared nature, it allows him to assess the likely effect of his (named) actions on others. This access to shared definitions coupled with the capacity of self-objectification is what allows the individual actor freedom of choice in deciding his action. However, the possession of shared meanings does not guarantee consensus as to action, nor does it preclude individuality. Although the individual takes account of the expectation of others, his action is not a directly determined response to them—we may know what others mean, but decide that their expectations of us are inappropriate. In any case, in a complex society expectations are rarely uniform among all parties to an activity, and may be challenged and/or mutually altered.

In the 'symbolic' model of man then, human conduct proceeds via the exchange and appraisal of symbols, and consistency of action is guaranteed by the sharing of these symbols. Society is not in this view a determinant set of structures which interact in predictable ways but rather a collection of individuals who interact with each other on the basis of shared symbols, and thereby create a viable 'working' consensus (Goffman, 1959).

The main weakness to the 'symbolic' approach is highlighted by Foote in his critique of their analysis of motive:

Their analysis calls attention to the function of language . . . but leaves the reader with an uncomfortable feeling of an unanalysed hiatus between words and acts . . . (Foote, 1951:14).

Whereas in the sociologistic approach the individual is 'dissolved' in social structure in the symbolic approach he tends to become 'dissolved' in the communicative processes analysed. While I am in sympathy with the emphasis on man's ability to construct his world, nevertheless I feel that it leaves the 'substance' of man as much out of the picture as does the more traditional 'sociologistic' approach.

It is now generally accepted that man's social life developed in interaction with, and partly as a result of, his biological evolution (for a brief review see Bruner's selection). One of the central features in this development was the development of a new kind of skill—what Leslie White (1949) has called 'symboling'. This skill is dependent on, and is located in, the complex physiological transformations in Man's evolution, especially the development and transformation of the auditory and vocalic systems, and the transformation of the cerebral cortex. (On this see Lenneberg, 1967). Yet it is clear that the symbolic capacity of man, which receives its clearest expression in language, is similar in many respects to the cognitive capacity of animals. It is clear that most animals *organize* their world by a process of *categorization* (however this proceeds), and that the primates at least (and probably other mammals too) have the capacity to respond to the relations *between* things as well as directly to the things themselves. Such categorization and 'relational response' involve the processes of differentiation (or discrimination), and the interrelating of categories, i.e. the perception of and tolerance for transformations. This process of conceptualization is not necessarily conscious or aware; indeed, most writers would argue that it is not. Rather, it depends on the presence of the objects to be related to—memory/conceptualization is immediate and enactive whereas in man it has a degree of permanence and stability independent of immediately perceivable objects which is lacking in other animals.

The evidence from animal psychology suggests that although animals have the capacity to respond to relations between things, they cannot conceptualize such relations without the presence of the things to be related to. As the work of Piaget has so aptly demonstrated, (Flavell, 1963, Piaget and Inhelder, 1969), the initial world of the human infant is of this nature. It is only gradually that the human child develops its innate cognitive capacities of differentiation and interrelation via its manipulation of objects, and develops first iconic (or 'pictive') and finally symbolic communicative orders. The continuity and interdependence of these modes of cognition is clearly brought out in Bruner's selection. Bruner also shows what a powerful 'tool' language is in his review of a series of inventive experiments with children at different levels of language competence. While man is unique in his use of symbolic communication, it is clear that it is not the concept-formation aspect of symbolization which is unique. The activity of naming (or symboling) may be seen as the human peculiarity to make explicit the process that is universal among (at least) higher animals, that is, the organization and categorization of sensory data. The 'symbolic function' thus appears to be dependent on cognitive functioning which characterizes all animate life forms, and is merely one end of a continuum of categorization.

As man's 'distinctive attribute' is so firmly rooted in his biological nature, and as it is in fundamental respects continuous with general 'animalic' biologically based characteristics, we may expect to find that man's biological nature is also important in other fundamental ways. This in fact seems to be the case with respect to the 'active' nature of man. Support for this idea is to be found in the work of Piaget (Piaget and Inhelder, 1969; Furth, 1969, esp. pp. 12-21, 167-202; See also White, 1959). Piaget sees intelligence as a particular instance of biological adaptation, and stresses that it must be seen in terms of the interlocking interaction between the organism and the environment. As Piaget puts it himself:

It has always seemed to me that a valid interpretation of cognitive functions and their development must take into account biological considerations . . . (there is) an indissociable interaction between interior structures and the stimu- lations of the external environment. A stimulus cannot be active unless it is assimilated to schemes of reactions which provoke the response. (Furth, 1969).

Neither the 'sociologistic' nor the 'symbolic' approaches adequately come to grips with this notion of man as being both *shaped by* and *shaping* his environment at the same time.

It is through the adaptation of the child to its environment via the gradual building up of structures of knowing about the world on the basis of its initial simple reflex actions that the child moves from a state of *being* in the world, characterized by lack of differentiation between itself and its environment, to a state of *acting* in the world, characterized by differentiation of itself both physically and socially from its environment. This development is gradual and cumulative and goes forward by the child's actions on and experiences in its environment. Now, for the child to respond to the world implies that not only is it responding to something, but also that there is something within it which provides the basis for such a response. To give a simple example; until a child can discriminate shapes visually it will be unable to differentiate between a ball (which rolls) and a box (which doesn't). It may therefore try to roll the box. It is as the result of such 'mistakes' that it comes to recognize and discriminate different aspects of its environment. However, as in this example, such differentiation can only occur if there are already existing structures in terms of which such experiences can be comprehended. Not only then are responses *to* something, they are also in terms *of* something: they are constructed partly in terms of the characteristics of what is being responded to and partly in terms of determinants which are intrinsic to the structure of the respondent.

According to Piaget the initial 'schemes' of response upon which the structures of human behaviour are built are the sucking and grasping reflexes. It is through these that the child begins to explore his environment and it is these which provide the basis of the initial apprehensions which serve as preparation for what later becomes open to reflexive thought. As Piaget documents thoroughly in the many published reports of his research, it is through the progressive elaboration of reflexes, through the learning of the nature of the world and of its own capacities for response by interaction with it, that the child develops into a symbolic and social actor. This development entails the construction of adaptation to new realities, and always starts at the surface of both the individual and the 'reality'. For example, we first learn about shape, mass, volume and weight by coming into contact physically with objects which have various sizes, shapes and weights. It is not until after such 'enactive' experience that we can proceed to abstract symbolic ideas about mass, volume and weight. It seems, then, that cognitive development proceeds via the interiorization of action, and that the individual develops from an originally undifferentiated, unco-ordinated, self-centred and enactive mode of being in the world to a condition which is characterized by the reversible, organized and symbolic nature of action. Man, in this picture, appears as *both* passive and active—as doing *and* undergoing. The two main activities involved in such development are play—the repetition of known activity in an unstressful situation; and imitation. In play what is already known is produced and mastered and, incidentally (but crucially), new discoveries are made about the world: the discovery of 'differences in sameness'. For example, Weir (1962) describes the way in which the pre-sleep word play of her 2½-year-old son seemed to involve active experimentation with the ordering and sequencing of the words the child knew, leading as a result to his mastery of phonetics and grammar. Play is present at all ages (we are all familiar with 'rehearsing' or 'playing out' our roles prior to an important event such as a first date or first formal speech) and across a wide range of situations.[2]

Imitation is reciprocal to play and is concerned with the mastery of new situations and, according to Piaget, is a key process in the development of man's symbolic capacity (Piaget and Inhelder, 1969; 53-6). It seems that imitation is one way of responding to new situations and mastering new actions. Imitation provides a clear guide to how things should be done, and

[2] For some other examples of the important function play serves in development see Piaget (1932); Mead (1934: 149-158); White (1959); Stone (1970); and Herron and Sutton-Smith (1971).

does not require prior comprehension of the activity. We often find that before we can understand a new situation or action we first have to gain mastery over the relevant activities involved. The development of such mastery often proceeds through the imitation of others. Indeed, for a wide range of motor and social skills imitation is the main source of learning and instruction in such areas (e.g. learning to drive a car) is, in its initial stages, no more than guided imitation. For example, this is clearly the case in the child's acquisition of language. What Brown calls 'imitation-with-expansion' seems to play an important part in the development of the child's language. This type of 'instruction by imitation' involves the re-presentation to the child by an adult of the child's utterance but with the insertion of the appropriate modifiers and qualifiers; e.g. 'Eve lunch', 'Eve is having lunch'. Clearly, the function of such imitative expansions is to amplify the child's utterance and thereby to direct its attention to 'abstract' aspects of activity (such as time, duration, possession) which it may not have been aware of. (For one account of this see Brown and Belugi, 1966.) Imitation and play are thus important activities in the development of the child and although they may be later superseded by other modes of action they remain important processes in human conduct throughout the individual's life.

Having looked at the biological basis to man's active nature, let us turn to consideration of the social aspects of human action. Central to any consideration of this, is the concept of 'role' which has been seen as the integrating concept *par excellence* spanning and bridging the gap between the 'social system' on the one side and the individual on the other. (See for example Parsons, 1951.) In practice, however, sociologists using the concept have tended to describe role requirements in social system terms and have either failed to look at individual role players, or have treated them as isomorphic copies of the organization which is being studied. A number of the selections explore the constructive element in role playing, and show that the active nature of man in constructing his conduct must be considered for an adequate sociological understanding of human conduct.

In his selection Flavell discusses the general characteristics of role-taking, and suggests the main elements involved in its development. Flavell is concerned with the development of the child's thinking about its social environment, and is concerned to construct a general model of this by drawing on the works of Mead, Piaget and Vigotsky. Throughout he is concerned to trace the development of the child from a state of generalized egocentrism, where the child is a prisoner of its own point of view and is unable, by virtue of this 'imprisonment', to comprehend or understand the role of the others, to a position of sociocentrism where the child is able to communicate effectively with others. Flavell see this development as dependent upon the development of general perceptual-cognitive and linguistic capabilities. Without the development of such abilities role-taking, and hence human social interaction, would clearly be impossible.

As role-taking is dependent on these capabilities it is relevant to enquire about the social conditions which facilitate or hinder their development. The Hess and Shipman selection is also concerned with the relationship of language to cognitive development and, by implication, to role-playing and the development of self-conceptions. Their study investigates and supports Bernstein's suggestion (1972) that patterns of speech (that is, language in *use* as distinct from the formal characteristics of language *per se*) are initially dependent on the patterns of social relationships characteristic of the social group in which language is acquired, particularly the family context. Once learnt, these habitual forms of speech exercise an influence on other forms of social life. Bernstein locates two main types of speech use, which he calls the 'restricted' and the 'elaborated' codes, and suggests that these two types of code have definite cognitive consequences for their habitual users. He suggests that the restricted code, which is characterized by a restricted range of alternatives and consequently a high degree of predictability, is primarily characteristic of social groups which in Durkheim's terms we would characterize as mechanically solidary (Durkheim, 1960). That is, they are characterized by a high degree of cohesion and use imperative modes of control. The elaborated code, which is characterized by a high range of alternatives and consequently is not very predictable, is more flexible and enables its user to act more flexibly and in a greater range of situations than the restricted code user. This code derives from a social group which is characterized more by something akin to Durkheim's organic solidarity. That is, social groups which emphasize 'individuality'.

The selection by Ford *et al* is in many ways a continuation of this theme. Ford and her associates argue that the ability to separate and assert one's individuality over the roles which one habitually performs largely depends on the nature and character of these roles. They are concerned to show that the expression of what Goffman has called 'role distance' (Goffman, 1961) and Turner 'role-making' (Turner, 1962) is allowed and/or constrained by the nature of the roles themselves. It may well be that role behaviour entails the two aspects of role taking and role making (Turner, 1962) since roles, even in formal organizations, are not (indeed cannot be) explicitly and rigidly defined. It is also true that behaviour is consistent only by virtue of its relatedness to the expectation of others and that 'taking the role of the other' inevitably involves an active element of creation (or role making). However, the degree of role-making which individuals can engage in is not arbitrary, but inheres (to a certain extent at least) in the nature of the roles themselves. Ford convincingly argues that the setting and type of roles open to the working class is such that the working class individual never develops the same degree of autonomy of action as middle class individuals.

It seems, then, that role performance depends on two interrelated aspects: the possession of the prerequisite general capabilities discussed by Flavell, and the nature of the role itself. Both these aspects seem to be influenced by the social contexts within which roles are located. However, it seems that there is a general sequential development which characterizes the learning and performance of all roles. This development essentially entails the sort of movement which Flavell characterizes as the shift from egocentrism to sociocentrism, and has been well depicted by Goffman in his description of the role of the merry-go-round rider (Goffman, 1961: 105-9). The initial stage is that of role-immersion, characterized by complete immersion in the role as the individual strives for mastery over the basic role-tasks. Next there is the stage of role-display where the individual portrays (shows off) his mastery over and excellence in the role. At this stage the individual is expressing himself through the role. Finally, there is the stage of 'role distance' or 'role-making', characterized by the expression of one's individuality within the context of the role by the introduction of personal embellishments or reference to other roles. This stage depends on a good knowledge of the role's requirements and the mastery of its tasks for it is only when the role is well mastered that it can become a backdrop for the display of individuality. The extent to which roles may be used in this way will vary. For example, the potential allowed for the elaboration and display of self are vastly different between the clearly specified role tasks and expectations of the man on the assembly line and the ambiguously defined role of the research worker in 'pure' science. The ways in which social settings condition role-taking and role-playing are considered in some detail by Layder and Ashton in their selections.

It is impossible to talk about role without either implicitly or explicitly referring to the self-conceptions of the role-players. Indeed, one of the few points on which protagonists of the 'sociologistic' and the 'symbolic' approaches agree is that self-conceptions develop via role-taking and role-playing. Our ability to treat ourselves as objects, and to take into account others' expectations (i.e. to role-take) is crucial to the smooth functioning of social life. Stability and predictability in social conduct is possible not only because of such role-taking ability, but also because we each develop the ability to recognize ourselves as a particular human being with a distinctive set of attributes, that is, to develop a fairly consistent conception of self. To the degree that this conception (or its elements) is aware, it exercises regulatory control over behaviour. It is therefore important to explore the part played by the individual's conceptions of himself in human social action.

The development of self starts at birth. In the initial stages the process is beyond the conscious control of the individual, although his actions are obviously salient to the way he is responded to. (We respond to a quiet baby in a different way from a noisy one.) As Stone puts it (Stone, 1962) identities are invested or imposed upon the child by others e.g. on the basis of its sex.[3]

---

[3] I distinguish between 'identity' and 'self-conception'. By identity I mean the social location or placement of an individual. Such identification or placement is a central part of human life, and is 'objective' and open to knowledge by others. Self-conceptions are based on such identities but are essentially subjective and unknowable. They refer to the ideas we have of ourselves, and consist in part of the ranking of 'objective' identities in some sort of order of importance.

The body is very important in this connection for it provides the concrete 'objective' basis for the location of self in terms of these 'invested' identities e.g. in terms of sex or skin colour. To a certain extent this investment of identities continues all our life, although we are likely to gain a measure of control over such definitions of self by others. In addition to providing a basis for the location of identities the body is also important for the part it plays in the development of self-awareness. Before a social awareness of oneself can be developed a physical awareness of oneself as an object in a world of objects must first have been established. This develops via the child's initial physical encounters with its environment. As it bumps up against and manipulates the objects in its world it begins to learn the parameters of its body, and to locate the edges between itself and other objects. Crucial in this, as Piaget's work documents so clearly, is the co-ordination of the various sensory schemes whereby it apprehends and makes contact with its world. In the course of its actions the child learns that it is a 'locus of cause' in the world (White, 1959)—not only do things happen *to* it, but it can *do* things to the world, and can cause things to happen.

With the development of language (as Bruner suggests) its capacity for such 'effective' causation becomes greatly amplified and more controllable. One of the most important consequences of language acquisition for the development of self is the development of naming capacity. As Foote (1951) and Stone (1962) argue naming is crucial for the establishment of identity, of oneself as well as of others. The acquisition of a name serves to provide a basis for the development and elaboration of awareness about one's social self in much the same way that the body provides the basis for the development and elaboration of one's awareness of oneself as a physical object. Names sum up identities, particularly when coupled with titles, and to that extent provide others with a degree of control over the named. (This applies not only to individuals, but also to situations.) However, names also have a subjective element for nobody knows in detail what his name really means to the individual. In this sense a name epitomizes the reciprocity between the social and the individual.

Another important element in the development of self is the individual's actions. We have already seen the centrality of activity for the development of ideas of oneself as a physical object and locus of causation. We are also held responsible for our actions—'you did this you bad boy'—and they are linked to us. Over time our ability to control our actions effectively builds up into some sort of balance and gives rise to the development of a certain level of self-esteem. A number of the selections, in particular that of Franks, suggest that this sort of belief in one's abilities is a crucial element in human behaviour. This belief stems partly from the effectiveness of the child in its exchanges with its environment, and partly from the responses of others to his actions. Coopersmith, on the basis of his empirical investigation of families and their children, confirms the importance of such self-esteem or efficacy for individual conduct and suggests that it is best generated in situations 'marked by high levels of activity, strong and independent convictions and differences of opinion that contribute to self-definition, provide social stimulation, and lead to increased communication between family members'.

The ideas we have of ourselves are important elements which guide and control our behaviour in subtle and varied ways. Gergen's selection explores some of these subtle influences and shows how the responses of others to our behaviour, the actions we engage in, and the situations in which we act, serve to create, sustain and change the conceptions we hold of ourselves. It is clear that while self-conceptions guide behaviour they are in turn influenced and shaped in the course of the very behaviour they are affecting.

One of the continuing themes in both sociology and psychology is the question of why it is that people behave in the way they do. This question has often been answered by the imputation of something 'inside' the individual which drives or propels action. In addition to this inner source of momentum many scholars have been concerned with the shaping and moulding of the individual by 'external' variables which become incorporated within the individual and are somehow fused with the internal drives. For example, Parsons sees that the simple Durkheimian position that the individual is constrained by social factors external to him and beyond his control is inadequate, and that an element of 'voluntarism' must be introduced into any analysis of social behaviour (Parsons, 1949). However, to introduce the consideration of 'free choice' by the actors poses an immediate problem. How is it that the individual acts predictably? Parson's answer is that by virtue of the overlaying of primary motivational drives with secondary social drives the individual is motivated to act in the way in which it is necessary for him to act if the social system is to continue functioning. The individual 'internalizes' the appropriate beliefs and values during his early socialization, and these function to motivate him to act appropriately: the individual wants to act in the way he has to act (Parsons, 1951).

This sort of position has been attacked by followers of the 'symbolic' approach. (See Stone and Farberman, 1970 Part 8.) They argue that the problem of motives and motivation cannot usefully be thought of in terms of inner drives or instincts which stir or initiate action in the passive individual. Rather, motives are best seen as socially structured and acceptable linguistically mediated reasons for acting which are operable and understandable only in specific contexts of action. Their assumption is that man acts, and that is all there is to it; and they therefore focus their attention on the way in which motive statements facilitate and allow the continuance of social interaction, particularly when a person's action is called into question. As Scott and Lyman put it 'excuses and justifications are socially approved vocabularies which neutralize an act or its consequences when one or both are called into question' (Scott and Lyman, 1968). This emphasis on the facilitating nature of speech is consonant with much work in the sociological enterprise, and bears a resemblance to Weber's definition of motive in terms of a 'complex of subjective meaning which seems to the actor himself or to the observer as an adequate ground for the conduct in question' (Weber, 1947: 98). This approach to motive assumes that, for the sociologist at least, it is sufficient to explore how 'vocabularies of motive' work and it is not really relevant to ask questions about internal sources making the individual act in the way he does. In other words, they argue that it is whether or not action is acceptable, and if it is *not* acceptable how the unacceptability of such action is dealt with, which is the main focus of interest for the sociological understanding of human conduct.

The selection by Franks addresses just these problems, and suggests that it is important and useful to investigate the motivational factors inherent in man's nature. He argues that for an individual to function adequately he must have developed a certain belief in himself, and an awareness of his ability to affect the world in predictable ways. He suggests that Robert White's notion of 'competency motivation' (White, 1959) provides the basis for the investigation of this aspect of man's nature. This emphasis on competency motivation and inner self-esteem as a motivating force in man is not intended to contradict the emphasis by the 'symbolic' approach on the social nature of motive statements. The aim is rather to provide an empirically grounded basis for the 'active' nature of man which their explanations assume.

While Franks' selection confronts the basic problem of 'motive as cause', the selection by Kanter focuses on wider social parameters of motive and shows how the structuring of Utopian communities in nineteenth century USA operated to generate individual commitment to and involvement in these communities. She shows how the historical continuity of these communities was dependent upon their ability to generate such motivational structures and identifies some of the structural mechanisms involved.

This discussion of the social aspects of human action has stressed the interplay between the individual actor and the setting within which such action takes place. This interplay forms the focus of attention in the selections from Glaser and Strauss, Layder, and Ashton. All of these are concerned with the development of action over time, and with both how individuals construct their activities within organizational constraints and with how these constraints affect the individuals. That is, they are concerned with the development of careers. This concept is used here in a wider way than the reader may be used to. The concept derives from the field of work, and specifically from the analysis of its 'upper' levels, e.g. management and the professions. In its original sense it was used to refer to a scheduled set of status changes governed by fairly well defined rules whereby the individual passed through a series of prescribed stages. The career was regarded as hierarchical (one proceeded 'up' the ladder) and its outline and the prescribed ways of completing (or qualifying) each stage were defined by the organization. As Layder's selection shows this model is too rigid and inflexible to describe even the range of middle class work careers. However, if we take the concept to refer generally to any movement through a series of stages not only does it become more useful for the analysis of work careers, but it also assumes a wide range of applicability in the analysis of other areas of social life (Roth, 1963: Ch. 5). There are two main uses to the concept thus redefined. First, its focus on recurrent socially structured benchmarks which exist in most (if not all) areas of human social action. Second, it points up the permanence of process and the variability of structure. For example, the processes of and the stages in the acquisition of language are essentially the same for all children yet the particular languages which are learnt vary widely in their grammatical structure: the same process produces widely differing structures. Some of the general properties of careers are discussed by Glaser and Strauss at the end of their analysis of dying as a 'career'.

The interplay between individuals and social settings is clearly brought out by Ashton in his exploration of the ways in which childhood experiences at school and in the family lead to the development of perspectives which serve to 'commit' the school-leaver to a certain type of job choice. (See Becker, 1960 for a general discussion of commitment.) Such commitments result from a variety of other sources as well: from generalized cultural expectations concerning school performance; from bureaucratic regulations concerning qualifications; from the adjustments to and expectations of the work experience. Ashton shows not only how these factors vary by social background, but also that they have differential saliency and impact on self-conceptions, frames of reference and 'career choices'.

*   *   *   *   *

Let me now summarize the main points of this introduction. In man (as with other organisms) the physiological structure places certain limits on the types of behaviour which are possible, while at the same time allowing a great range and flexibility of response. This great range of flexibility allows for the very great elaboration of man's basic reflexive actions and the building up of very complex patterns of behaviour, initially through play and imitation. When this potential for behaviour over a wide range of activities is added to man's biologically based symbolic capacity and the generic 'animalic' tendency to explore the environment (White, 1959), all the ingredients are present for the development of the complex patterns of behaviour characteristic of human social action. The early action-based ways of knowing and being in the world provide the essential basis for the later more complex and abstract 'symbolic' mode which is crucial for human behaviour. However, this mode of knowing is equally based upon the actions (although not necessarily aware actions) of the individual in his world, and on the structure of his environment. Human behaviour at all levels demonstrates aspects of construction which derive partly from the internal states or structures of the individual (both learned and inherited) and partly from the nature of the external environment. This internal structuring aspect is what provides the basis for the knowing, meaningful, self-referring and other-regarding behaviour characteristic of human social action. It is of course possible, as most sociologists do, to take these aspects of man's nature for granted. However, knowledge and awareness of them allow a better understanding of human conduct.

I have argued, then, that the 'active' capacity of man is a biologically founded aspect of his nature which provides the dynamic for the development of the cognitive and communicative skills necessary for human social action to be possible. Although the potential for the development of these skills may be the same for most people, their realization is conditioned by a whole range of factors. Each individual is born into a specific social situation which is characterized by certain types of typical activities and the accompanying regulations, interpretations, and legitimations which make sense of these activities. There are, however, certain recurrent elements and processes which cut across the great variety of social situations. The first part of the book focuses on the general features of human social action, while in the second attention is on the impact of the social contexts on such action.

References

Becker, H. S., 1960, Notes on the concept of commitment, *American Journal of Sociology*, [66] 32-40.

Bernstein, B., 1972, *Class, Codes and Control*, London: Routledge and Kegan Paul.

Blumer, H., 1969, *Symbolic Interactionism: Perspective and Method*, Englewood Cliffs, N.J.: Prentice Hall.

Brown, R. and Bellugi, U., 1966, Three processes in the child's acquisition of syntax. In E. H. Lenneberg (ed.), *New Directions in the Study of Language*, Cambridge, Mass.: The M.I.T. Press Paperback, pp. 131-61.

Dahrendorf, R., 1961, Democracy without liberty: an essay on the politics of other-directed man. In S. M. Lipset and L. Lowenthal (eds.), *Culture and Social Character*. New York: Free Press, pp. 175-206.

Durkheim, E., 1950, *The Rules of Sociological Method*, Glencoe, Ill: Free Press.

Durkheim, E., 1952, *Suicide: A Study in Sociology*, London: Routledge and Kegan Paul.

Durkheim, E., 1960, *The Division of Labour in Society*, Glencoe, Ill: Free Press.

Flavell, J. H., 1963, *The Developmental Psychology of Jean Piaget*, Princeton, N.J.: Van Nostrand.

Foote, N. N., 1951, Identification as a basis for a theory of motivation, *American Sociological Review*, [16] 14-21.

Furth, H. G., 1969, *Piaget and Knowledge*, Englewood Cliffs, N.J.: Prentice Hall.

Goffman, E., 1959, *The Presentation of Self in Everyday Life*, New York: Doubleday.

Goffman, E., 1961, *Encounters*, Indianapolis: Bobbs-Merrill.

Herron, R. and Sutton-Smith, B. (eds.), 1971, *Childs Play: Collected Readings on the Biology, Ecology, Psychology and Sociology of Play*, New York: J. Wiley & Sons.

Lenneberg, E. H., 1967, *The Biological Foundations of Language*, New York: John Wiley & Sons.

Mead, G. H., 1934, *Mind, Self and Society*, Chicago. University of Chicago Press.

Parsons, T., 1949, *The Structure of Social Action*, Glencoe Ill.: Free Press.

Parsons, T., 1951, *The Social System*, Glencoe, Ill.: Free Press.

Piaget, J., 1932, *The Moral Judgement of the Child*, London: Routledge and Kegan Paul.

Piaget, J. and Inhelder, B., 1969, *The Psychology of the Child*, London: Routledge and Kegan Paul.

Roth, J., 1963, *Timetables,* Indianapolis: Bobbs-Merrill.

Scott, M. B. and Lyman, S. M., 1968, Accounts, *American Sociological Review,* [33] 46-62.

Stone, G. P., 1962. Appearance and the self. In A. M. Rose (ed.), *Human Behaviour and Social Processes,* London: Routledge and Kegan Paul, pp. 86-118.

Stone, G. P., 1970, The play of little children. In G. P. Stone and H. A. Farberman (eds.), *Social Psychology Through Symbolic Interaction,* Waltham, Mass.: Ginn-Blaisdell.

Stone, G. P. and Farberman, H. A. (eds.), 1970, *Social Psychology Through Symbolic Interaction,* Waltham, Mass.: Ginn-Blaisdell.

Turner, R., 1962, Role taking: process versus conformity. In A. M. Rose (ed.), *Human Behaviour and Social Processes,* London: Routledge and Kegan Paul, pp. 20-40.

Weber, M., 1947, *The Theory of Social and Economic Organization,* New York: Free Press (originally published by Oxford University Press).

Weir, R., 1962, *Language in the Crib,* The Hague: Mouton & Co.

White, L. A., 1949, The symbol: the origin and basis of human behaviour. In his *The Science of Culture,* Farrar, Straus and Cudaby.

White, R. W., 1959, Motivation reconsidered: the concept of competence, *Psychological Review* [66] 298-333.

Part one

The Social Actor

Jerome S. Bruner
The Center for Cognitive Studies, Harvard University

The Course of Cognitive Growth[1]

Jerome S. Bruner, The course of cognitive growth, *American Psychologist*, 1964 [19] 1-15.

The ideas and experiments reported in this article are dealt with more fully in Jerome S. Bruner, 1966, *Studies in Cognitive Growth*, New York, J. Wiley & Sons. D.F.

I shall take the view in what follows that the development of human intellectual functioning from infancy to such perfection as it may reach is shaped by a series of technological advances in the use of mind. Growth depends upon the mastery of techniques and cannot be understood without reference to such mastery. These techniques are not, in the main, inventions of the individuals who are 'growing up'; they are, rather, skills transmitted with varying efficiency and success by the culture—language being a prime example. Cognitive growth, then, is in a major way from the outside in as well as from the inside out.

Two matters will concern us. The first has to do with the techniques or technologies that aid growing human beings to represent in a manageable way the recurrent features of the complex environments in which they live. It is fruitful, I think, to distinguish three systems of processing information by which human beings construct models of their world: through action, through imagery, and through language. A second concern is with integration, the means whereby acts are organized into higher-order ensembles, making possible the use of larger and larger units of information for the solution of particular problems.

Let me first elucidate these two theoretical matters, and then turn to an examination of the research upon which they are based, much of it from the Center for Cognitive Studies at Harvard.

On the occasion of the One Hundredth Anniversary of the publication of Darwin's *The Origin of Species*, Washburn and Howell (1960) presented a paper at the Chicago Centennial celebration containing the following passage:

[1] The assistance of R. R. Olver and Mrs Blythe Clinchy in the preparation of this paper is gratefully acknowledged.

It would now appear ... that the large size of the brain of certain hominids was a relatively late development and that the brain evolved due to new selection pressures *after* bipedalism and consequent upon the use of tools. The tool-using, ground-living, hunting way of life created the large human brain rather than a large brained man discovering certain ways of life. [We] believe this conclusion is the most important result of the recent fossil hominid dis-coveries and is one which carries far-reaching implications for the interpreta-tion of human behaviour and its origins. ... The important point is that size of brain, insofar as it can be measured by cranial capacity, has increased some threefold subsequent to the use and manufacture of implements. ... The uniqueness of modern man is seen as the result of a technical-social life which tripled the size of the brain, reduced the face, and modified many other structures of the body. (p.49 f.).

This implies that the principal change in man over a long period of years—perhaps 500,000 thousand—has been alloplastic rather than autoplastic. That is to say, he has changed by linking himself with new, external implementation systems rather than by any conspicuous change in morphology—'evolution-by-prosthesis', as Weston La Barre (1954) puts it. The implement systems seem to have been of three general kinds—*amplifiers of human motor capacities* ranging from the cutting tool through the lever and wheel to the wide variety of modern devices; *amplifiers of sensory capacities* that include primitive devices such as smoke signaling and modern ones such as magnification and radar sensing, but also likely to include such 'software' as those conventional-ized perceptual short-cuts that can be applied to the redundant sensory environ-ment; and finally *amplifiers of human ratiocinative capacities* of infinite variety ranging from language systems to myth and theory and explanation. All of these forms of amplification are in major or minor degree conventionalized and transmitted by the culture, the last of them probably the most since ratiocinative amplifiers involve symbol systems governed by rules that must, for effective use, be shared.

Any implement system, to be effective, must produce an appropriate internal counterpart, an appropriate skill necessary for organizing sensorimotor acts, for organizing percepts, and for organizing our thoughts in a way that matches them to the requirements of implement systems. These internal skills, represented genetically as capacities, are slowly selected in evolution. In the deepest sense, then, man can be described as a species that has become specialized by the use of technological implements. His selection and survival have depended upon a morphology and set of capacities that could be linked with the alloplastic devices that have made this later evolution possible. We move, perceive, and think in a fashion that depends upon techniques rather than upon wired-in arrangements in our nervous system.

Where representation of the environment is concerned, it too depends upon techniques that are learned—and these are precisely the techniques that serve to amplify our motor acts, our perceptions, and our ratiocinative activities. We know and respond to recurrent regularities in our environment by skilled and patterned acts, by conventionalized spatioqualitative imagery and selective perceptual organization, and through linguistic encoding which, as so many writers have remarked, places a selective lattice between us and the physical environment. In short, the capacities that have been shaped by our evolution as tool users are the ones that we rely upon in the primary task of representation—the nature of which we shall consider in more detail directly.

As for integration, it is a truism that there are very few single or simple adult acts that cannot be performed by a young child. In short, any more highly skilled activity can be decomposed into simpler components, each of which can be carried out by a less skilled operator. What higher skills require is that the component operations be combined. Maturation consists of an orchestration of these components into an integrated sequence. The 'distractability', so-called, of much early behaviour may reflect each act's lack of imbeddedness in what Miller, Galanter, and Pribram (1960), speak of as 'plans'. These integrated plans, in turn, reflect the routines and subroutines that one learns in the course of mastering the patterned nature of a social environment. So that integration, too, depends upon patterns that come from the outside in—an internalization of what Roger Barker (1963) has called environmental 'behaviour settings'.

If we are to benefit from contact with recurrent regularities in the environment, we must represent them in some manner. To dismiss this problem as 'mere memory' is to misunderstand it. For the most important thing about memory is not storage of past experience, but rather the retrieval of what is relevant in some usable form. This depends upon how past experience is coded and processed so that it may indeed be relevant and usable in the present when needed. The end product of such a system of coding and processing is what we may speak of as a representation.

I shall call the three modes of representation mentioned earlier enactive representation, iconic representation, and symbolic representation. Their appearance in the life of the child is in that order, each depending upon the previous one for its development, yet all of them remaining more or less intact throughout life—barring such early accidents as blindness or deafness or cortical injury. By enactive representation I mean a mode of representing past events through appropriate motor response. We cannot, for example, give an adequate description of familiar sidewalks or floors over which we habitually walk, nor do we have much of an image of what they are like. Yet we get about them without tripping or even looking much. Such segments of our environment—bicycle riding, tying knots, aspects of driving—get represented in our muscles, so to speak. Iconic representation summarizes events by the selective organization of percepts and of images, by the spatial, temporal, and qualitative structures of the perceptual field and their transformed images. Images 'stand for' perceptual events in the close but conventionally selective way that a picture stands for the object pictured. Finally, a symbol system represents things by design features that include remoteness and arbitrariness. A word neither points directly to its referent here and now, nor does it resemble it as a picture. The lexeme 'Philadelphia' looks no more like the city so designated than does a nonsense syllable. The other property of language that is crucial is its productiveness in combination, far beyond what can be done with images or acts. 'Philadelphia is a lavendar sachet in Grandmother's linen closet', or $(x + 2)^2 = x^2 + 4x + 4 = x(x + 4) + 4$.

An example or two of enactive representation underlines its importance in infancy and in disturbed functioning, while illustrating its limitations. Piaget (1954) provides us with an observation from the closing weeks of the first year of life. The child is playing with a rattle in his crib. The rattle drops over the side. The child moves his clenched hand before his face, opens it, looks for the rattle. Not finding it there, he moves his hand, closed again, back to the edge of the crib, shakes it with movements like those he uses in shaking the rattle. Thereupon he moves his closed hand back towards his face, opens it, and looks. Again no rattle; and so he tries again. In several months, the child has benefited from experience to the degree that the rattle and action become separated. Whereas earlier he would not show signs of missing the rattle when it was removed unless he had begun reaching for it, now he cries and searches when the rattle is presented for a moment and hidden by a cover. He no longer repeats a movement to restore the rattle. In place of representation by action alone—where 'existence' is defined by the compass of present action —it is now defined by an image that persists autonomously.

A second example is provided by the results of injury to the occipital and temporal cortex in man (Hanfmann, Rickers-Ovsiankina, & Goldstein, 1944). A patient is presented with a hard-boiled egg intact in its shell, and asked what it is. Holding it in his hand, he is embarrassed, for he cannot name it. He makes a motion as if to throw it and halts himself. Then he brings it to his mouth as if to bite it and stops before he gets there. He brings it to his ear and shakes it gently. He is puzzled. The experimenter takes the egg from him and cracks it on the table, handing it back. The patient then begins to peel the egg and announces what it is. He cannot identify objects without reference to the action he directs toward them.

The disadvantages of such a system are illustrated by Emerson's (1931) experiment in which children are told to place a ring on a board with seven rows and six columns of pegs, copying the position of a ring put on an identical board by the experimenter. Children ranging from 3 to 12 were examined in this experiment and in an extension of it carried out by Werner (1948). The child's board could be placed in various positions relative to the experimenter's : right next to it, 90 degrees rotated away from it 180 degrees rotated, placed face to face with it so that the child has to turn full around to make his placement, etc. The older the child, the better his performance. But the younger children could do about as well as the oldest so long as they did not have to change their own position vis-à-vis the experimenter's board in order to make a match on their own board. The more they had to turn, the more difficult the task. They were clearly depending upon their bodily orientation toward the experimenter's board to guide them. When this orientation is disturbed by having to turn, they lose the position on the board. Older children succeed even when they must turn, either by the use of imagery that is invariant across bodily displacements, or, later, by specifying column and row of the experimenter's ring and carrying the symbolized self-instruction back to their own board. It is a limited world, the world of enactive representation.

We know little about the conditions necessary for the growth of imagery and iconic representation, or to what extent parental or environmental intervention affects it during the earliest years. In ordinary adult learning a certain amount of motoric skill and practice seems to be a necessary precondition for the development of a simultaneous image to represent the sequence of acts involved. If an adult subject is made to choose a path through a complex bank of toggle switches, he does not form an image of the path, according to Mandler (1962), until he has mastered and overpractised the task by successive manipulation. Then, finally, he reports that an image of the path has developed and that he is now using it rather than groping his way through.

Our main concern in what follows is not with the growth of iconic representation, but with the transition from it to symbolic representation. For it is in the development of symbolic representation that one finds, perhaps, the greatest thicket of psychological problems. The puzzle begins when the child first achieves the use of productive grammar, usually late in the second year of life. Toward the end of the second year, the child is master of the single-word, agrammatical utterance, the so-called holophrase. In the months following, there occurs a profound change in the use of language. Two classes of words appear—a pivot class and an open class—and the child launches forth on his career in combinatorial talking and, perhaps, thinking. Whereas before, lexemes like *allgone* and *mummy* and *sticky* and *bye-bye* were used singly, now for example *allgone* becomes a pivot word and is used in combination. Mother washes jam off the child's hands he says *allgone sticky*. In the next days, if his speech is carefully followed (Braine, 1963), it will be apparent that he is trying out the limits of the pivot combinations, and one will even find constructions that have an extraordinary capacity for representing complex sequences—like *allgone bye-bye* after a visitor has departed. A recent and ingenious observation by Weir (1962) on her $2\frac{1}{2}$-year-old son, recording his speech musings after he was in bed with lights out, indicates that at this stage there is a great deal of metalinguistic combinatorial play with words in which the child is exploring the limits of grammatical productiveness.

In effect, language provides a means, not only for representing experience, but also for transforming it. As Chomsky (1957) and Miller (1962) have both made clear in the last few years, the transformational rules of grammar provide a syntactic means of reworking the 'realities' one has encountered. Not only, if you will, did the dog bite the man, but the man was bitten by the dog and perhaps the man was not bitten by the dog or was the man not bitten by the dog. The range of reworking that is made possible even by the three transformations of the passive, the negative, and the query is very striking indeed. Or the ordering device whereby the comparative mode makes it possible to connect what is *heavy* and what is *light* into the ordinal array of *heavy* and *less heavy* is again striking. Or, to take a final example, there is the discrimination that is made possible by the growth of attribute language such that the global dimension *big* and *little* can now be decomposed into *tall* and *short* on the one hand and *fat* and *skinny* on the other.

Once the child has succeeeded in internalizing language as a cognitive instrument, it becomes possible for him to represent and systematically transform the regularities of experience with far greater flexibility and power than before. Interestingly enough, it is the recent Russian literature, particularly Vygotsky's (1962) book on language and thought, and the work of his disciple, Luria (1961), and his students (Abramyan, 1958; Martsinovskaya, undated) that has highlighted these phenomena by calling attention to the so-called second-signal system which replaces classical conditioning with an internalized linguistic system for shaping and transforming experience itself.

If all these matters were not of such complexity and human import, I would apologize for taking so much time in speculation. We turn now to some new experiments designed to shed some light on the nature of representation and particularly upon the transition from its iconic to its symbolic form.

Let me begin with an experiment by Bruner and Kenney (1966) on the manner in which children between 5 and 7 handle a double classification matrix. The materials of the experiment are nine plastic glasses, arranged so that they vary in 3 degrees of diameter and 3 degrees of height. They are set before the child initially, as in Figure 1, on a 3 × 3 grid marked on a large piece of cardboard. To aquaint the child with the matrix, we first remove one, then two, and then three glasses from the matrix, asking the child to replace them. We also ask the children to describe how the glasses in the columns and rows are alike and how they differ. Then the glasses are scrambled and we ask the child to make something like what was there before by placing the glasses on the same grid that was used when the task was introduced. Now we scramble the glasses once more, but this time we place the glass that was formerly in the southwest corner of the grid in the southeast corner (it is the shortest, thinnest glass) and ask the child if he can make something like what was there before, leaving the one glass where we have just put it. That is the experiment.

The results can be quickly told. To begin with, there is no difference between ages 5, 6, and 7 either in terms of ability to replace glasses taken from the matrix or in building a matrix once it has been scrambled (but without the transposed glass). Virtually all the children succeed. Interestingly enough, *all* the children rebuild the matrix to match the original, almost as if they were copying what was there before. The only difference is that the older children are quicker.

Matrix Procedure

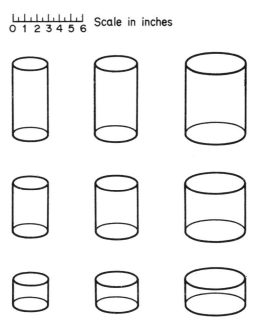

Figure 1 Array of glasses used in study of matrix ordering (Bruner and Kenney, 1966)

Now compare the performance of the three ages in constructing the matrix with a single member transposed. Most of the 7-year-olds succeed in the transposed task, but hardly any of the youngest children. Figure 2 presents the results graphically. The youngest children seem to be dominated by an image of the original matrix. They try to put the transposed glass 'back where it belongs', to rotate the cardboard so that 'it will be like before', and sometimes they will start placing a few glasses neighbouring the transposed glass correctly only to revert to the original arrangement. In several instances, 5- or 6-year-olds will simply try to reconstitute the old matrix, building right over the transposed glass. The 7-year-old, on the other hand, is more likely to pause, to treat the transposition as a problem, to talk to himself about 'where this should go'. The relation of place and size is for him a problem that requires reckoning, not simply copying.

Now consider the language children use for describing the dimensions of the matrix. Recall that the children were asked how glasses in a row and in a column were alike and how they differed. Children answered in three distinctive linguistic modes. One was *dimensional*, singling out two ends of an attribute— for example, 'That one is higher, and that one is shorter'. A second was *global* in nature. Of glasses differing only in height the child says, 'That one is bigger

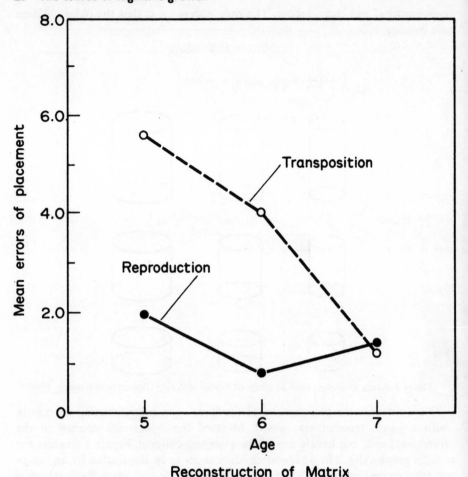

Reconstruction of Matrix

Figure 2 Mean number of errors made by children in reproducing and transposing a 3 × 3 matrix (Bruner and Kenney, 1966)

and that one is little'. The same words could be used equally well for diameter or for nearly any other magnitude. Finally, there was *confounded* usage: 'That one is tall and that one is little', where a dimensional term is used for one end of the continuum and a global term for the other. The children who used confounded descriptions had the most difficulty with the transposed matrix. Lumping all ages together, the children who used confounded descriptions were twice as likely to fail on the transposition task as those who used either dimensional or global terms. *But the language the children used had no relation whatsoever to their performance in reproducing the first untransposed matrix.* Inhelder and Sinclair[2] in a recent communication also report that confounded

[2] Bärbel Inhelder and Mimi Sinclair, personal communication, 1963.

language of this kind is associated with failure on conservation tasks in children of the same age, a subject to which we shall turn shortly.

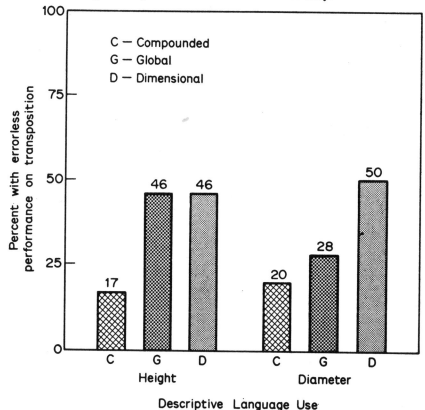

Figure 3 Percentage of children (aged 5–7) using different language patterns who reproduced transposed matrix without error (Bruner and Kenney, 1966)

The findings of this experiment suggest two things. First, that children who use iconic representation are more highly sensitized to the spatial-qualitative organization of experience and less to the ordering principles governing such organization. They can recognize and reproduce, but cannot produce new structures based on rule. And second, there is a suspicion that the language they bring to bear on the task is insufficient as a tool for ordering. If these notions are correct, then certain things should follow. For one thing, *improvement* in language should aid this type of problem solving. This remains to be investigated. But it is also reasonable to suppose that *activation* of language habits that the child has already mastered might improve performance as well—a hypothesis already suggested by the findings of Luria's students (e.g., Abramyan, 1958). Now, activation can be achieved by two means: one is by having the child 'say' the description of something before him that he must deal with symbolically. The other is to take advantage of the remoteness of reference that is a feature of language, and have the child 'say' his description in the absence of the things to be described. In this way, there would be less likelihood of a perceptual-iconic representation becoming dominant and inhibiting the operation of symbolic processes. An experiment by Françoise Frank (1966) illustrates this latter approach—the effects of saying before seeing.

Conservation Tests

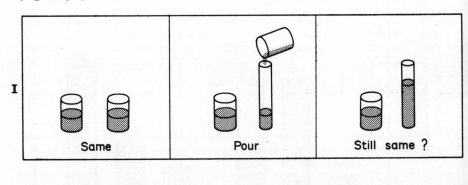

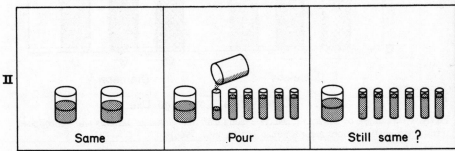

Figure 4 Two Geneva tests for conservation of liquid volume across transformations in its appearance (Piaget and Inhelder, 1962)

Piaget and Inhelder (1962) have shown that if children between ages 4 and 7 are presented two identical beakers which they judge equally full of water, they will no longer consider the water equal if the contents of one of the beakers is now poured into a beaker that is either wider or thinner than the original. If the second beaker is thinner, they will say it has more to drink because the water is higher; if the second beaker is wider, they will say it has less because the water is lower. Comparable results can be obtained by pouring the contents of one glass into several smaller beakers. In Geneva terms, the child is not yet able to conserve liquid volume across transformations in its appearance. Consider how this behaviour can be altered.

Françoise Frank first did the classic conservation tests to determine which children exhibited conservation and which did not. Her subjects were 4, 5, 6, and 7 years old. She then went on to other procedures, among which was the following. Two standard beakers are partly filled so that the child judges them to contain equal amounts of water. A wider beaker of the same height is introduced and the three beakers are now, except for their tops, hidden by a screen. The experimenter pours from a standard beaker into the wider beaker.

Screening Prediction and Feedback: Part III

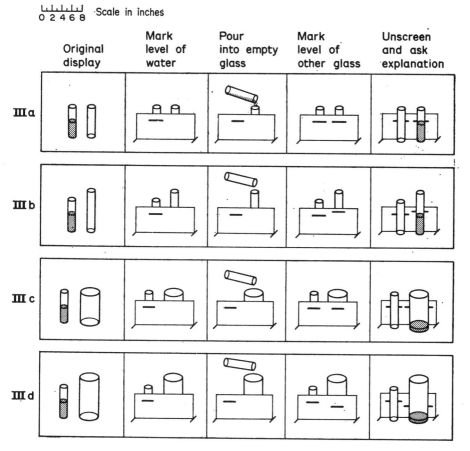

Figure 5 One procedure used in study of effect of language activation on conservation (Frank, 1966)

The child, without seeing the water, is asked which has more to drink, or do they have the same amount, the standard or the wider beaker. The results are in Figure 6. In comparison with the unscreened pre-test, there is a striking increase in correct equality judgments. Correct responses jump from 0% to

50% among the 4s, from 20% to 90% among the 5s, and from 50% to 100% among the 6s. With the screen present, most children justify their correct judgment by noting that 'It's the same water', or 'You only poured it'.

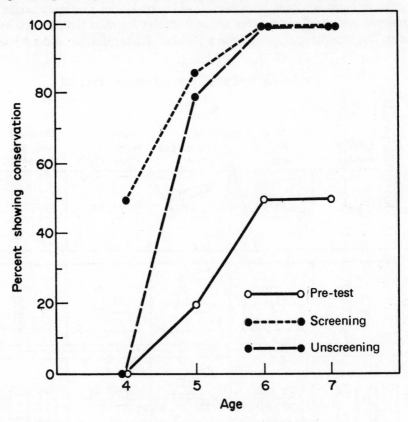

Conservation and Screening

Figure 6 Percentage of children showing conservation of liquid volume before and during screening and upon unscreening of the displays (Frank, 1966)

Now the screen is removed. All the 4-year-olds change their minds. The perceptual display overwhelms them and they decide that the wider beaker has less water. But virtually all of the 5-year-olds stick to their judgment, often invoking the difference between appearance and reality—'It looks like more to drink, but it is only the same because it is the same water and it was only poured from there to there', to quote one typical 5-year-old. And all of the 6s and all the 7s stick to their judgment. Now, some minutes later, Frank does a post-test on the children using a tall thin beaker along with the standard ones, and no screen, of course. The 4s are unaffected by their prior experience : none of them is able to grasp the idea of invariant quantity in the new task. With the 5s, instead of 20% showing conservation, as in the pre-test, 70% do.

With both 6s and 7s, conservation increases from 50% to 90%. I should mention that control groups doing just a pre-test and post-test show no significant improvement in performance.

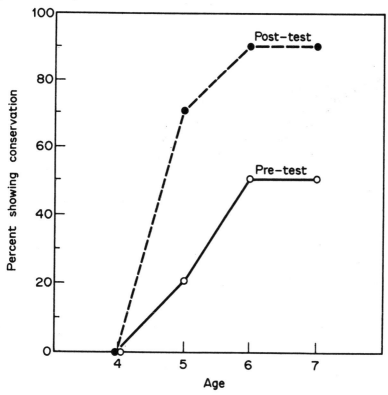

After—Effects of Screening

Figure 7 Percentage of children showing conservation of liquid volume in identical pre-test and post-test run after completion of experiment (Frank, 1966)

A related experiment of Nair's (1963) explores the arguments children use when they solve a conservation task correctly and when they do not. Her subjects were all 5-year-olds. She transferred water from one rectangular clear plastic tank to another that was both longer and wider than the first. Ordinarily, a 5-year-old will say there is less water in the second tank. The water is, of course, lower in the second tank. She had a toy duck swimming in the first container and when the water was poured into the new container, she told the child that 'The duck was taking his water with him'.

Three kinds of arguments were set forth by the children to support their judgments. One is perceptual—having to do with the height, width, or apparent 'bigness' of the water. A second type has to do with action: the duck took the water along, or the water was only poured. A third one, 'transformational' argument, invokes the reversibility principle: if you poured the water

back into the first container, it would look the same again.[3] Of the children
who thought the water was not equal in amount after pouring, 15% used nonperceptual arguments to justify their judgment. Of those who recognized the
equality of the water, two-thirds used nonperceptual arguments. It is plain that
if a child is to succeed in the conservation task, he must have some internalized
verbal formula that shields him from the overpowering appearance of the
visual displays much as in the Frank experiment. The explanations of the
children who lacked conservation suggest how strongly oriented they were to
the visual appearance of the displays they had to deal with.

Consider now another experiment by Bruner and Kenney (1966) also
designed to explore the border between iconic and symbolic representation.
Children aged 5, 6, and 7 were asked to say which of two glasses in a pair was
fuller and which emptier. 'Fullness' is an interesting concept to work with, for
it involves in its very definition a ratio or proportion between the volume of a
container and the volume of a substance contained. It is difficult for the iconic-
ally oriented child to see a half-full barrel and a half-filled thimble as equally
full, since the former looms larger in every one of the attributes that might be
perceptually associated with volume. It is like the old riddle of which is
heavier a pound of lead or a pound of feathers. To make a correct judgment of
fullness or emptiness, the child must use a symbolic operation, somewhat like
computing a ratio, and resist the temptation to use perceptual appearance—
that is, unless he finds some happy heuristic to save him the labour of such a
computation. Figure 8 contains the 11 pairs of glasses used, and they were
selected with a certain malice aforethought.

There are four types of pairs. In type I (Displays 4, 9a, and 9b), the glasses
are of unequal volume, but equally, though fractionally, full. In Type II
(Displays 2, 7a, and 7b) again the glasses are of unequal volume, but they are
completely full. Type III (Displays 3, 8a, and 8b) consists of two glasses of
unequal volume, one filled and the other part filled. Type IV consists of
identical glasses, in one case equally filled, in another unequally (Displays 1
and 5).

All the children in the age range we have studied use pretty much the same
criteria for judging *fullness*, and these criteria are based on directly observable
sensory indices rather than upon proportion. That glass is judged fuller that has
the great apparent volume of water, and the favoured indication of greater
volume is water level; or where that is equated, then width of glass will do;
and when width and water level are the same, then height of glass will prevail.
But now consider the judgments made by the three age groups with respect to
which glass in each pair is *emptier*. The older children have developed an
interesting consistency based on an appreciation of the complementary relation

[3] Not one of the 40 children who participated in this experiment used the compensation
argument—that though the water was lower it was correspondingly wider and was,
therefore, the same amount of water. This type of reasoning by compensation is said by
Piaget and Inhelder (1962) to be the basis of conservation.

Ratio Procedure

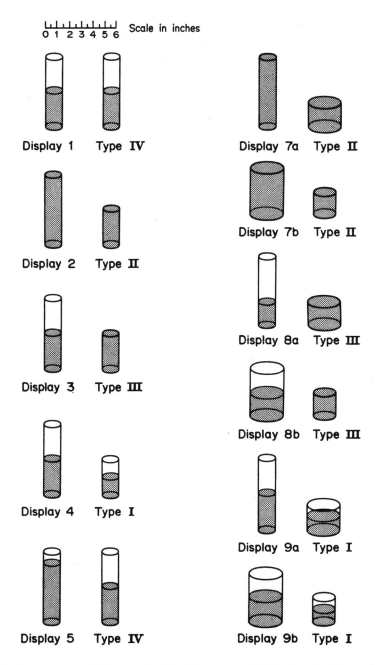

Scale in inches
0 1 2 3 4 5 6

Display 1   Type IV

Display 2   Type II

Display 3   Type III

Display 4   Type I

Display 5   Type IV

Display 7a   Type II

Display 7b   Type II

Display 8a   Type III

Display 8b   Type III

Display 9a   Type I

Display 9b   Type I

Figure 8 Eleven pairs of glasses to be judged in terms of which glass is fuller and which emptier (Bruner and Kenney, 1966)

of filled and empty space—albeit an incorrect one. For them 'emptier' means the glass that has the largest apparent volume of unfilled space, just as 'fuller' meant the glass that had the largest volume of filled space. In consequence, their responses seem logically contradictory. For the glass that is judged fuller also turns out to be the glass that is judged emptier—given a large glass and a small glass, both half full. The younger children, on the other hand, equate emptiness with 'littleness': that glass is emptier that gives the impression of being smaller in volume of liquid. If we take the three pairs of glasses of Type 1 (unequal volumes, half filled) we can see how the judgments typically distribute themselves. Consider only the errors. The glass with the larger volume of empty space is called emptier by 27% of the erring 5-year-olds, by 53% of the erring 6-year-olds, and by 72% of erring 7-year-olds. But the glass with the smallest volume of water is called emptier by 73% of the 5-year-olds who err, 47% of the 6s, and only 28% of the 7s. When the children are asked for their reasons for judging one glass as emptier, there is further confirmation : most of the younger children justify it by pointing to 'littleness' or 'less water' or some other aspect of diminutiveness. And most of the other children justify their judgments of emptiness by reference to the amount of empty space in the vessel.

Table 1 Percentage of erroneous judgments of which of two glasses is emptier based on two criteria for defining the concept

Criteria for 'emptier' judgment	Age		
	5	6	7
Greatest empty space	27%	53%	72%
Smallest volume of liquid	73%	47%	28%
	100%	100%	100%
Percentage correct	9%	8%	17%
$N =$	30	30	30

Note—Criteria are greater volume of empty space and lesser volume of water. From Bruner and Kenney (1966).

The result of all this is, of course, that the 'logical structure' of the older children seems to go increasingly awry. But surely, though Figure 9 shows that contradictory errors steadily increase with age (calling the same glass fuller and emptier or equally full but not equally empty or vice versa), the contradiction is a by-product of the method of dealing with attributes. How shall we interpret these findings? Let me suggest that what is involved is a translation difficulty in going from the perceptual or iconic realm to the symbolic. If you ask children of this age whether something can be fuller and also emptier, they

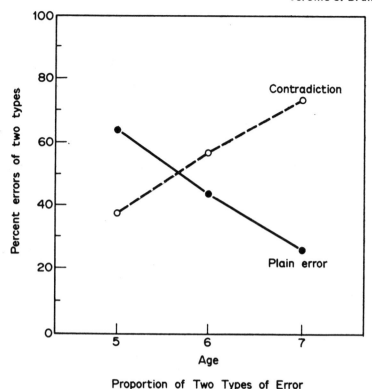

Proportion of Two Types of Error

Figure 9 Percentage of children at three ages who make contradictory and plain errors in judging which of two glasses is fuller and which emptier. (A contradictory error is calling the same glass both fuller or emptier or calling them equally full but not equally empty or vice versa. A plain error is calling one glass fuller and the other emptier, but incorrectly. From Bruner and Kenney, 1966)

will smile and think that you are playing riddles. They are aware of the contrastive nature of the two terms. Indeed, even the very young child has a good working language for the two poles of the contrast : 'all gone' for completely empty and 'spill' or 'tippy top' for completely full. Recall too that from 5 to 7, there is perfect performance in judging which of two identical beakers is fuller and emptier. The difference between the younger and the older child is in the number of attributes that are being attended to in situations involving fullness and emptiness: the younger child is attending to one—the volume of water; the older to two—the volume of filled space and the volume of empty space. The young child is applying a single contrast pair—full-empty—to a single feature of the situation. The older child can attend to two features, but he does not yet have the means for relating them to a third, the volume of the container *per se*. To do so involves being able to deal with a relation in the perceptual field that does not have a 'point-at-able' or ostensive definition. Once the third term is introduced—the volume of the glass—then the symbolic concept of proportion can come to 'stand for' something that is not present perceptually. The older child is on the way to achieving the insight, in spite of his contradictions. And, interestingly enough, if we count the number of children who justify their judgments of fuller and emptier by pointing to *several* rather than a single attribute, we find that the proportion triples in both cases between age 5 and age 7. The older child, it would seem, is ordering his perceptual world in such a way that, shortly, he will be able to apply concepts of relationship that are not dependent upon simple ostensive definition. As he moves toward this more powerful 'technology of reckoning' he is led into errors that seem to be contradictory. What is particularly telltale is the fact, for example, that in the Type III displays, younger children sometimes seem to find the judgment easier than older children—pointing to the fuller by placing their finger on the rim of the full member and pointing to the emptier with the remark that 'It is not to the top'. The older child (and virtually never the younger one) gets all involved in the judgment of 'fuller by apparent filled volume' and then equally involved in the judgment of 'emptier by apparent empty volume' and such are his efforts that he fails to note his contradiction when dealing with a pair like Display 8b.

Table 2 Percentage of children who justify judgments of 'fuller' and 'emptier' by mentioning more than a single attribute

Age	*'Fuller' judgments*	*'Emptier' judgments*	N
5	7.2%	4.1%	30
6	15.6%	9.3%	30
7	22.2%	15.6%	30

Turn now to a quite different experimental procedure that deals with the related concept of equivalence—how seemingly different objects are grouped into equivalence classes. In the two experiments to be cited, one by Olver (1961), the other by Rigney (1962), children are given words or pictures to sort into groups or to characterize in terms of how they are alike. The two sets of results, one for words, the other for pictures, obtained for children between 6 and 14, can be summarized together. One may distinguish two aspects of grouping—the first has to do with the features or attributes that children use as a criterion for grouping objects: *perceptual features* (the colour, size, pattern, etc.), *arbitrary functional features* (what I can do with the objects regardless of their usual use: you can make noise with a newspaper by crumpling it and with a book by slamming it shut, etc.), *appropriate functional features* (potato, peach, banana, and milk are characterized 'You can eat them'). But grouping behaviour can also be characterized in terms of the syntactical structure of the equivalence sets that the child develops. There are, first, what Vygotsky (1962) has called *heaps:* collections put together in an arbitrary way simply because the child has decided to put them together that way. Then there are *complexes :* the various members of a complex are included in the class in accordance with a rule that does not account uniformly for the inclusion of all the members. Edge matching is one such rule: each object is grouped into a class on the basis of its similarity with a neighbouring object. Yet no two neighbouring pieces may be joined by the same similarity. Another type of complexive grouping is thematic: here objects are put together by virtue of participating in a sentence or a little story. More sophisticated is a key ring in which one organizing object is related to all others but none of those to each other. And finally, considerably more sophisticated than heaps and complexes, there are *superordinate concepts,* in which one universal rule of inclusion accounts for all the objects in the set—all men and women over 21 are included in the class of voters provided they meet certain residence requirements.

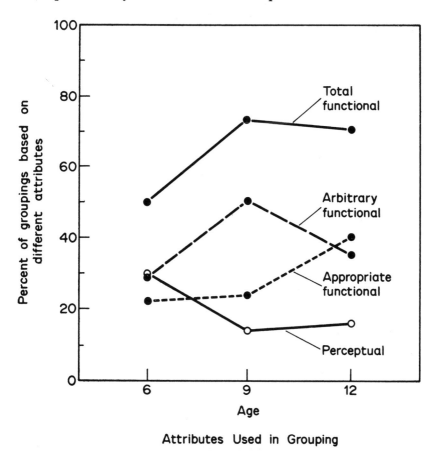

Attributes Used in Grouping

Figure 10 Features of objects used by children of different ages as a basis for placing the objects in equivalence groups (Olver, 1961)

The pattern of growth is revealing of many of the trends we have already discussed, and provides in addition a new clue. Consider first the attributes or features of objects that children at different ages use as a basis for forming equivalence groups. Figure 10 indicates, the youngest children rely more heavily on perceptual attributes than do the others. As they grow older, grouping comes to depend increasingly upon the functional properties of things —but the transitional phase is worth some attention, for it raises anew the issue of the significance of egocentrism. For the first functional groupings to appear are of an arbitrary type—what 'I' or 'you' can do to objects that renders them alike rather than what is the conventional use or function to which objects can be put. During this stage of 'egocentric functionalism', there is a corresponding rise in the use of first- and second-person personal pronouns: 'I can do thus and so to this object; I can do the same to this one,' etc. Gradually, with increasing maturity the child shifts to an appropriate and less egocentric form of using functional groupings. The shift from perceptual to functional groupings is accompanied by a corresponding shift in the syntactical structure

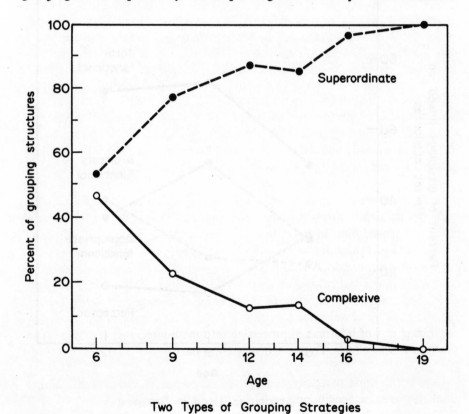

Two Types of Grouping Strategies

Figure 11 The use of two rules of equivalence grouping found in children of different ages (Olver, 1961)

of the groups formed. Complexive groupings steadily dwindle; superordinate groupings rise, until the latter almost replace the former in late adolescence. It is difficult to tell which is the pacemaker in this growth—syntax or the semantic basis of grouping.

Rigney reports one other matter of some interest. Her young subjects formed groups of any size they wished, choosing pictures from a display board of several dozen little water colours. She observed that the most perceptually based groups and the ones most often based on complexive grouping principles were pairs. A count of these revealed that 61% of all the groups made by 6-year-olds were such pairs, 36% of those made by 8-year-olds, and only 25% of the groupings of 11-year-olds.

On the surface, this set of findings—Olver's and Rigney's alike—seems to point more to the decline of a preference for perceptual and iconic ways of dealing with objects and events, particularly with their grouping. But closer inspection suggests still another factor that is operating. In both cases, there is evidence of the development of hierarchical structure and rules for including objects in super-ordinate hierarchies. Hierarchical classification is surely one of the most evident properties of the structure of language—hierarchical grouping that goes beyond mere perceptual inclusion. Complexive structures of the kind described earlier are much more dominated by the sorts of associative principles by which the appearance of objects leads to their spontaneous grouping in terms of similarity or contiguity. As language becomes more internalized, more guiding as a set of rules for organizing events, there is a shift from the associative principles that operate in classical perceptual organization to the increasingly abstract rules for grouping events by the principles of inclusion, exclusion, and overlap, the most basic characteristics of any hierarchical system.

We have said that cognitive growth consists in part in the development of systems of representation as means for dealing with information. The growing child begins with a strong reliance upon learned action patterns to represent the world around him. In time, there is added to this technology a means for stimultanizing regularities in experience into images that stand for events in the way that pictures do. And to this is finally added a technology of translating experience into a symbol system that can be operated upon by rules of transformation that greatly increase the possible range of problem solving. One of the effects of this development, or possibly one of its causes, is the power for organizing acts of information processing into more integrated and long-range problem solving efforts. To this matter we turn next.

Consider in rapid succession three related experiments. All of them point, I think, to the same conclusion.

The first is by Huttenlocher (1966), a strikingly simple study, performed with children between the ages of 6 and 12. Two light switches are before the child;

each can be in one of two possible positions. A light bulb is also visible. The child is asked to tell, on the basis of turning only one switch, what turns the light on. There are four ways in which the presentations are made. In the first, the light is off initially and when the child turns a switch, the light comes on. In the second, the light is on and when the child turns a switch, it goes off. In the third, the light is on and when the child turns a switch, it stays on. In the fourth and final condition, the light is off and when the child turns a switch, it stays off. Now what is intriguing about this arrangement is that there are different numbers of inductive steps required to make a correct inference in each task. The simplest condition is the off-on case. The position to which the switch has just been moved is responsible for the light going on. Intermediate difficulty should be experienced with the on-off condition. In the on-off case, two connected interferences are required: the present position achieved is rejected and the original position of the switch that has been turned is responsible for lighting the bulb. An even larger number of consecutive acts is required for success in the on-on case: the present position of the turned switch is rejected, the original position as well and the present position of the *other* switch is responsible. The off-off case requires four steps : rejecting the present position of the turned switch, its original position, and the present position of the other switch, finally accepting the alternative position of the unturned switch. The natures of the individual steps are all the same. Success in the more complex cases depends upon being able to integrate them consecutively.

Huttenlocher's results show that the 6-year-olds are just as capable as their elders of performing the elementary operation involved in the one-step case: the on-off display. They, like the 9s and 12s, make nearly perfect scores. But in general, the more inferential steps the 6-year-old must make, the poorer his performance. By age 12, on the other hand, there is an insignificant difference between the tasks requiring one, two, three, or four connected inferences.

An experiment by Mosher (1962) underlines the same point. He was concerned with the strategies used by children from 6 to 11 for getting information in the game of Twenty Questions. They were to find out by 'yes-no' questions what caused a car to go off the road and hit a tree. One may distinguish between connected constraint-locating questions ('Was it night-time?' followed up appropriately) and direct hypothesis-testing questions ('Did a bee fly in the window and sting the man on the eye and make him go off the road and hit the tree?'). From 6 to 11, more and more children use constraint-locating, connected questioning. Let me quote from Mosher's account:

We have asked children . . . after they have played their games, to tell us which of two questions they would rather have the answer to, if they were playing the games again—one of them a typical constraint-seeking question ('Was there anything wrong with the man?') and the other a typical discrete test of an hypothesis ('Did the man have a heart attack?'). All the eleven-year-olds and all the eight-year-olds choose the constraint-seeking question, but only 29% of the six-year-olds do. [p. 6].

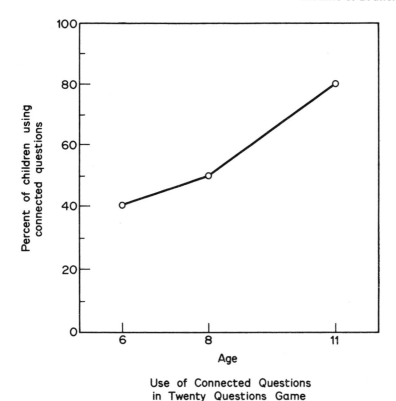

Use of Connected Questions
in Twenty Questions Game

Figure 12 The proportion of children at different ages who use connected questions in a Twenty Questions game (Mosher, 1962)

The questions of the younger children are all one-step substitutes for direct sense experience. They are looking for knowledge by single questions that provide the answer in a finished form. When they succeed they do so by a lucky question that hits an immediate, perceptible cause. When the older child receives a 'yes' answer to one of his constraint-locating questions, he most often follows up by asking another. When, on the rare occasions that a younger child asks a constraint question and it is answered 'yes', he almost invariably follows it up with a specific question to test a concrete hypothesis. The older child can accrete his information in a structure governed by consecutive inference. The younger child cannot.

Potter's (1966) study of the development of perceptual recognition bears on the same point. Ordinary coloured photographs of familiar scenes are presented to children between 6 and 12, the pictures coming gradually into focus. Let me sum up one part of the results very briefly. Six-year-olds produce an abundance of hypotheses. But they rarely try to match new hypotheses to previous ones. 'There is a big tower in the middle and a road over there and a big ice cream cone through the middle of the tower and a pumpkin on top.'

It is like a random collage. The 9-year-old's torrent of hypotheses, on the other hand, shows a sense of consistency about what is likely to appear with what. Things are in a context of likelihood, a frame of reference that demands internal consistency. Something is seen as a merry-go-round, and the child then restricts later hypotheses to the other things to be found in an amusement park. The adolescent operates under even more highly organized sequential constraints: he occasionally develops his initial hypotheses from what is implied by the properties of the picture, almost by intersection—'It is red and shiny and metallic: It must be a coffee-pot.' Once such constraints are established, the order of hypotheses reflects even more the need to build up a consistent world of objects—even to the point of failing to recognize things that do not fit it.

What shall we make of these three sets of findings—that older children are able to cumulate information by asking questions in a directed sequence leading to a fine goal, and that they are capable of recognizing visual displays in a manner governed by a dominating frame of reference that transcends momentary and isolated bits of information? Several points seem apparent. The first is that as children mature, they are able to use indirect information based on forms of information processing other than the act of pointing to what is immediately present. They seem, in short, to make remote reference to states and constraints that are not given by the immediate situation, to go beyond the information given. Second, and this is a matter that has already been discussed, they seem to be able to cumulate information into a structure that can be operated upon by rules that transcend simple association by similarity and contiguity. In the case of Twenty Questions, the rule is best described as implication—that knowing one thing implies certain other things and eliminates still others. In the experiments with the light switches, it is that if the present state does not produce the effect, then there is a system for tracing back to the other states that cause the light to go on. Where perceptual recognition is concerned, the rule is that a piece of information from one part of the display implies what other parts might be. The child, in sum, is translating redundancy into a manipulable model of the environment that is governed by rules of implication. It is this model of the environment that permits him to go beyond the information before him. I would suggest that it is this new array of cognitive equipment that permits the child to transcend momentaneity, to integrate longer sequences of events.

Let me urge, moreover, that such a system of processing environmental events depends upon the translation of experience into symbolic form. Such a translation is necessary in order for there to be the kind of remoteness of reference as is required when one deals with indirect information. To transcend the immediately perceptual, to get beyond what is vividly present to a more extended model of the environment, the child needs a system that permits him to deal with the nonpresent, with things that are remote in space, qualitative similarity, and time, from the present situation. Hockett (1959), in describing the design features of language includes this feature as crucial. He is referring to human speech as a system of communication. The same point can be made about language as an instrument of thought. That humans have the *capacity* for using speech in this way is only part of the point. What is critical is that the capacity is *not* used until it is coupled with the technology of language in the cognitive operations of the child.

The same can be said for the models of the environment that the child constructs to go beyond present information. This is not to say that non-verbal animals cannot make inferences that go beyond the present stimulus: anticipatory activity is the rule in vertebrates. But the models that the growing child constructs seem not to be anticipatory, or inferential, or probabilistic-frequency models. They seem to be governed by rules that can more properly be called syntactical rather than associative.

My major concern has been to examine afresh the nature of intellectual growth. The account has surely done violence to the richness of the subject. It seems to me that growth depends upon the emergence of two forms of competence. Children, as they grow, must acquire ways of representing the recurrent regularities in their environment, and they must transcend the momentary by developing ways of linking past to present to future—representation and integration. I have suggested that we can conceive of growth in both of these domains as the emergence of new technologies for the unlocking and amplification of human intellectual powers. Like the growth of technology, the growth of intellect is not smoothly monotonic. Rather, it moves forward in spurts as innovations are adopted. Most of the innovations are transmitted to the child in some prototypic form by agents of the culture: ways of responding, ways of looking and imaging, and most important, ways of translating what one has encountered into language.

I have relied heavily in this account on the successive emergence of action, image, and word as the vehicles of representation, a reliance based both upon our observations and upon modern readings of man's alloplastic evolution. Our attention has been directed largely to the transition between iconic and symbolic representation.

In children between 4 and 12 language comes to play an increasingly powerful role as an implement of knowing. Through simple experiments, I have tried to show how language shapes, augments, and even supersedes the child's earlier modes of processing information. Translation of experience into symbolic form, with its attendant means of achieving remote reference, transformation and combination, opens up realms of intellectual possibility that are orders of magnitude beyond the most powerful image forming system.

What of the integration of intellectual activity into more coherent and interconnected acts? It has been the fashion, since Freud, to see delay of gratification as the principal dynamism behind this development—from primary process to secondary process, or from assimilation to accommodation, as Piaget would put it today. Without intending to question the depth of this insight, let me suggest that delay of immediate gratification, the ability to go beyond the moment, also depends upon techniques, and again they are techniques of representation. Perhaps representation exclusively by imagery and perceptual organization has built into it one basic operation that ties it to the immediate present. It is the operation of pointing—ostensiveness, as logicians call it. (This is not to say that highly evolved images do not go beyond immediate time and given place. Maps and flow charts are iconic in nature, but they are images that translate prior linguistic and mathematical renderings into a visual form.) Iconic representation, in the beginning, is built upon a perceptual organization that is tied to the 'point-at-able' spatioqualitative properties of events. I have suggested that, for all its limitations, such representation is an achievement beyond the earlier stage where percepts are not autonomous of action. But so long as perceptual representation dominates, it is difficult to develop higher-order techniques for processing information by consecutive inferential steps that take one beyond what can be pointed at.

Once language becomes a medium for the translation of experience, there is a progressive release from immediacy. For language, as we have commented, has the new and powerful features of remoteness and arbitrariness: it permits productive, combinatorial operations in the *absence* of what is represented. With this achievement, the child can delay gratification by virtue of representing to himself what lies beyond the present, what other possibilities exist beyond the clue that is under his nose. The child may be *ready* for delay of gratification, but he is no more able to bring it off than somebody ready to build a house, save that he has not yet heard of tools.

The discussion leaves two obvious question begging. What of the integration of behaviour in organisms without language? And how does language become internalized as a vehicle for organizing experience? The first question has to be answered briefly and somewhat cryptically. Wherever integrated behaviour has been studied—as in Lehrman's (1955) careful work on integrated instinctive patterns in the ringdove, it has turned out that a sustaining external stimulus was needed to keep the highly integrated behaviour going. The best way to control behaviour in subhuman species is to control the stimulus situation. Surely this is the lesson of Lashley's (1938) classic account of instinctive behaviour. Where animal learning is concerned, particularly in the primates, there is, to be sure, considerable plasticity. But it too depends upon the development of complex forms of stimulus substitution and organization—as in Klüver's (1933) work on equivalence reactions in monkeys. If it should seem that I am urging that the growth of symbolic functioning links a unique set of powers to man's capacity, the appearance is quite as it should be.

As for how language becomes internalized as a programme for ordering experience, I join those who despair for an answer. My speculation, for whatever it is worth, is that the process of internalization depends upon interaction with others, upon the need to develop corresponding categories and transformations for communal action. It is the need for cognitive coin that can be exchanged with those on whom we depend. What Roger Brown (1958) has called the Original Word Game ends up by being the Human Thinking Game.

If I have seemed to underemphasize the importance of inner capacities—for example, the capacity *for* language or *for* imagery—it is because I believe that this part of the story is given by the nature of man's evolution. What is significant about the growth of mind in the child is to what degree it depends not upon capacity but upon the unlocking of capacity by techniques that come from exposure to the specialized environment of a culture. Romantic clichés like 'the veneer of culture' or 'natural man', are as misleading if not as damaging as the view that the course of human development can be viewed independently of the educational process we arrange to make that development possible.

References

Abramyan, L. A., 1958. Organization of the voluntary activity of the child with the help of verbal instruction. Unpublished diploma thesis, Moscow University. Cited by A. R. Luria, *The role of speech in the regulation of normal and abnormal behavior.* New York: Liveright, 1961.

Barker, R. G., 1963. On the nature of the environment. Kurt Lewin Memorial Address presented at American Psychological Association, Philadelphia, September.

Braine, M. D., 1963. On learning the grammatical order of words. *Psychol. Rev.,* [70], 323-348.

Brown, R., 1958. *Words and things.* Glencoe, Ill.: Free Press.

Bruner, J. S. and Kenney, Helen, 1966. The development of the concepts of order and proportion in children. In J. S. Bruner, *Studies in cognitive growth.* New York: Wiley.

Chomsky, N., 1957. *Syntactic structures.* S'Gravenhage, Netherlands: Mouton.

Emerson, L. L., 1931. The effect of bodily orientation upon the young child's memory for position of objects. *Child Develpm.,* [2], 125-142.

Frank, Françoise, 1966. Perception and language in conservation. In J. S. Bruner, *Studies in cognitive growth.* New York: Wiley.

Hanfmann, Eugenia, Rickers-Ovsiankina, Maria and Goldstein, K., 1944. Case Lanuti: Extreme concretization of behavior due to damage of the brain cortex. *Psychol. Monogr.,* [57] (4, Whole No. 264).

Hockett, C. F., 1959. Animal 'languages' and human language. In J. N. Spuhler, *The evolution of man's capacity for culture.* Detroit: Wayne State Univer. Press. Pp. 32-39.

Huttenlocher, Janellen, 1966. The growth of conceptual strategies. In J. S. Bruner, *Studies in cognitive growth.* New York: Wiley.

Klüver, H., 1933. *Behavior mechanisms in monkeys.* Chicago: Univer. Chicago Press.

La Barre, W., 1954. *The human animal.* Chicago: Univer. Chicago Press.

Lashley, K. S., 1938. Experimental analysis of instinctive behavior. *Psychol. Rev.,* [45], 445-472.

Lehrman, D. S., 1955. The physiological basis of parental feeding behaviour in the ring-dove (*Streptopelia risoria*). *Behavior,* [7], 241-286.

Luria, A. R., 1961. *The role of speech in the regulation of normal and abnormal behavior.* New York: Liveright.

Mandler, G., 1962. From association to structure. *Psychol. Rev.,* [69], 415-427.

Martsinovskaya, E. N., 1961. Research into the reflective and regulatory role of the second signalling system of pre-school age. Collected papers of the Department of Psychology, Moscow University, undated. Cited by A. R. Luria, *The role of speech in the regulation of normal and abnormal behavior.* New York: Liveright.

Miller, G. A., 1962. Some psychological studies of grammar. *Amer. Psychologist,* [17], 748-762.

Miller, G. A., Galanter, E. and Pribram, K. H., 1960. *Plans and the structure of behavior.* New York: Holt.

Mosher, F. A., 1962. Strategies for information gathering. Paper read at Eastern Psychological Association, Atlantic City, N.J., April.

Nair, Patricia, 1963. An experiment in conservation. In Center for Cognitive Studies, *Annual Report.* Cambridge, Mass.: Author.

Olver, Rose R., 1961. A developmental study of cognitive equivalence. Unpublished doctoral dissertation, Radcliffe College.

Piaget, J., 1954. *The construction of reality in the child.* (Trans. by Margaret Cook). New York: Basic Books.

Piaget, J. and Inhelder, Bärbel, 1962. *Le développement des quantités physiques chez l'enfant.* (2nd rev. ed.) Neuchâtel, Switzerland: Delachaux & Niestlé.

Potter, Mary C., 1966. The growth of perceptual recognition. In J. S. Bruner, *Studies in cognitive growth.* New York: Wiley.

Rigney, Joan C., 1962. A developmental study of cognitive equivalence transformations and their use in the acquisition and processing of information. Unpublished honours thesis, Radcliffe College, Department of Social Relations.

Vygotsky, L. S., 1962. *Thought and language.* (Ed. & trans. by Eugenia Hanfmann & Gertrude Vakar) New York: Wiley.

Washburn, S. L., & Howell, F. C., 1960. Human evolution and culture. In S. Tax, *The evolution of man.* Vol. 2. Chicago: Univer. Chicago Press.

Weir, Ruth H., 1962. *Language in the crib.* The Hague: Mouton.

Werner, H., 1948. *Comparative psychology of mental development.* (Rev. ed.) Chicago: Follett.

John H. Flavell
Institute of Child Development, University of Minnesota

The development of role-taking and communication skills in children

This is an edited version of pp. 4-21. D.F.

The nature and development of role-taking and communication skills

As they grow and develop, children typically acquire a wide array of knowledges and skills with respect to the objects in their milieu, both human and nonhuman. An important subset of their acquisitions regarding human objects, that is, in the area of social learning, undoubtedly includes that complex of abilities which have been variously called *role taking, role perception, role playing, role enactment, empathy, person perception,* and the like. Piaget (1926) long ago argued that the child is at first an *egocentric* organism, unwittingly the prisoner of his own individual perspective and largely ignorant of and unconcerned with the differing perspectives of other people. One of the principal purposes of our research programme was to examine in detail the developmental progression from this initial egocentrism toward the acquisition of various skills of the role-taking variety.

Just what are these 'various skills of the role-taking variety' for which there appear to be so many confusing near-synonyms in the literature? Our own analysis closely follows that given in Sarbin's review of the area (1954), although diverging from it at certain points.[1] The basic and essential ingredient of any sort of skill sequence in this area appears to us to be that process in which the individual somehow cognizes, apprehends, grasps—whatever term you prefer—certain attributes of another individual. The attributes in question are primarily of the type that could be described as inferential rather than directly perceptible, for example, the other's needs, his intentions, his opinions and beliefs, and his emotional, perceptual or intellectual capacities and limitations. Tagiuri and Petrullo have in mind the same class of attributes in their definition of person perception:

[1] Sarbin's masterful survey also offers a detailed treatment of aspects of role theory which are not immediately relevant to our research and are therefore not included in the present analysis, for example, a discussion of social roles and an account of the development of the self.

Indeed, when we speak of person perception or of knowledge of persons, we refer mostly to the observations we make about *intentions, attitudes, emotions, ideas, abilities, purposes, traits*—events that are, so to speak, inside the person. (1958, p. x).

The role taker's estimate of these attributes is normally a synthesis of information from two sources: (a) his knowledge of people and their behaviour in various situations (including, perhaps, some previous knowledge of this particular other and his habits); (b) perceptual input from the overt behaviour of the other or from other cue sources in the immediate situation. Using Sarbin's terminology, we would say that the estimate is thus based on an integration of the subject's pre-existing *role expectations* and his current *role perception* (1954). And finally, the estimate-taking process may be a deliberate and conscious action on the subject's part, but it need not and frequently will not be; likewise, the process may be either very brief or considerably extended in time. This basic process of obtaining information about the other's internal events needs a title which will distinguish it from other processes in the role-taking domain. We prefer to call it the *discrimination of role attributes* in the other: *discrimination* is a suitably noncommittal name for the little-understood cognitive and perceptual activities through which the subject gains his information about the other, and *role attributes* is abstract enough to cover the host of inferrable properties of the other about which information may be sought.

We believe that the discrimination of role attributes is most profitably conceptualized as an act or process which forms a part, but *only* a part, of a larger context of motives and behaviour. The context itself may vary considerably, however, and it is this variation which makes both for a proliferation of terms in this area (*role taking, role playing*, etc). and for their all too frequent vagueness. The discrimination of role attributes is normally an initial instrumental act within the context, a first step in a chain of events directed toward some ulterior goal. Thus, we discriminate another's role attributes, not for its own sake, but for some reason, and what we do next with the information so obtained will depend upon what that reason was. An adequate overview of behaviour in the general role-taking domain therefore requires an examination, not of role-attribute discrimination alone, but also of the variety of context in which it is observed.

Sarbin (p. 282) has made a good beginning classification of such contexts. He makes an important distinction between *role enactment* and *role taking*. In the former, the subject actually takes on the role attributes of the other and behaves overtly in accordance with them (for example, the child who plays the mother's role vis-à-vis her dolls, or the man who acts the part of an executive once he is promoted to this position). The latter refers to the more covert, more exclusively cognitive process of adopting the perspective or attitude of another, silently 'putting yourself in his shoes' in a given situation. More generally, a distinction can be made between two major types of contexts in which role-attribute discrimination figures as an initial, instrumental response.

First, there are those cases (Sarbin's *role enactment*) where the discrimination process is followed by a literal and overt assumption of those attributes of the other which the process has uncovered; that is, one first determines the nature of the other's role (be it a socially defined, enduring role or some transistory one which the culture has not named), and then one proceeds to fulfill that role oneself. As Sarbin has shown (pp. 232-235), there is considerable variation among contexts of this type. They vary, for example, in the extent to which the whole self participates in the enactment of the role: there are casual roles (for example, customer in a supermarket) which one assumes with minimal organismic involvement; there are others in which the involvement is extremely intense and well-nigh complete (for example, states of ecstasy, or of taking the role of a moribund person in cases of Voodoo death); and there are numerous intermediate subtypes. There is also variation in the extent to which the role behaviour one has adopted is carried out overtly. Sarbin points out, for example, that the empathic response, normally a more or less covert affair, *can* become overt (for example, one may shudder and grimace when another recounts a painful or terrifying experience he has had); cognitive behaviour in the role-taking area will sometimes 'spill over' into action, as he puts it (p. 232). As a further complication regarding the overtness-covertness dimension, Maccoby (1959) has suggested that many adult social roles (for example, that of 'mother') are initially practised covertly during childhood, preparatory to later, overt enactment.

The second major type includes all the remaining contexts and is the one most pertinent to our research. Here, the subject begins as usual by discriminating the other's role attributes and will frequently go beyond this to assume these attributes, but only briefly and covertly (Sarbin's *role taking*). However, this role assumption does not then progress very far toward overt role enactment and, above all, the *motives* for doing the discriminating and temporary assuming are something *other* than those which prompt full-fledged role enactment. That is, the goal behaviour is not role enactment *per se*, with whatever rewards normally accrue to it (see Maccoby, 1959, for a discussion of some instigating conditions for role enactment). Rather, the subject seeks out the other's role attributes, not to *play out* his role, but to *understand* it—and understand it from his own, still active role position vis-à-vis the other.

In some cases this act of understanding is itself the only immediate objective, and does not serve as an instrumental response to other actions immediately following. For example, most of us sometimes play the part of observers of the human scene, simply curious about how person X sees the world, about 'what makes him tick', with no thought of doing anything more useful with what we discover than satisfying our curiosity. The information-seeking motive is a powerful one in human beings, and it can be directed toward role attributes as well as toward other events in the milieu.

Often, however, the act of understanding does serve as a means to one's subsequent behaviour, the latter generally being in some sense complementary to the behaviour of the other. For example, the other is our opponent in some kind of a contest, perhaps a competitive game, and our understanding of his role attributes helps to govern our own strategy and tactics. Or the other is, on the contrary, our collaborator or fellow team member in some joint enterprise, and our knowledge of his role attributes and derivative behaviours will again maximize the effectiveness of our own actions in furthering the enterprise. Or the other is trying to convey a subtle, hard-to-characterize feeling he has experienced, and your ability to grasp how it felt to him will determine your next response and, perhaps, the whole course of the subsequent interchange between you (psychotherapy is a familiar prototype here).

There are obviously many everyday examples of this general type: in all cases, the essential process consists of discriminating the other's role attributes for the purpose of—a vague but inclusive expression is needed here— 'behaving appropriately' toward him, within the confines of one's *own* role. One important subtype to which we have given considerable research attention in the present investigation is the case where role-attribute discrimination facilitates effective verbal communication directed toward the other. Piaget called attention to this apparent dependence of effective communication on role-taking skills in his early writing (1926), and also gave the relationship a developmental cast by arguing that the younger child's egocentrism seriously hampers his ability to communicate with others. Our analysis here is essentially an elaboration of his. To the extent that the child fails to discriminate those role attributes of the other which are relevant to the sort of message the child should send to the other, in the latter's role as listener, to that extent is the message likely to be ill-adapted to the other's informational needs and hence inadequately communicative. Conversely, to the extent that the child does take an accurate measure of the other's listener role attributes, and then actively uses this knowledge to shape and adapt his message accordingly, to that extent ought the communication be an effective, nonegocentric one. An important part of what is involved in effective communicating might be conceptualized as a coding-then-recoding process, in which the recoding component is 'monitored', so to speak, by role-taking activity. An ineffective, egocentric communication, on the other hand, is essentially arrested at the initial, coding step of the process. The following is a schematization of the probable microdevelopment involved in each type of communication.

Egocentric communication

1. *S* (speaker) cognizes X (data) and covertly codes them so that they are meaningful and 'communicable' to himself.

2. *S* sends *L* (listener) a message about X. The message is in all important respects unrecoded, that is, it is essentially a simple externalization without modification of his private coding and is hence an egocentric communication (see Figure 1).

Figure 1 Schema of egocentric communication

Nonegocentric communication

1. *S* cognizes X and covertly codes it for himself, just as in step 1 above.

2. Prior to and/or during his communication to *L* (step 3 below), *S* attempts to discriminate those role attributes of *L* which appear to be pertinent to *L*'s ability to decode communicative input regarding X.

3. *S* recodes X and externalizes it as a message to *L* about X. This recoding-and-externalization process occurs under the aegis of two concurrent (and

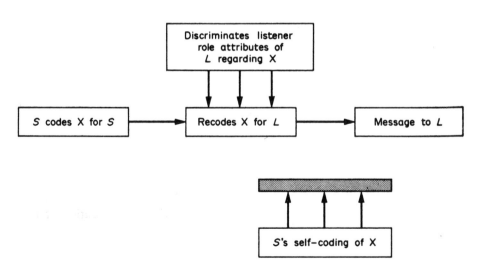

Figure 2 Schema of nonegocentric communication

related) activities: (a) S uses the information gained in step 2 to shape and fashion the message in such a way as to maximize the likelihood that it will meet L's communicative needs; (b) S actively suppresses the insistent and recurring tendency to allow his message to drift or 'regress' toward the initial coding of step 1 (the egocentric error), a tendency which exists by virtue of the fact that this initial coding is both continuously and intrusively present in S's consciousness and, by definition, is communicatively adequate for him, that is, communicatively satisfying from his point of view (see Figure 2).

The schematization just presented is of course a simplified one, and there are other important factors which qualify and complicate it. In the first place, the aim of a communicative message is not always simply to *inform* the listener, as the preceding discussion would imply. For example, some communications are intended to be *persuasive*, that is, to move the listener toward some specified course of action.

Second, the sequences of events shown in Figures 1 and 2 and described above probably do no more than approximate what happens in real-life communicative acts. In the first place, it seems likely that the major components of nonegocentric, affective communication do not really occur in a single, fixed sequence, but rather alternate and interweave in diverse ways throughout the course of the entire communicative act. For instance, after a part of the message has already been sent, the speaker may return to the data, code some hitherto unnoticed aspect, recode it, perhaps reject that recoding on the basis of a further look at the listener's role attributes, recode again, externalize this recoding as a new addition to the message, return again to the data, etc., etc. Also, the basic distinction we have made between coding for self and recoding for other may itself not always be a clear one. Zajonc (1960) has shown, for example, that if the subject is aware that the information he is coding is to be communicated later, he will tend to code it in a particular way, presumably for easier recoding when it comes time to construct his message; under these conditions, the initial coding seems already to approach a recoding, is already a kind of 'prerecoding'. Our model of egocentric communication may likewise be too simple. In particular, it may well be that the child's private and covert coding must always differ *somewhat* from its externalized expression as a message to another person, no matter how incognizant he may be of the other's role attributes, *qua* listener.[2] If this be true, the situation given in Figure 1 is best regarded as an idealized one which egocentric communications approach, but never quite reach.

There is a final qualification which is especially important to keep in mind: although it is our view that role-attribute discrimination ordinarily lends a powerful assist to the communicative process, in the manner previously des-

2 Vygotsky's (1962) interesting speculations about the differences between covert and overt coding are relevant to this point, and will be discussed in the next section of this chapter.

cribed, we do not regard it as a *sufficient* condition for the construction of an effective message nor, in certain special cases perhaps, even a *necessary* one. It cannot be a sufficient condition because there are other, what appear to be different, skills which also contribute. For example, the subject can scarcely communicate data X adequately if his perceptual and cognitive abilities are inadequate to code it properly for himself at the outset; that which cannot be discriminated can manifestly not be communicated. In the same way, an effective verbal message obviously presupposes a set of already-developed verbal skills, for example, an adequate vocabulary, and the ability to construct clear sentences and arrange them in a communicatively useful sequence. This is not to suggest that perceptual-cognitive skills, verbal skills, and the disposition and ability to discriminate role attributes comprise three distinct and noninteracting behaviour domains. Just how difficult it is to set boundary lines here will be pointed out in the next section in connection with Piaget's theory. Nonetheless, the reference to sufficient conditions here is still worth making, at least as a general principle. However frequent or rare its occurrence in reality, one can at least imagine the case where the speaker has probingly discriminated all relevant role attributes in the listener and nonetheless cannot communicate effectively because he lacks the requisite perceptual, cognitive, or verbal equipment.[3]

There is also a situation where role-attribute discrimination ought not even be necessary for effective communication, namely, where the listener role attributes of speaker and listener coincide; here, the speaker's externalized self-coding should in principle be as communicable to the listener as it is to himself. Although this situation may never quite be realized in everyday life, it certainly must be approached at times. The fact of its existence has an interesting methodological implication for research on the development of a functional liaison between role-attribute discrimination and communicative behaviour. The implication is that one can *only* detect the workings of the former on the latter in experimental situations where the role attributes of speaker and listener are certain to *differ* in some substantial way. If they do so differ, one has the possibility of distinguishing, on the basis of what the communicative product looks like, those subjects who have been attending to the listener's attributes from those who, in egocentric fashion, have not. If the two sets of role attributes are similar, on the other hand, one can make no such distinction, since there will be no inferential basis for it in the com-

---

[3] In order to keep things at a manageable level of complexity, we have been assuming a more or less constant input capacity on the listener's part. In reality, however, this capacity is, of course, another vital determinant of the success or failure of a given communication. In the example above, for instance, it may be the listener, rather than the speaker, who lacks the necessary tools to make the message successful; or conversely, his superior 'communicative receptors' may yet save the day in the case of an unendowed speaker. See Piaget (1926, ch. 3) and Fry (1961) for a more extended discussion of the listener's role in the communicative interaction.

munication protocols (that is, the one message is just as likely to be adapted to the listener's input needs as the other).

Previous theoretical contributions

Our conceptualization of role-taking and communication behaviour and development has a number of theoretical ancestors . . . Although choices here are a little arbitrary, there appear to be three individuals whose writings in this area are of particular importance: Mead, Piaget and Vygotsky. . . .

According to Mead, the fundamental human acquisition is the capacity to utilize what he calls *significant symbols* (Mead, 1947; Smith, 1946). The basic paradigm is a two-person, communicative interaction in which person A makes a gesture which B perceives (the term 'gesture' is used in the broadest possible sense to include any observable behaviour on A's part, but with special attention given to verbal communication). This gesture is a significant symbol if it calls out the same response (or the covert analogue thereof) in A that it calls out in B, that is, if A shares B's cognition—'takes his role'—with respect to that gesture. By this definition, a dog who growls menacingly at another dog is making a gesture which is not a significant symbol, since there is no reason to infer that the gesture is a stimulus for the same response in the first dog as it is for the second (for example, fear and withdrawal). Thus, meaningful human communication, entailing significant symbols:

. . . involves not only communication in the sense in which birds and animals communicate with each other, but also an arousal in the individual himself of the response which he is calling out in the other individual, a taking of the role of the other, a tendency to act as the other person acts.
(Mead, 1947, p. 183).

And again:

Gestures become significant symbols when they implicitly arouse in an individual making them the same responses which they explicitly arouse, or are supposed to arouse, in other individuals, the individuals to whom they are addressed . . :
(*ibid.*, p. 180).

Mead appears to make this process of significant symbol formation the cornerstone of the development of all behaviour which is uniquely human. Initially, the child only apprehends the attitude of particular others towards his own gestures, but gradually they coalesce for him into the attitudes which whole groups in the society possess in common, that is, into the attitudes of what Mead calls the *generalized other*:

I have pointed out, then, that there are two general stages in the full development of the self. At the first of these stages, the individual's self is constituted simply by an organization of the particular attitudes of other individuals toward himself and toward one another in the specific social acts in which he participates with them. But at the second stage in the full development of

the individual's self that self is constituted not only by an organization of these particular individual attitudes, but also by an organization of the social attitudes of the generalized other or the social group as a whole to which he belongs.
(*ibid.*, p. 186).

As this passage suggests, the formation of the self system is one of the 'uniquely human' acquisitions founded on this process. Another is effective social interaction of all types including, of course, verbal communication. Still another, but less obvious, derivation is that thinking itself is a kind of role-taking affair, involving the same basic process as other, more public and social activities. Mead describes thinking as an 'internalized conversation of gestures' and suggests that the most 'generalized' of generalized others, the reference group which includes the most members, is that defined by the 'logical universe of discourse', consisting of the community of rational thinkers (*ibid.*, p. 185).

The relevance of Mead's theory to our own conception is apparent. In the first place, he has in his notion of the significant symbol provided a rough but useful definition of intentional, deliberate communication, as distinguished from the plethora of other situations—often loosely called 'communicative'—where the behaviour of one individual is the stimulus for a response by another. And second, it is obviously relevant because of the central place accorded to communication and role taking in the development of human behaviour—the primitive situation in which the significant symbol arises, it will be recalled, is none other than a communicative one, and moreover, a communicative one in which something like role-attribute discrimination is deeply implicated. Mead's writings have thus made it difficult for all subsequent theorists, both to ignore the importance of communication processes in human development, and to ignore the importance of role taking in communicative processes.

However, one should not read more into Mead's theory than it actually asserts, and there are in fact several crucial things which one cannot readily draw from it in constructing an adequate picture of role taking and communication. It is hard to convey what the theory lacks in this respect without caricaturing it, that is, without making it appear more simplistic and oblivious to important problems than is really the case. However, the basic difficulty can be described as follows. Although the theory is, as we have shown, vitally concerned with role taking and communication, it curiously enough does *not* provide—*qua* theory—for role-taking and communication *difficulties* or *errors* in the individual performing these acts, and hence does not really deal with the developmental process by which the difficulties are gradually surmounted and the errors gradually diminished.

Although Mead, of course, acknowledges the fact of individual differences in adult attributes (1947, p. 189), his theoretical constructs (significant symbols and generalized others) are basically mechanisms for generating sameness, for creating interindividual homogeneity. Because of this, there are important interpersonal paradigms of which Mead the theorist cannot take due account. In particular, there is the situation where A and B have markedly different role attributes; here, any role taking and communication which A carries out vis-à-vis B must have a problem-solving character, if the former process is to be accurate and the latter process to be effective. That is, A must actively search out the crucial differences between his own orientation and B's and, if a communication to B is in order, use the fruits of this search in forging an informative, recoded message. By virtue of the ubiquitousness of adult differences in role attributes—momentary, situational ones as well as the more enduring, characterological ones—this kind of situation is the rule rather than the exception in adult human interactions. In consequence, accurate discrimination of role attributes and effective communication will still pose problems, will still require the utilization of certain skills, even after the incorporation of the generalized other has taken place. The question then remains, whence come these skills? Although Mead's theory has developmental aspects to it, they do not explicitly pertain to the development of *these* skills. The capacity to make use of significant symbols, for example, is indeed a developmental affair (Mead, 1947, pp. 179-182), but it appears to entail a development which is different from and prior to the one of which we speak, although obviously related to it. The two-year-old who looks at his mother, points to the household pet, and says 'Doggie' has met at least the minimal requirements for Mead's acquisition. The ten-year-old who can picture to himself how an object in front of him appears to a friend standing on the opposite side of it, and who simplifies his message when explaining something to his three-year-old brother—he is well on the way to acquiring the kind of skills we have in mind. Mead defines a significant symbol as a gesture which arouses the same response in both A and B; what he does not deal with is how A acquires the ability to discern B's qualities as a responder generally, and in particular how he acquires the ability to select those gestures which will, in fact, arouse the same response in B.

It would be redundant to present an extended discussion of Piaget's views (for example, Piaget, 1926; Flavell, 1963), since they have in large measure already been expressed in the previous section's conceptualization of role taking and communication. It is enlightening, however, to contrast them on key points with those of Mead. First, Mead took the communication situation as his theoretical point of departure and derived from it, among other things, a conception of thinking (thought is an internalized conversation of gestures, etc.). Piaget, on the other hand, drew his notions about communication from a prior analysis of cognition. As indicated earlier, he asserted that a fundamental and pervasive quality of the young child's thought is its egocentrism, consisting of a general incognizance of the notion of 'points of view', and hence a lack of awareness of how the child's own may differ from other people's. His cognitive field of vision includes the data thought about, but not the process of thinking itself. Insensitive to the very fact that the way he construes the data is only one construction among many possible (because the construing process itself never becomes an object of thought), it follows that he can scarcely check for cognitive bias in his own view of events, can scarcely inquire about the difference between this and other views, and so on. Thus, intellectual egocentrism is fundamentally an inability to take roles; it is an inability, in our terms, to search out the role attributes of others, compare them with one's own, and make effective use of the comparison in any of a variety of adaptions.

The variety of adaptations is indeed large: Piaget suggests that egocentrism taints the child's efforts in virtually all spheres of activity. For example, his primitive conceptions about the physical world (among which are animistic beliefs) are thought to be an egoncentric product (Flavell, 1963, ch. 8). In the same way, egocentrism gives rise to curious attitudes about moral-ethical phenomena (*ibid*.). And finally, it casts its shadow over the spectrum of inter-personal activities which require role-taking ability including, of course, verbal communication:

> There is no reason to believe that cognitive egocentrism, marked by unconscious preferential focusing, or by a lack of differentiation of viewpoints, has no application to the field of interpersonal relations, in particular those which are expressed in language. To take an example from adult life, every beginning instructor discovers sooner or later that his first lectures were incomprehensible because he was talking to himself, so to say, mindful only of his own point of view. He realizes only gradually and with difficulty that it is not easy to place oneself in the shoes of students who do not yet know what he knows about the subject matter of his course. (Piaget, 1962, p. 5).

It is clear from the above that Piaget also differs from Mead in attending to the disparity in role attributes which may exist between individuals, and hence to the fact that role-taking and communication situations are frequently problem-solving situations requiring considerable skill for their solution. And from this it is but a short step to the view that such skills are slowly acquired during childhood, with corresponding developmental changes in role-taking and communication behaviour. In contrast to Mead, Piaget expended both a great deal of thought and some ingenious experimentation (for example, Piaget, 1926; Piaget and Inhelder, 1956) on this developmental problem. His research evidence led him to believe that the inroads of egocentrism on communication and related interpersonal skills are especially pronounced up to the early school years:

> How then are we to characterize the stage of understanding between children before the age of 7 or 8? It is no paradox to say that at this level, understanding between children occurs only in so far as there is contact between two identical mental schemas already existing in each child . . . [in other words, in those cases which demand no role taking on the speaker's part]. In all other cases the explainer talks to the empty air. He has not, like the adult, the art

c

of seeking and finding in the other's mind some basis on which to build [in our terms, recode] anew.
(Piaget, 1926, p. 133).

After age 7-8, the child gradually rids himself of the egocentric illusion, and begins to use role-taking techniques to make his communications adaptive. The decline in egocentrism is believed to result from reinforcements—often negative ones, it appears—issuing from interactions with peers:

. . . social interaction is the principal liberating factor, particularly social
interaction with peers. In the course of his contacts (and especially, his conflicts
and arguments) with other children, the child increasingly finds himself forced
to reexamine his own percepts and concepts in the light of those of others,
and by so doing, gradually rids himself of cognitive egocentrism.
(Flavell, 1963, p. 279).

We alluded earlier to the problem of distinguishing among the various factors which contribute to the quality of a communicative message—especially, role-taking skills versus perceptual, cognitive, and linguistic ones. Piaget's conceptualization sheds some light on this difficult problem. His analysis implies that the child's role-taking deficiencies (that is, his egocentrism), may contribute to the inadequacy of the final message in two ways. First, there is the straight-forward effect we have been discussing all along, that is, these deficiencies prevent the child from assessing listener role attributes for the purpose of adapting the message to the listener's needs. Second, they are regarded as also influencing the perceptual, cognitive and linguistic factors themselves; this is the intellectual versus the social side of Piaget's egocentrism concept. According to Piaget, the fact that the child is continually a prisoner of his own point of view adversely affects his perceptual and cognitive discriminations, and also his comprehension and use of the language. Since these factors are, as we have said, of undoubted importance in shaping both the child's initial self-coding and his ability to recode, we have here a second, more indirect effect of role-taking deficiencies on the final communicative output. The causal structure here can be illustrated by a simple diagram. Figure 3 depicts the two 'routes' by which the child's generalized egocentrism could affect this output. At the top, there is its direct and concrete expression in the form of insensitivity to the listener's role attributes. The first diagonal arrow represents its contribution to deficiencies in the perceptual, cognitive and linguistic skills which, in addition to sensitivity to role attributes, are presumed necessary for the construction of an effective message (the two diagonal arrows on the right). It would be too extreme to suppose that egocentrism is the *only* factor which sets limits on these skills, hence the lower, left-hand box in the diagram. Since the origin of nonrole-taking factors in communication is not of central interest to us, we shall not try to speculate about these 'other causal variables'; presumably, they would be of the genre of insufficient practice and experience in making discriminations, in linguistic coding and recoding, and the like.

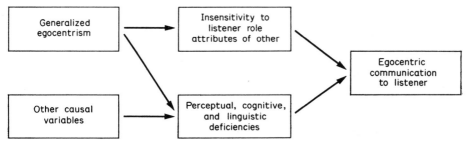

Figure 3 Causal structure of egocentric communication

If this formalization of Piaget's views is correct, it has an interesting implication for the interpretation of communication data. It makes one susceptible at once to an overestimation and an underestimation of the contributions of role-taking skills to any overt communicative product. Take the case of an inadequate communication which a child has produced in one of our task situations. These situations were deliberately constructed to highlight insensitivity to listener role attributes as a factor in such communications, and it usually seemed easy enough to infer its machinations. For example, one could often see that the child failed to say something which this particular listener needed to know, despite the fact that its inclusion in the message would *appear* not to have been beyond the child's perceptual-cognitive and linguistic capabilities. In other words, it *seemed,* at least, that he could and would have said it if *only* he had attended to the listener's informational needs, if *only* he had put himself in the listener's place. But appearances can be deceiving, and it may be that our data interpretations throughout this monograph can be justly criticized as allotting too large a causal role to this factor and too small a one to the others. We had an interpretative bias at the outset, after all, and it may have led us consistently to overestimate role-taking inadequacy. On the other hand, there is the indirect effect of egocentrism to be reckoned with (that is, on the child's perceptual, cognitive, and linguistic capabilities), the neglect of which leads to a systematic underestimation of the potency and pervasiveness of role-taking deficiency as a causal agent here. For instance, Piaget makes a persuasive case for the view that a generalized egocentrism would have to play a vital part in the child's initial self-coding of the communication's raw materials. It would seem, then, that there are interpretative hazards on either side of the midline, and that 'nothing but' arguments of both varieties— communication failure is due to 'nothing but' inadequate perceptual-cognitive-verbal equipment, or to 'nothing but' an inability to discriminate the other's listener role attributes—are bound to be off the mark.

Although Piaget assumed that the viewpoints of self and other regarding data X are apt to differ markedly (and that the egocentric child does not recognize this fact), he did not try to work out any general principles by which these differences in viewpoint could be described. In particular, he did not try to describe the typical characteristics of what we have called the communicator's initial self-coding of data X, as contrasted with its subsequent recoding in an overt, public message. Vygotsky (1962, especially ch. 7), however, did include an analysis of this problem as part of a general theoretical account of the development of language and cognition. His analysis is highly germane to our schema of communication and role taking, inasmuch as it asserts that one's private self-coding of events is a decidedly unedited, communicatively inadequate affair, and that an extensive recoding is usually necessary if it is to become an adequate, public communication. According to Vygotsky, speech in the early, preschool years is at once private and social, with no real differentiation between self-coding and coding for others. All of his speech is overt, and equally personal and public in orientation. With development, however, the two functions gradually diverge. Social, communicative speech remains overt and is presumed to become progressively elaborate and complex, as mastery of the language increases. Private speech becomes progressively covert and, as it does so, undergoes certain alterations in its formal characteristics.

It is these alterations in form which make *inner speech*, as Vygotsky calls it, an unfit vehicle for communication. In particular, it is said to become highly abbreviated and condensed, in comparison with social speech. This abbreviation and condensation is due primarily to the fact that sentence subjects tend to be discarded, leaving only predicates or pieces thereof. Thus, the inner-verbal expression of 'I guess I'll go there tomorrow' might be 'go tomorrow' or simply 'tomorrow'; since the subject of the action is already understood, the whole meaning is 'carried' by one or more parts of the predicate. As Vygotsky states it:

This tendency (predication), never found in written speech and only sometimes in oral speech, arises in inner speech always. Predication is the natural form of inner speech; psychologically, it consists of predicates only. It is as much a law of inner speech to omit subjects as it a law of written speech to contain both subjects and predicates.
(*ibid.*, p. 145).

Inner speech, then, appears to be a special type of verbal coding, largely made up of a few of what would be the 'key words' in a public utterance; it seems to be an efficient and optimally nonredundant language for communicating data to and for oneself, via a kind of 'minimal-cueing' or prompting technique. If this is really the language of self-coding, it is clear how great a linguistic metamorphosis must occur behind the scenes in a full and effective public communication. And it is also obvious why an egocentric externalization without recoding (see again Figure 1), or anything approximating it, is so unlikely to meet the listener's informational requirements. Vygotsky's conceptions, perhaps even more than Piaget's, point up the wide gulf which is liable to exist between speaker and listener, with the corollary that the everyday business of bridging this gulf in adult communication entails no mean skill.

References

Flavell, J. H., 1963. *The Developmental Psychology of Jean Piaget.* Princeton, N.J.: Van Nostrand.

Fry, C. L., 1961. The effects of training in communication and role perception on the communicative abilities of children. Unpublished doctoral dissertation, University of Rochester.

Maccoby, E. E., 1959. Role-taking in childhood and its consequences for social learning. *Child Develpm.,* [30], 239-252.

Mead, G. H., 1947. Language and the development of the self. In T. M. Newcomb and E. L. Hartley (eds), *Readings in Social Psychology,* New York: Henry Holt. Pp. 179-189.

Piaget, J., 1926. *The Language and Thought of the Child.* New York: Harcourt, Brace.

Piaget, J., 1962. Comments on Vygotsky's critical remarks concerning *The Language and Thought of the Child,* and *Judgment and Reasoning in the Child.* Attachment to L. S. Vygotsky, *Thought and Language,* Cambridge, Mass. and New York,: M.I.T. Press and Wiley.

Piaget, J., and Inhelder, B., 1956. *The Child's Conception of Space,* London: Routledge and Kegan Paul.

Sarbin, T. R., 1954. Role theory. In G. Lindzey (ed.)., *Handbook of Social Psychology,* Vol. 1. Cambridge, Mass: Addison-Wesley. Pp. 223-258.

Smith, M., 1946. Communicative behavior. *Psychol. Rev.,* [53], 294-301.

Tagiuri, R., and Petrullo, L., (eds), 1958. *Person Perception and Interpersonal Behavior.* Stanford: Stanford University Press.

Vygotsky, L. S., 1962. *Thought and Language.* Cambridge, Mass. and New York: M.I.T. Press and Wiley.

Zajonc, R. B., 1960. The process of cognitive tuning in communication. *J. Abnorm. Soc. Psychol.,* [61]), 159-167.

Stanley Coopersmith
Department of Psychology, University of California

The antecedents of self-esteem

What summary statements and conclusions can we make about the conditions associated with the development of high self-esteem? Or, more exactly, what differentiates the antecedent conditions and personal characteristics associated with the occurrence of high self-esteem from those associated with less favourable self-appraisals? The most general statement about the antecedents of self-esteem can be given in terms of three conditions: total or nearly total *acceptance* of the children by their parents, clearly defined and enforced *limits*, and the *respect* and latitude for individual action that exist within the defined limits. In effect, we can conclude that the parents of children with high self-esteem are concerned and attentive toward their children, that they structure the worlds of their children along lines they believe to be proper and appropriate, and that they permit relatively great freedom within the structures they have established. Examination of this combination of conditions reveals some general relationships between childrearing practices and the formation of self-esteem. The most notable of these deal with parental behaviour and the consequences of the rules and regulations that parents establish for their children. These relationships indicate that definite and enforced limits are associated with high rather than low self-esteem; that families which establish and maintain clearly defined limits permit *greater* rather than less deviation from conventional behaviour, and freer individual expression, than do families without such limits; that families which maintain clear limits utilize *less* drastic forms of punishment; and that the families of children with high self-esteem exert greater demands for academic performance and excellence. Taken together, these relationships indicate that, other things being equal, limits and rules are likely to have enhancing and facilitating effects and that parental performance within such limits is likely to be moderate, tolerant, and generally civilized. They suggest that parents who have definite values, who have a clear idea of what they regard as appropriate behaviour, and who are able and willing to present and enforce their beliefs are more likely to rear children who value themselves highly. Parents who can act this way apparently have less need to treat their children harshly, and, from all indications, are viewed with greater affection and respect by their offspring.

There is, of course, an underlying question about the nature and enforcement of the limits and rules espoused by the parents of children with high-esteem. Two sources of evidence lead us to believe that the limits established are reasonable, rational, and appropriate to the age of the child, and are not arbitrary and inflexible. The first basis for this belief is the consistent and marked acceptance of their offspring that these parents express. They are concerned for their welfare, are willing to exert themselves on their behalf, and are loyal sources of affection and support. They express their acceptance in a variety of ways, with expressions of interest and concern being perhaps the major underlying feature of their attitudes and behaviours. The second reason for believing that the limits are moderate and reasonable comes from our evidence concerning the parents. Our study indicates that the parents of children with high self-esteem are themselves active, poised, and relatively self-assured individuals who recognize the significance of childrearing and believe they can cope with the increased duties and responsibilities it entails. The parents generally appear to be on relatively good terms with one another and to have established clear lines of authority and responsibility. Both father and mother lead active lives outside the family and apparently do not rely upon their families as the sole or necessarily major sources of gratification and esteem. The concern that these parents show for their children, the attention they give them, and their calm, realistic, and assured demeanour lead us to believe that they would be unlikely to impose harsh or extreme restrictions, or to behave in a capricious manner; firm, clear, but extensive limits appear to be much more consistent with their personalities. There are no indications—and several contraindications—that these (high self-esteem) parents are harsh, vindictive, emotional, or power seeking. They apparently believe strongly in the validity of their perceptions and values and guide the lives of their children accordingly, yet at the same time accept and tolerate dissent within the limits that have been established.

Why well-defined limits are associated with high self-esteem can be explained in several ways. First and foremost we should note that well-defined limits provide the child with a basis for evaluating his present performance as well as facilitating comparisons with prior behaviour and attitudes. The limits serve to define the social geography by delineating areas of safety and hazards, by indicating means of attaining goals, and by pointing out the landmarks that others use to judge success and failure. When the map drawn by the parents is a realistic and accurate depiction of the goals accepted by the larger social community and the means used to reach them, it serves as a guide to the expectations, demands, and taboos of that community. As such, the map clarifies the ambiguities and inconsistencies of social behaviour and also endows such behaviour with a sense of meaning and purpose. If provided early, and accurately enough, and if it is upheld by behavioural as well as

verbal reinforcement, limit definition gives the child the conviction that there
is indeed a social reality that makes demands, provides rewards, and punishes
violations. Imposition of limits is likely to give the child, on a rudimentary
nonverbal and unconscious level, the implicit belief that a definition of the
social world is possible and that the 'real' world does indeed impose restrictions and demand compliance with its norms. On this level limits result in
differentiation between one's self and the environment and thus serve to
increase self-definition. In sum, imposition of limits serves to define the expec-,
tations of others, the norms of the group, and the point at which deviation
from them is likely to evoke positive action; enforcement of limits gives the
child a sense that norms are real and significant, contributes to self-definition,
and increases the likelihood that the child will believe that a sense of reality
is attainable.

That persons with high self-esteem come from homes notable for their
definition of limits raises the question whether persons with positive self-
attitudes are likely to be more rigid, submissive, and insensitive. In more
neutral and descriptive terms the question is whether persons reared under
clear, enforced limits are likely to comply automatically with the desires of
others, lose their initiative, and assume a pedestrian and simple way of perceiving and thinking. The issue, in effect, is whether the gains of self-esteem
that flow from definite standards may be offset by inflexible opinions, sancti-
monious convictions of personal correctness, and a closeminded insensitivity
to possibilities and alternatives. From the evidence available to us, the
response to this question would appear to be generally negative. We find that
individuals with high self-esteem who are reared under strongly structured
conditions tend to be more, rather than less, independent and more creative
than persons reared under more open and permissive conditions. From other
indications (Coopersmith, 1967) it appears that children reared within definite
limits are also more likely to be socially accepted as peers and leaders by
their associates and also more capable of expressing opinions and accepting
criticism. Thus many of the presumably negative effects of limit definition are
not supported by empirically derived evidence. Once the loaded terms and
value judgments are cast aside and specific behavioural indices are employed,
it appears that parents who are less certain and attentive of their standards are
likely to have children who are more compliant to the will of their peers and
less likely to perceive alternatives—as well as lower in self-esteem.

Psychologically, the distinctive feature of the home in which limits are
clearly defined is that the standards, information, and cues it provides are
cognitively clear. This clarity enables a child to judge for himself whether he
has attained a desired goal, made progress, or deviated. In a home where
standards are ambiguous, a child requires the assistance of others to decipher
its cues, recognize its boundaries, and understand its relationships. In the
cognitively clear world he learns to rely upon his own judgments and interpretations of events and consequences; the locus is internal and personal

rather than external and social. Detailed definition of standards, and their consistent presentation and enforcement, present the child with a wealth of information that he himself can employ to appraise and anticipate the consequences of his actions. A psychological world that provides sparse, ambiguous, or inconsistent information makes it difficult for the child to make rational decisions—that is, decisions with predictable outcomes—and increases the likelihood that he will either continually seek aid in interpreting his environment or will gradually withdraw from it: in neither case will he come to believe that he can, by himself, interpret his environment and guide himself through the thickets of its ambiguities.

Despite the benefits that they confer, would cognitively clear limits have beneficial effects upon children without the warmth and respect expressed by their parents? In more specific terms we may ask whether our results indicate that a *pattern* of conditions is necessary to produce high self-esteem, whether any single condition or set of conditions plays a greater role than others, and whether the self-esteem of the parents is invariably related to the child's self-esteem and to parental patterns of behaviour. Although our results do not permit a definitive empirical answer to all of these questions they do provide the basis for a tentative response. First, and foremost, we should note that there are virtually no parental patterns of behaviour or parental attitudes that are common to all parents of children with high self-esteem. Examination of the major indices and scales of acceptance, limit definition, respect, and parental self-esteem provides explicit support for the view that not all of these conditions are essential for the formation of high self-esteem. Thus, we find that 21.2 percent of mothers of children with high self-esteem rate low on acceptance, 12.1 percent of them do not enforce limits carefully, 19.4 percent do not believe that children should be permitted to dissent from their parent's views, and 24.3 percent are themselves rated as below average in self-esteem. The other side of this analysis—that is, examination of the attitudes and actions of parents whose children have low self-esteem—is equally revealing: 56.7 percent of them rate high on acceptance, 60.0 percent enforce definite limits, 50.0 percent tolerate dissent and expression, and 56.7 percent have high self-esteem. These findings apparently indicate that although we have established the general conditions associated with producing high self-esteem, not all of these conditions (or others) are essential to its development in any given individual nor is any single one of them sufficient to produce marked enhancement. Even though errors of measurement, scaling, and so on may contribute to the distribution of responses in any single analysis and the distributions differ for different analyses, it nonetheless appears that the apparent basic conditions of parental treatment and personal characteristics are not individually necessary nor sufficient to produce high self-esteem. This would suggest that combinations of conditions are required—more than one but less than the four established by this study (acceptance, limit definition, respect, and parental self-esteem). In addition it is likely that a minimum of devaluating conditions—that is, rejection, ambiguity, and disrespect—is required if high self-esteem is to be attained.

At least in theory, two combinations are likely to occur with considerable frequency: high parental self-esteem is likely to be associated with acceptance; firm limit definition is likely to be found in concert with respect for individual expression. The rationale for the relationship between high parental self-esteem, acceptance, and the child's high self-esteem stems from the findings of other investigators of the process of identification (Bateson, 1944; Sears, 1957; Whiting, 1954). Their general conclusion appears to be that the child's identification with his parents is markedly increased and to a great extent derives from parental acceptance. A close affective tie apparently establishes the desire to emulate, and also the likelihood that parentally approved behaviours will be expressed. In effect, the child is more likely to follow in the footsteps of his parents and accede to their desires if they indicate their approval of him than if they disapprove of him and treat him in a punitive, rejecting manner. Doll play, used as an index of underlying attitudes, reveals that parental nurturance is positively associated with preference for adult dolls (Levin, 1952) : a child is less likely to adopt an adult role when he is physically punished or rejected. Studies of institutionally reared children (Goldfarb, 1945; Bowlby, 1951) suggest that persons who have not had a history of nurturant experience with a parental figure tend to be socially immature and shallow in their emotional responses. Our own results indicate that children with high self-esteem are more likely than others to be close to their parents, to confide in them, to respond to the punishments they administer, to be socially skilled and emotionally responsive. This leads us to the initial conclusion that, to the extent that identification plays a role in the formation of self-esteem, children with high self-esteem are more likely to identify, as well as more likely to have a favourable model with which to identify.

The second suggestion—that clear, enforced limits are related to respect for individual expression—stems from the observation that openly expressed rules and restraints provide a framework for discussion and hence require less supervision and restriction. From a purely structural viewpoint, rules that are fixed and accepted make it possible, although not certain, that persons exercising authority will be less concerned and threatened by differences of opinion. If such rules of conduct do not exist, persons in authority are more likely to consider that differences of opinion threaten their position. An external code of specified practices and rights that is enforced provides those governed by it with at least some degree of assurance against arbitrary actions and also permits those who exercise authority to be more casual in their treatment of dissent; it engenders a more relaxed attitude for those who must administer social organizations as well as for those who must live within them.

The relation between parental self-esteem and the child's self-esteem indicates that unconscious identification and conscious modeling may well underlie the self-evaluations of many individuals. These processes need not contribute equally to the history of each person but there does appear to be a general relationship between the parents' self-esteem and the manner in which he treats his children. Parents with high self-esteem are generally more accepting of others, decisive, inclined to lead active personal lives, and convinced of their powers. They presumably have less need to gain vicarious successes from the accomplishments of their children and are able to provide their children with a definite idea of what they expect and desire. The parent with low self-esteem who is accepting of his child may provide a negative model for esteem building but at the same time the pattern of his actions may well lead the child to a higher level of self-appraisal than he has himself attained. The combination of a high self-esteem model and an enhancing pattern of treatment should provide the highest and most stable levels of positive self-evaluation. Some recent attempts to modify the antisocial actions of adolescents suggest that an effective, rewarding model establishes the motivation for change and provides the specific cues for desirable action patterns.

References

Bateson, G., 1944. Cultural Determinants of Personality. In J. McVickers Hunt (ed.)., *Personality and the Behavior Disorders,* Vol. 11, New York: Ronald Press.

Bowlby, J., 1951. *Maternal Care and Mental Health.* World Health Organization Monograph No. 2.

Coopersmith, S., 1967. *The Antecedents of Self Esteem.* W. H. Freeman & Co.

Goldfarb, W., 1945. Psychological privation in infancy and subsequent adjustment, *Am. J. Orthopsychiatry,* [15]), 247-225.

Levin, H., 1952. Permissive child rearing and adult role behavior in children. Paper delivered at Eastern Psychological Association, Atlantic City, March 28.

Sears, R. R., 1957. Identification as a form of behavioral development. In D. B. Harris (ed.), *The Concept of Development,* Minneapolis: University of Minnesota Press.

Whiting, J. W., 1954. (Symposium Paper) in J. M. Tanner and B. Inhelder (eds), *Discussions on Child Development II.,* New York: International Universities Press.

David D. Franks
Department of Sociology, University of Denver

Current conceptions of competency motivation and self-validation

---

This is an original article prepared especially for this reader. D.F.

I

More than a decade ago Dennis Wrong pointed a crook'd finger at sociologists for painting an oversocialized view of man (1961). Evidence that Wrong's statement indeed struck a responsive chord among American sociologists can be seen in the frequency with which his article appears in edited readers and footnotes in professional journals. The implicit recognition of his point has not been matched, however, by attempts to remedy the problem—at least not in the context posed by Wrong.

Wrong's criticism focused on how sociological explanations had developed since their original attempts to explain the problem of social order. These explanations existed on two levels: the societal and the social psychological, though problems in their explanatory power were of course inter-related. Marx illustrated the first level of explanation asking how societies regulated potentially destructive conflicts between groups. On the social psychological level it was Hobbes who had first phrased the problem of order with maximum clarity: given man's propensity towards unpredictability, violence and deceit, how is he nonetheless so amenable to the influence of social norms and commonly held values? Why, instead of a 'war of all against all', is there as much regularity and consensus in society as there is? Durkheim had viewed the structural question of order, first answered by Marx, as calling for an identification of 'the sources of social cohesion', whereas the problem at the Hobbesian level was essentially: how is it that man becomes tractable to social discipline? Wrong felt that sociology has an *overintegrated* view of society in its answer to the question on the structural level and an *oversocialized* view of man in its answer on the social psychological level. (Wrong, 1961: 123). The present article follows Wrong's in its concentration on the oversocialized dimension of the problem.

The first social psychological motif to come under Wrong's attack was a simplistic view of the socialization process as a rote internalization of culturally given norms. One difficulty with this conceptualization revolved around the way rules were perceived by the actor being socialized. Thus norms were not perceived as external obstacles in the environment constraining him to conform against his own desires, but rather goals and values exhibited by the outside culture became absorbed into the very psychic constitution of the actor and indeed became *self* imposed. Internalization as the key mechanism of socialization left the individual as an empty vessel whose only relevant substance was what his culture poured into him through this process. Wrong's criticism is certainly well taken, at least for a significant number of cases. For example, Ruth Benedict's brilliant little book, *Patterns of Culture*, dealt a telling blow to the notion of a substantive *a priori* human nature. She described the amazingly wide varieties of cultural forms into which men could be successfully socialized. This view of man as a blank tablet on which culture impressed its substance was further fortified by interpretations of the Sapir-Whorf hypothesis in which even one's private perceptions of the world were seen as being determined by the grammatical rules of his language (Whorf, 1956). Rather than seeing social behavior as a result of the interaction between factors having their source in our physical heritage and factors having their source in culture 'sui generis', emphasis lay on culture alone. Men could be socialized to accept any way of life since there was nothing outside of culture to allow a strain between its dictates and a dubious, if not recalcitrant, human being. If a social system, as it was presently constructed, needed warriors and slaves, men willing to be warriors and slaves were created by that system's socialization process. Regularity in social life was thus assured by the theory.[1] Non-conformists were the result of an abnormality of some type since a normal socialization process guaranteed willing incorporation of societal norms. There was no way in this picture that a respectably normal man could at the same time be significantly deviant.

The implicit model of motivation shared by a significant number of sociologists was the second motif identified by Wrong as producing a view of man incapable of explaining the disorder that nonetheless existed in society: man conforms to normative expectations because of his deep desire to win the approval of others. Here he cites Hans Zetterberg who offered the following hypothesis as a strong contender for the major motivational theorem in sociology:

An actor's actions have a tendency to become dispositions that are related to the occurrence of favoured uniform evaluations of the actor and/or his actions in his social system. (1957:188).

[1] Actually Wrong was arguing that we had forgotten the original question (the problem of order) since the answers given made everything *but* order seem inconceivable. What is often ignored by readers of Wrong's article is his insistence that sociological answers never completely solve the questions . . . that packed into our answer to the problem of social order should be also an answer to how disruption can occur. Thus Wrong points admiringly to the *dialectic* thread in Thomas Hobbes' answer to the problem while—as sociologists must—he rejects the content of the answer. Nonetheless, 'the war of all against all is not simply effaced with the creation of political authority: it remains an ever-present potentiality in human society, at times quiescent, at times erupting into open violence.' (1961:124) The whole tenor of his thought is to see the war of all against all and Leviathan dialectically, as coexisting and interacting opposites.

The generalized import of this theorem, at least in Zetterberg's mind, is illustrated by his statement that 'the maximization of favourable attitudes from others would thus be the counterpart in sociological theory to the maximization of profit in economic theory' (as quoted in Wrong, 1961: 128). Wrong questions whether people are so profoundly sensitive to the expectations of others that action is inevitably guided by these expectations.

Certainly both motifs are partially valid; both point to significant phenomena involved in the achievement of social order—to the extent that such order does exist. The core of the disagreement revolves around the nature of the facts to be explained. To sociologists who take as fact that one can deviate from the culturally prescribed norms and yet not be abnormal, the oversocialized theories are of insufficient generality for they simply cannot explain such phenomenon. As a matter of fact one has difficulty in conceiving how disorder comes about at all, and in explaining the problem of order *too well* they are incapable of explaining the disorder that does in fact exist without resorting to some model of abnormality. What is needed is a motivational model that explains more adequately why some men ignore—at least in their behaviour—the responses of others to them.

Frequently this is explained by difficulties involved in the role-taking process and no room is left for the person who role-takes correctly—who recognizes that people will disapprove of his behaviour and for other reasons (not satisfactorily specified in the theory) go their own way regardless. On the other hand the motivational theory emphasizing as it does the importance of the approval of others to the individual self, stands non-plussed when faced with the fact that some people, though highly validated consistently by various reference groups, nonetheless feel painful doubts regarding their own self worth. The frequently recorded phenomena of people committing suicide at the virtual pinnacle of their career is swept under the carpet with a deft left hand since it threatens the theory with serious embarrassment.

It seems timely then to continue in the direction that Wrong pointed by identifying certain concepts that would be useful in describing a view of man in which the animal has substance, which enables him to stand, if you will, over against his socialization process and over against the opinions of his fellow man—enabling 'the individual always (to) seek to preserve a part of himself from the intrusions of society.' (See Stone and Farberman, 1970: 14).[2]

---

[2] In the volume cited above, Stone and Farberman offer four frameworks in sociology that can avoid Wrong's charge: (1) Mead's 'I'; (2) Sullivan's parataxic distortion; (3) Goffman's role distance, and (4) human intention and value. The first will hardly be acceptable to those of an empirical bent as will be discussed later. The second carries the connotation of abnormality which is just what Wrong is attempting to avoid in his insistence on the dialectic. It is *normal* for man to be less than completely socialized! (Becker, 1965: 112 and Wrong, 1961: 131) Goffman emphatically does not deal with the man behind the mask (for an exception see the tragic quote, Goffman, 1961: 235). Role distance is achieved by bringing in another role—the discussion never gets to the substantial man beyond it. The present article will broach part of the last alternative—that of intentions. (See Franks, 1972 for a more detailed discussion of these points.)

Understanding of the present state of affairs in sociology, however, may be enriched if consideration is first given to some factors that prevented a more active substantial man from entering the social psychological scene in an effective way. For good reason, Wrong could not turn to the social psychology distinctive of his own discipline when trying to repair the inadequacies that he saw its model of man. Strauss, (1959) Blumer, (1969) Turner, (1962) and other current symbolic interactionists[3] energetically criticize structural sociology for their passive view of man as simply being the result of norms and other external forces. However, on close inspection the framework, as it is usually presented today, exhibits a strange ambivalence in its portrayal of man: at once active, but only ethereally so, individual (insofar as the 'I' is concerned) but lacking a substantial individuality of his own to pit against the 'stings and arrows' of the reflected appraisals of others. It is to an analysis of action in this framework we shall now turn.

II

The stimuli given off by one's external environment are so enormous that any attempt to impartially attend to all of it would be impossible. Clear and meaningful perception depends on blocking out or minimizing those sensations that are not relevant for our subjective purposes. Not to do so would be to lack concentration—to be distracted. Thus a commonly held tenet in social psychology is that all perception is selective. From this position an important question emerges: by what criterion does the organism determine what is relevant and/or irrelevant? The question is critical because this process lies at the very base of the theory of perception. The answer in the framework of symbolic interaction, is found in *action*. According to George Herbert Mead, perception—indeed cognition and meaning itself, is built up—constructed—in the act. The initiation of an act is the impulse. Persons who are hungry see things in terms of food; persons who are angry themselves, interpret even kindly gestures as malevolent. ('He's trying to manipulate me.') One does not perceive and then act, rather one's action interests function as a spotlight in the intellectual darkness offered by a sea of almost infinite stimuli. This spotlight brings certain attributes of objects into focus, leaves others on a dim periphery, and leaves stimuli irrelevant to a particular impulse shut out in total blackness. Because of this selective process, objects as perceived by humans are not offered by nature alone, but are partially created out of something initiated by the actor himself—his particular impulse to act. Perception

3 Symbolic interaction is a perspective that has developed from a distinctly sociological frame of reference. It was given telling impetus in the United States by G. H. Mead aided by other American pragmatists such as Dewey and James. Social psychology, placed as it is between disciplines, tends to be handled differently depending on whether it comes from a psychological or sociological framework. Though sociologists differ in the mode of social psychology they find useful, there can be little quarrel that symbolic interaction is derived from a distinctively sociological perspective.

then is transactional in the sense that its source lies in the action intent of the individual as much as the properties inherent in environmental stimuli. In the pragmatic tradition informing the framework of symbolic interaction, the actor himself was firmly implanted in the process of perception. 'The animal is thus not a passive robot merely reacting to the environment of stimuli . . . so much as he has an impulse to act that influences which stimuli in his environment come to his attention.' (McCall and Simmons, 1966). Action in this scheme is paramount. Perception, human cognition and/or meaning, subserve action, not the other way around. Concepts and percepts clear the way for effective action. Thus action is the beginning and end of the scheme. The viewpoint remains truly transactional, however, despite the emphasis on the actor himself and the creative nature of the process. In his discussion of the universal, Mead accepted the assumption that stimuli existed independently of humanly constructed meanings and that there were outside limits as to what could be successfully worked into any action impulse (Mead, 1934).

The creative aspect of the process is seen most clearly in the symbolic construction of social objects having no determinant physical structure, e.g., school grades, kinship and occupational positions, academic degrees, days of the week, etc. Sounds available to our senses may act as vehicles to communicate these meanings but the meanings themselves are independent of physically determined stimuli and the senses. No one seriously asks what 'Tuesday' smells, tastes, looks or feels like. Such 'objectifications' are symbolically constructed and only exist in a specifiable 'universe of discourse', i.e., through a shared matrix of communicated meanings. Even symbolically given concepts, however, are seen not as coming from the heavens detached from human activities, but as born in human interaction and moulded by the action interests of the group.

In summaries of symbolic interaction (see for example Rose, 1962; Manis and Meltzer, 1967; Blumer, 1969) the interpretive nature of human perception is stressed as a key emphasis in the perspective. This point becomes even more crucial when interactionists stress that the distinguishing feature of human life is that the person becomes a self-conscious object to himself allowing social rather than biological directives to his behaviour. This process of self-perception is as creative and interpretive then as any of those described above and the place of action is just as critical. This allows Herbert Blumer, for example, to make one of his most noteworthy points: Man is more than the passive result of forces lodged in the makeup of society conceived in terms of social structure, collective representations, and social situations. Man is constantly interpreting rather than reacting to these forces. Social structure, according to a significant number of symbolic interactionists, is advisory, not determinant. In Blumer's terms, 'the human being stands over against the world, or against alters, with such a process and not with mere ego,' (Blumer, 1969: 81).

Suffice it to say that action and its corollary—creativity—is crucial to the framework presented here. If the environment perceived by the actor is sickled over by the action impulses of the individual, and if the very creation of meaning is placed in the act itself, then one would expect an appropriate amount of attention be given to the queries—what is the source of these all important impulses that operate as the first stage of the act? What makes the human individual creative in the sense that he manipulates and constructs his world according to his purposes? If he is not a passive reactor, what is it that he brings to his world in order to transact with it? However, we find that answers to these questions are unsatisfactory. The result of this gap in the theory is that its view of sources of self-validation becomes the epitomy of the oversocialized, other directed, model of motivation articulated by Wrong.[4]

When initiating dialogues on the subject of motivation, Symbolic Interactionists frequently feel that they must wipe away any attempt to seek explanations *inside* the physiological makeup of the individual as irrelevant to social action. (See Stone and Farberman, 1970: 467). Man is regarded as active naturally—as Dewey asserts—and any attempt to explain this is unnecessary. The strategy behind this is clear enough even if the justification is not: if questions concerning the *inner* well-spring of action in man can be explained away as simply 'in his nature' then attention is free to roam into the realm of external processes of social interaction—motives become solely socially derived 'linguistic designations of intents' moving interaction forward by providing the necessary clues to keep actors cued in to each others' lines of action. Substantial—extra linguistic man—is written off by assertion. His body gives nothing but random action impulses pulled into sensible lines by other persons who insist that he have specific motives. This enables other actors to role-take with him enabling them to generate a meaningful response. There is little doubt that such a framework operates well in analysing co-operative joint action where a premium is placed on sensitivity to others. The point is that by limiting the study of motives to situated, particular motive *statements,* other factors involved in social action that are *not* keyed necessarily to cooperativeness are left outside of the focus.

Once the symbolic interaction framework has diverted attention away from an intrinsic well-spring of action it is hardly surprising that an oversocialized model of man follows. All that is relevant in regard to motivation has its

---

4 This has the great advantage, as Becker has seen, in easing our 'liberal' consciences while our social institutions determine more and more what man should be; for no compelling directives outside of the needs of the organization itself can be brought to bear on their activities . . . not while man remains an illusion—a totally pliable creature who has no significant substance and separability from the reflected appraisals of others. The argument here is not for unbridled concern over individual wants but a strain—a dialectic balance between what is good for man and what is necessary for the maintenance of *his* institutions. If the ideological bias here is evident as it should be, it is also evident in the oversocialized model of man still current in American sociology, for it doggedly ignores available fact and theory (Becker, 1964).

source in the social structure. Blumer's words not withstanding, a picture is created wherein there is no private dimension to motivation which is, in part at least, autonomous from society. How then can man, in terms of motivation, 'stand against his world and other alters'? Furthermore, the position is not founded on empirical grounds but by quoting a mere assertion: according to Dewey 'man is active by nature and that is all to be said on that score!' There is a great deal more to be said on this score which besides being founded on a host of experimental evidence and observations from numerous frameworks has the function of escaping the problems of the oversocialized view of man in the symbolic interactionist perspective on motivation.

For Mead, self was directly rooted in otherness. The individual self emerged as the child obtained a reflexive perspective on his own action through imaginatively taking the role of others in monitoring his own behaviour. This process of social control was at the same time a process of self-construction. In order for conjoint interaction to emerge, one had to invest (nearly) the same meanings on his own behaviour as did others. Thus self (or more precicsely, self-consciousness was merely linguistic. Since self emerged out of communicative acts a mechanism was needed to connect the self with the active dimension of experience. Mead saw this as the 'I'. Thinking was an internal conversation between the 'I' and the 'me' seen as distinct phases of this inner communication. Whatever the vagaries attached to the 'I', it was in theory connected with active impulse, creativity, change and unpredictableness. The 'me' was seen as those perspectives on one's self learned from others' responses toward the actor. Derived as it is from the responses of others, the 'me' is in theory observable. The 'I' is the knower, the 'me' the object as known.

If there is agreement in the field about the origin of the 'me' in the reflected appraisals of others, there is a striking disagreement in regard to the 'I'.[5] Such disagreement is perhaps a function of the metaphysical nature of the concept. Regardless, the point is clear: if autonomy, spontaneity and creativity belong to the 'I', and if there is so much disagreement in regard to its nature,

[5] Stone and Farberman quote Mead as stating the 'me' is a 'me' which was an 'I' at an earlier time. Mead himself in other places warned against a time sequence approach. Observing the 'I' is impossible, even to the actor, since the know*er* when observed *becomes* the known. It is like trying to catch oneself falling asleep—impossible by definition. As Weigart argues (1970), 'If we have no way of knowing the self as "I", how can we know that a later "me" was in fact an earlier "I".' McCall and Simmons warn against a time series model arising when one thinks of the inner conversation as 'a simple dialogue between something called the "I" and something called the "me".' . . . ordinarily, one's mind is reacting to what one is saying or thinking *as one is saying or thinking it.* Finally, Rose (1962) opts for the 'I' as *self-conception* built up on the individual 'me's. He also sees in the 'I' a creative thrust independent of one's environment. The 'I' comprises attitudes assigned by the individual to himself, not necessarily expected in the culture. The disagreement about the 'I' should be evident in these selected examples.

the active component of man as an important part of the theory is decidedly weakened.

Kolb, a writer sympathetic with the Meadian tradition, argues that Mead clearly specifies the nature of the 'me' but in effect labels the 'I' as simply the 'not me' aspect of the self (Kolb, 1967). A residual category cannot be expected to become a compelling part of a theory to scholars at large.

In any event, Mead seemed to recognize that there was a creative spontaneous push to man. He took *as fact* that man was naturally like this analytically prior to and independent of socialization. The 'I' was brought into the analytic framework to describe, not explain this. Though it was on the periphery of the spotlight cast by the framework, he obviously thought it was too consequential to ignore. But the 'I' remained simply descriptive— a stop-gap term in his theory to keep something in that was important to an accurate view of man with adequate generality.

When one explains the source of an impulse to action as the 'I' he has indulged in a game of words rather than empirical explanation. Since the framework has not offered empirical researchers an operational definition of the 'I', concepts making up their tested hypotheses must focus on the 'me', or the passive factors involved in the self. Regardless of its descriptive assumptions regarding the 'I' and Blumer's remarks about creativity, such a theory leaves only one source of self-validation on the empirical level: the reflected appraisals of others. Ironically, then, in practice, symbolic interaction research lies squarely in the camp of the oversocialized view of motivation portrayed by Wrong. Wrong's plea for a reversal in the field of what he refers to as an oversocialized view of man has, I think, simply remained a plea (albeit with a great deal of support from the field) that has not as yet become translated into empirical research because concepts needed to guide such research are lacking.

III

In this section I will argue that Robert White's conception of *Competency Motivation* should be seriously considered by sociologists as providing a forward thrust—indeed an intentionality—independent of language acquisition emanating from factors inherent in the mammalian heritage of man yet not reducible to fixed drives resulting from physiological tissue deficits. Furthermore, it provides a dimension to self-development and maintenance that is separable from consensual validations of others and allows for a realm of autonomy from the looking glass self of modern sociology. This results in a man of substance with a nature that can either be violated or nurtured by his social institutions. Without appealing to dogmatic assertion or an essentially non-empirical rhetoric, it can replace Mead's 'I' as an explanation on a general level for the manipulative exploratory thrust behind action impulses. Firmly embedded in a psychological framework of the autonomously functioning ego[6] the concept is congruent with self-conscious, purposeful action and at the same time preserve the spontaneous, creative character of man captured in the 'I'.

White (1963) presents the interesting proposal that if one were to ask any reasonably reflective person to tell us what kind of experiences would seriously threaten his self-esteem, he would most likely describe some combination of (1) failure in his own actions, and (2) fall in the esteem of other people. We would not expect informants, he says, to reject one source altogether but we would expect variations in replies.[7] Perhaps White's quote (1963) from Silverberg express this idea most concisely:

> Throughout life self-esteem has two sources: an inner source, the degree of effectiveness of one's own aggression; and an external source, the opinions of others about oneself. Both are important, but the former is the steadier and more dependable one; the latter is alway more uncertain. Unhappy and insecure is the man who, lacking an adequate inner source for self-esteem, must depend for this almost wholly upon external sources. It is the condition seen by the psychotherapist almost universally among his patients. (Silverberg, 1952:29).

'The effectiveness of one's own aggression' is taken very broadly here as the intentions of the ego to affect a certain consequence on the world. A truly interactive theory of self-evaluation will emphasize these two sources of self-esteem. Inner self-esteem is gained from successfully manipulating an impartial environment through our own efficacious actions, be it on a social or physical level. Intention and action are the crucial elements here, *not* which type of environment is involved. Inner self-esteem is not a random, but an earned validation. Knowledge (including knowledge on one's own competence) is pragmatic at this point in the sense that it is gained through the 'several consequences of our several actions'. It is a knowledge of action possibilities, i.e., what can I do to make such and such happen? (See White, 1965: 200-201). Inner validation does not necessarily come from the praise of others but

---

[6] Similar to Mead's 'I', Competency Motivation can only explain the general source of a generalized push into action. Neither concept explains why one has one specific action impulse rather than another. Important to the character of spontaneity and creativity that informs a truly active model of man, is the autonomy of the impulse from the fixed drives of sex, hunger, thirst, elimination, and sleep that are physiologically determined. Unlike the traditional learning theory model that sees all behaviour as reducible to drives, Ego psychology postulates a realm of ego that transcends these drives. Both Mead's 'I' and White's Competency Motivation assume such an autonomously functioning ego structure.

[7] Throughout this section I have borrowed extensively from White since the purpose is mainly to accurately describe his concept rather than emphasize my own points. The following sources have been used and may provide a useful directive for the interested student: White, 1959, 1960 and 1963. A provocative application of competency motivation to the field of mental health appears in Smith (1968). An application to schizophrenia in particular, was made by White himself (1965).

from the actor's own assessment of how the consequences of his actions mesh with his intents. A person whose goal is to kick a football 65 yards with a perfect spiral only gets his intentions confirmed if he hits it correctly. The validation is in the consequences of his actions and no other person need give him applause. Not *necessarily*, that is! The saliency of this 'non-social' validation depends greatly on his balance on one side of the inner-outer pole of self-esteem. For some people, as Silverberg points out, satisfaction is minimized unless an audience is there to give acclaim.

In the pure case, outer self-esteem is validation by others, that is independent of our intents and purposes. It is not earned by a specific action. Unqualified mother-love is a case in point. People who validate our specific actions in an ingratiating way because of a powerful position achieved some time ago, are manipulating us rather than giving feedback because of our intents. Such validation—if it is perceived as such at all—would be mostly outer. The important point is that the term 'outer' does not mean simply social—it means validation given outside of our intents—not earned.[8] In the child as well as the adult effects produced without focalized attention, intention and directed effort are simply experienced in a different way from results that are not the consequences of our intended actions. The person who obtains praise that simply 'happens to him' does not feel these consequences as products of himself as effective agent. The feeling of self as an executive agent in the world must come from the inner pole of self-esteem (White, 1965: 203).

Whether a person is balanced on one side or the other may well be affected by the social environment of the actor according to White. He quotes, for example, the 'marketing orientation' described by Fromm with its vast impersonal markets, machine production, and business organizations which tends to shift the basis of self-esteem away from what one accomplishes objectively and toward how well one sells himself in the estimation of others. Much of this may depend on chance factors outside of the actor's control and his intents may give in to what just happens to result in positive responses from others. Certainly bureaucracies, insofar as some of them tend towards appearance rather than task orientation, may encourage emphasis on outer

---

[8] Both sources of self-esteem are needed by the child if he is to achieve optimum self-esteem (which few of us do). A balance of unqualified love and earned love is probably best for the child. White makes the point, however, that early self-esteem is usually dealt with as if it were wholly a question of how one is treated by other people. This is only true for outer self-esteem. The picture must be balanced by inner self-esteem which is truly interactional. 'A placid child who has always achieved generous narcissistic supplies, without doing much to earn them will enjoy an agreeable level of self-esteem, provided he never enters a harsher environment. Self-esteem will be more substantial, however, in the more active child who feels confident that he can elicit esteem from others by competent performances . . . ' (White, 1965: 201). The second child could have the benefit of both sources of self-esteem and be less at the mercy of his surroundings. In this view love is very important but not enough for the development of adequate ego strength. This presumably holds for the adult as well.

self-esteem.[9] Inner self-esteem is a derivative of Robert White's concept of competency motivation (1959, 1963). One advantage of White's proposal not shared by Mead's 'I' is that he used research evidence to argue against the passive model of man inherent in the established motivational models of his time.

White introduces his concept by pointing out that two very distinct fields—psychoanalytic ego psychology and animal psychology—were experiencing difficulty in fitting certain observed data into their homeostasis model. Both in human infants and other mammals, when all drives were satiated, when no 'tissue deficit' was there to propel them into action, they consistently *sought* new stimuli instead of basking in their temporary state of homeostasis. In addition the new stimulus was manipulated and explored in a way that produced learning. Without the necessary conditions postulated by drive theory the mammals (from rats to human children) clearly demonstrated the observable criteria for complex motivated behaviour, i.e., focus, intention and directed effort. Furthermore, the manipulatory behaviour—doing something *to* the environment, producing effects upon it and changes in it—seemed in many experiments to stand out as a reward in its own right. Chimpanzees, when faced with various play objects simultaneously, select those that lend themselves to manipulation, e.g., moved, changed, made to emit sounds, etc. No external stimuli producing a tissue deficit were needed to initiate the action and no external reward was needed to produce the behaviour. Both stimuli and reward were intrinsic in the makeup of the animal. Numerous studies and statements of researchers were used by White as evidence for his point (1959).

He then clarifies the significance of this for evolutionary theory. In organisms such as fish and insects, in which any given pair of individuals is capable of producing many millions of offspring in the course of their lifetime, there is an inevitability that at least one pair will survive out of the mass of babies produced. As we move to mammals and especially primates, the size of the production is sharply decreased and consequently much more depends on particular species members surviving. For each organism then, a premium is

9 One could think that a focus on being successful through pleasing others takes a certain degree of competency and this is probably true. One can find pure cases of inner and outer sources of self-esteem, but usually a continuum model fits the picture better— there is a combination of both with a balance on one side or the other. In pleasing others, the *focus*, however, shifts from being based mostly on the task one is attempting to achieve. Here, one will change his intents to obtain a gratifying response. This is very different from the person who makes pleasing people a subsidiary means to achieving his own intents. Winning the acceptance of others as an end in itself or as a means to an end are two different things. It is not a matter of 'either-or' but one of emphasis. An extreme emphasis on pleasing others places the locus of control outside of oneself and the feeling of self as agency is lost. In the outer directed person, if people reject him all is lost. The person buttressed with inner and outer self-esteem can survive the pain of rejection because he still has a sense of agency.

placed on learning to control the environment. They cannot forever be in a position of simple reactors, they must be in a context of *transaction* with their environment. This implies a measure of economy for each member; he cannot separately carry out a pre-established reactive pattern but must be able to produce new ones as the situations demand. Survival on this level no longer depends on chance and large numbers; it depends on a special kind of flexibility in learning and integration of learning relative to the physical properties of the environment. This results in a significant amount of control over it. Ability to produce offspring en masse is superseded by the ability of a few offspring to develop competency.

Basing his argument on experimental evidence from animal studies (corroborated by observational studies of children) and supported by evolutionary theory, White posits a type of motivation independent of drives manifesting itself in transactions with the environment. The result is a cumulative and broad knowledge about the nature of the environment and the organism's current and potential effectiveness on it. To distinguish this from drive theory he gave it the label 'effectence motivation'. If the homeostasis model proved insufficient to account for observed motivated behaviour on the part of higher animals when their drives were satiated, it is similarly insufficient for the accurate description of human infants and not less than drastically inappropriate for a broad description of the symbolic behaviour.

IV

Thinkers have long been sensitive to the interactive nature of the self on the two levels of action and thought. Ernest Becker (1965) has expressed this with clarity in his article on the convergence of C. W. Mills and Marx on the problem of alienation. Here he quotes Mills' use of Pierce: 'The realities of the world and the capacities of our own bodies are learned together; both come to us in terms of resistance and mastery, limitation and capacity.' And again, 'Consciousness proceeds on two spheres to make contact with the world and two kinds of human powers are brought into the plan: active organismic powers and more passive cognitive powers'. Baldwin is also seen by Becker as 'postulating that the sense of dualism of mind and body is something that develops as the child learns that he has an inside—a thought process—that is separate from the outer world of things'. Like White, Becker recognizes a difference between the self created by exercising his own powers, and that self image which is gained merely through reflected appraisal. A firm self is built up on both poles—inner and outer. The point is that there is a developmental psychic structure (portrayed by White) that exists prior to the self portrayed by Mead and later symbolic interactionists.

It is important that interactionists see a separation of knowledge and language on some level—especially with the infant. Apes can pile boxes together to reach an overhanging banana without resorting to simple trial and error in the arrangement of their boxes. The ape is able to solve problems 'in his head' and guide his overt behaviour by his *conceived* plan (White, 1959). Certainly Piaget's work indicates the same thing in babies prior to their acquisition of language:

When a 2-month-old baby sucks his thumb this cannot be called an intentional act because the coordination of the hand and of sucking is simple and direct. It therefore suffices for their child to maintain, by circular reaction, the favourable movements which satisfy his need, in order that this behaviour become habitual. On the other hand, when an 8-month-old child sets aside an obstacle in order to attain an objective, it is possible to call this intention, because the need set in motion by the stimulus of the act (by the object to be grasped) is only satisfied after a more or less lengthy series of intermediary acts (the obstacles to be set aside). Intention is thus determined by con-sciousness of desire, or of the direction of the act, this awareness being itself a function of the number of intermediary actions necessitated by the principal act.
(Piaget, 1963:147-8).

This early connection between intents, action, consequences and knowledge is crucial. Groos in 1901 perhaps summed up best the research of later workers in his classical analysis of play when he attached great importance to what he called the child's '*joy in being a cause*'. We 'demand a knowledge of effects,' he wrote, 'and to be ourselves the producers of effects. (Quoted in White, 1959: 316).

Current research has yet to uncover the intricate relationships that no doubt exist between inner self-esteem and validations that have their source in the responses of others to us independent of our intents. That the two types of validation are related but separate stems from the difference in their source. It seems reasonable, however, to suggest that competency motivation is not so automatically built into the human mammal that it cannot be submerged by pressures in the social environment. The experience of efficacy must remain the result of a transaction with the social environment.

V

To date, symbolic interactionists hesitate to address the substantial dimension of self built up through intentional action. When they deal with child development one wonders what was there in the first place to be socialized. Since babies cannot be totally overlooked by the interactionist, the very *least* is granted—random impulse only. We have seen that this is not true. Human babies as well as other mammals show behaviour characterized by consistency, direction and consummation long before the internalization of externally given symbols. Motivation, i.e., the tendency toward intentful action, comes *with* the mammal by virtue of being a mammal. Certainly the acquisition of language is necessary in order to develop distinctly human motives but motivational substance is there prior to socialization into significant symbols. The origin of inner self-esteem lies here. Rather than being replaced by symbolically given responses of others it is overlayed by the socially derived evaluations. What symbolic interaction has overlooked is the importance of the dialectic on the presocialization level and its dimension of independence from 'the looking glass self' originating in others. No 'other' has to teach a baby to enjoy causing things to happen—to be an effect—this is in him as well as in any other primate. Again this is not to deny that the symbolic overlay dependent on socialization can indeed submerge the intrinsic energies described above.

The dual, and truly interactional model of self-esteem presented here, shifts the sociological gestalt on man in a variety of ways. For example, blacks may not be so concerned about being 'accepted' by whites in America—but they may be very concerned about being *consequential*. Conformity to expectations may enter principally insofar as it is useful in the accomplishment of an objective rather than because of the 'need for acceptance' (See Turner, 1962). A conception of inner self-esteem allows us to understand how men who have betrayed their own values may suffer critical loss of self-esteem even though their peers as well as the public give consistently positive feedback. In this regard Erikson has warned that children:

... cannot be fooled by empty praise and condescending encouragement. They may have to accept artificial bolstering of their self-esteem in lieu of something better, but their ego identity gains real strength only from wholehearted and consistent recognition of real accomplishments.
(1950, p. 208).

If this is true for children it should apply to adults as well. Acceptance of others as *a* primary motivation may be true in many cases but is not of sufficient generality. Persons afraid to commit themselves to the achievement of their intentions and who simply attempt to *appear* as if they have achieved it (in the eyes of others) are robbing themselves of the firmly felt self built up through inner self-esteem. Outer sources of validation—though frantically sought—may never satisfy them. Finally, the concept of competence developed here has allowed a way out of the status quo bias inherent in the conception of mental health as social adjustment (See Smith, 1968: 273).

It would indeed be shameful if sociology, needful as it may be of a lever by which it might avoid the oversocialized view of man, would fail to consider the framework presented by White.

References

Allport, Gordon W., 1955. *Becoming*, New Haven: Yale University Press.
Becker, Ernest, 1964. *The Revolution in Psychiatry*. New York: Free Press.
Becker, Ernest, 1965. Mills' social psychology and the great historical convergence on the problem of alienation. In Irving L. Horowitz (ed.), *The New Sociology*, New York: Oxford University Press, pp. 108-133.

Benedict, Ruth 1934. *Patterns of Culture*. Boston and New York: Houghton Mifflin.
Blumer, Herbert, 1969. *Symbolic Interaction: Perspective and Method*. Englewood Cliffs, N.J.: Prentice-Hall, Inc.
Erikson, Erik, 1950. *Childhood and Society*. New York: W. W. Norton.
Franks, David, 1972. Symbolic interaction, the over-socialized view of man, and competency motivation: implications for mental health. Mimeo, University of Denver.
Goffman, Erving, 1961. *Encounters*. Indianapolis: Bobbs-Merrill.
Hobbes, Thomas, 1928. *Leviathan*. London: J. M. Dent and Sons.
Kolb, William L., 1967. A critical evaluation of Mead's 'I' and 'Me' concepts. In Jerome G. Manis and Bernard N. Meltzer (eds.), *Symbolic Interaction: A Reader in Social Psychology*. Boston: Allyn and Bacon, pp. 241-250.
McCall, George and Simmons, J. L., 1966. *Identities and Interactions*. New York: Free Press.
Manis, Jerome G., and Meltzer, Bernard N., (eds), 1967. *Symbolic Interaction: A Reader in Social Psychology,* Boston: Allyn and Bacon.
Mead, George H., 1934. *Mind, Self and Society*. Chicago: University of Chicago Press.
Piaget, Jean, 1963. *The Origins of Intelligence in Children*. New York: W. W. Norton.
Rose, Arnold M., (ed.), 1962. *Human Behavior and Social Processes*. Boston: Houghton Mifflin.
Silverberg, W. V., 1952. *Childhood Experiences and Personal Destiny*. New York: Springer.
Smith, M. Brewster, 1968. Competence and socialization. In John A. Clausen (ed.) *Socialization and Society*, Boston: Little, Brown, pp. 271-320.
Stone, Gregory P., and Farberman, Harvey A., (eds.), 1970. *Social Psychology Through Symbolic Interaction*. Waltham, Mass.: Ginn-Blaisdell.
Strauss, Anselm L., 1959. *Mirrors and Masks*. Glencoe, Ill.: Free Press.
Turner, Ralph H., 1962. Role-taking: process versus conformity. In Arnold Rose (ed.), *Human Behavior and Social Processes,* Boston: Houghton Mifflin, pp. 20-40.
Weigart, Andrew J., 1970. The substantive self. Paper presented to the Rocky Mountain Social Sciences Meetings, Fort Collins, Colorado.
White, Robert W., 1959. Motivation reconsidered: the concept of competence. *Psychological Review*, [66]: 297-333.
White, Robert W., 1960. Competence and the psychosexual stages of development. In M. Jones (ed.), *Nebraska Symposium on Motivation*. Lincoln: University of Nebraska Press, pp. 97-141.
White, Robert W., 1963. Ego and reality in psychoanalytic theory, *Psychological Issues*. International Universities Press.
White, Robert W., 1965. The experience of efficacy in schizophrenia. *Psychiatry*, [28], 199-211.
Whorf, Benjamin Lee, 1965. *Language, Thought and Reality*. Cambridge: Massachusetts Institute of Technology Press.
Wrong, Dennis, 1961. The oversocialized view of man in modern sociology. *American Sociological Review*, XXVI: 183-193.
Zetterberg, Hans L., 1957. Complaint actions. *Acta Sociologica,* [2], 179-201.

Kenneth J. Gergen
Department of Psychology, Swarthmore College

The self and interpersonal behaviour

Reproduced by arrangement with Holt, Rinehart & Winston, Inc., New York, from *The Concept of Self* by Kenneth J. Gergen, © 1971.

This is an edited version of pp. 65-86. D.F.

The true significance of any theory in the social sciences depends on its capacity to predict human behaviour. Here we shall explore several ways in which self-conception is integral to understanding and predicting the course of daily life. First, we shall deal with the core of human relations, the emotions, and see how self-conception is related to our feelings toward others. We shall then move to a second but equally important issue in social life, power and influence. In particular, we shall ask how self-conception influences the division of power in a relationship—who is more likely to initiate influence, who is more likely to be influenced. Third, we shall look at the way in which self-conception affects our goals in life and find that what we think of ourselves has much to do with our major aspirations as well as the effort we expend to reach our goals. We shall then turn to the dramatic aspect of self-conception, exploring the masks of identity used by people to achieve success.

Social attraction and the self

Persons may love or hate each other for a variety of reasons, but fundamental to the feelings we have for others are the feelings we have for ourselves. Depending on our self-esteem we may be predisposed not only to feel certain ways about others in general, but also to respond favourably or unfavourably to their actions towards us. Let us take a closer look at each of these dispositions.

Self-esteem and the acceptance of others

The noted psychoanalyst Erich Fromm was one of the first to observe the close connection between a person's evaluations of self and his feelings for others (1939). For Fromm, 'Hatred against oneself is inseparable from hatred against others.' On the basis of this observation, he considered low self-esteem, or excessive feelings of humility, to be a form of neurosis. Years later, Carl Rogers (1959) noted a similar phenomenon in many of his patients. Those who felt least capable of reaching their goals found it hardest to accept people around them.

There have subsequently been numerous attempts to document these observations more precisely. This research has been almost entirely correlational in nature, and almost without exception the results lend support to the earlier observations. Most typically, subjects or patients rate themselves on various tests of self-esteem and also evaluate other persons with whom they are acquainted. Positive correlations usually result, persons with high self-esteem showing greater acceptance of others.

Unfortunately, however, it is difficult to assess the significance of these results. Research on psychological assessment shows that people vary in their styles of filling out questionnaires or answering questions. For instance, some use extreme ends of scales while others tend to prefer more moderate answers. On tests of self-esteem and in rating other persons, extreme scorers tend to rate both themselves and others more positively (extremely negative scores are rare). Thus, positive correlations between self and other ratings could result from these stylistic modes of test-taking and have nothing to do with self-esteem *per se*. It seems, then, that although most of the available evidence corroborates the earlier observations, the crucial experiment remains to be done.

If self-esteem and esteem for others are indeed correlated, as the evidence suggests, we must ask why this should be so. Fromm has suggested that both feelings for self and feelings for others are based on the same set of childhood learning experiences. When children have been treated hostilely and their freedom has been spitefully curtailed, they develop a 'character conditioned hatred' toward both self and others. Unfortunately, Fromm does not complete his argument by specifying exactly why this disposition should include both self and others. If a child has received continuous hostility from his parents and peers, a negative reaction to himself is quite likely to result from reflected appraisal. At the same time that he learns to dislike himself, he develops hatred for his parents and/or his peers. His subsequent dislike for other people may constitute a generalization from earlier experiences. On a subjective level the feeling might be, 'I have always been treated badly, so what reason is there to suspect that others will be different?'

Rogers (1959) explains the relationship between self-esteem and acceptance of others in a slightly different way. For Rogers the regard received from others may be of two types: *conditional* or *unconditional*. Conditional regard is dependent on one's meeting the other's criteria of evaluation in order to be accepted; failure to meet his criteria leads to rejection. In contrast, unconditional regard is not dependent on the other's criteria of the evaluation. One is prized not for what he does but for his intrinsic value as a human being. Rogers observes that when regard is conditional, the person begins to evaluate himself conditionally—finding himself acceptable only if he meets certain criteria. When self-evaluation is conditional, the person defends against seeing himself in certain ways. He may distort his perception of self, avoid noticing certain of his actions, and, most important, be more defensive in social relationships. Since others may 'show him up for what he is', he may avoid close contact or discredit their views. In effect, others are viewed as threats. Rogers, logically, is much opposed to the use of conditional regard in human relationships.

Another explanation of the relationship between regard for self and regard for others is that the person who feels inferior may not wish to admit to himself that others have positive attributes. To acknowledge others' superiority is to suffer through social comparison; to see them as inferior is to boost one's self-esteem. Through biased scanning one can always find shortcomings in others and in this way show himself that he is really not so bad after all.

Finally, there is a generalized tendency, when we have little clear information about another person, to assume that he is like ourselves (see Gergen, in press). If we feel afraid when walking on a darkened street, we assume that this is probably normal and that most others would feel the same way. Similarly, the person low in self-esteem may make certain assumptions about others' 'true characteristics', assumptions that differ from those made by the person with high self-esteem. Which of these various factors produce the generally observed relationship between self-love and love for others and to what degree each is influential are questions for future research. Let us turn now to an aspect of attraction that has been more extensively studied.

Reactions to others' evaluations of self

Feelings toward self may not only influence our generalized feelings towards others, but may also predispose us to react in specific ways to their behaviour and evaluations of us. Typically, people tend to be attracted to those who evaluate them positively and to dislike those who appraise them negatively. There is considerable research to support this proposition; one example is a study by Jones, Gergen, and Davis (1962) in which undergraduate males were interviewed by advanced graduate students. After the interview half of the subjects learned that the graduate interviewer had a very positive opinion of them, while the other half learned that he disapproved of many of their personal characteristics. Subjects then evaluated the interviewer on a variety of dimensions. The results were clear : those receiving positive appraisals were overwhelmingly more positive in their evaluations of the interviewer.

In terms of self-theory, the reason for such results . . . (is) . . . that people are apt to incorporate positive facts about themselves more readily than negative facts, that they may accumulate goods in order to perceive themselves as superior to others, and that they tend to identify more completely with their roles when they receive positive reactions from others. All these observations point to the fact that self-esteem is all-important to the individual. Events or persons boosting one's esteem are gratifying and those which reduce it are abhorred. Rogers (1959) has spoken of a 'basic need for self regard', a need that leads one to seek the regard of others. He has noted that in some clinical cases the esteem of others seems more powerful a motive than physiological needs.

There is good reason to suspect that one's need for self-esteem develops in childhood. Essentially, it seems to depend on the close and frequent association between the reduction of physiological needs and feelings of being valuable. At the same time that a child is being fed he is also receiving the secondary message that he is valued. He may be fondled and caressed as an infant and may receive warm looks and affectionate talk as he grows older. He may be tickled when the wet, cold diaper is removed from his body and patted when a blanket is put over him to keep him warm. More subtly, by the very act of alleviating physical discomfort or increasing bodily pleasure, the other communicates to the child that he is esteemed.

The feeling of being valued or esteemed may be intrinsically neutral in tone. However, because of its frequent and continuous association with physical drive reduction, tactile pleasure, and the reduction of pain, it comes to have a learned value. As a result, the person learns to seek out the feeling of being esteemed for its own sake and to avoid the feeling of being valueless. To feel esteem for self is akin to one's most basic experience of well-being—the childhood experiences of being supported and nurtured by a benevolent environment. To be without esteem is symbolic of one's basic anguish in an unpredictable and uncontrollable world.

It follows from our discussion thus far that the more positive the appraisal we receive from another, the greater our attraction for him. However, let us turn to a study by Deutsch and Solomon (1959) and see how well this proposition holds up. In this experiment subjects worked together in groups to complete a difficult task. At a certain point in the procedure, each subject was given information indicating how much he had helped or hindered the group in reaching their goal. At random, half the subjects received information indicating that theirs had been one of the most outstanding contributions (success condition), while the other half learned that they had turned in the poorest performance in the group (failure condition). Although each subject received this information privately, he was led to believe that the others also knew of his rating. This manipulation was designed to create two groups, one with a temporary feeling of enhanced self-esteem and the other with a diminished regard for self.

Each subject then received a written evaluation from one of the other team members. By design, half the subjects in each of the above conditions received a positive evaluation. The fictitious team member praised them and said that he would be glad to have them on the team again (positive appraisal condition). The other half of the subjects received negative appraisals, wherein the team member criticized their performance and said that he would not like to have them continue on the team. All subjects then made a series of attraction ratings of the team member from whom they had received the appraisal. The major interest of the experiment was how attraction was affected by acceptance or rejection in state of high or low esteem.

Subjects who have succeeded (high self-esteem) react much as we have discussed. They are much more attracted to the person who appraises them positively than they are to a critic. But when subjects have failed (low self-esteem), they are more attracted to the critic than to the admirer. How can we account for this curious finding?

The one central feature of the condition in which low-esteem subjects are criticized is that the appraiser has been accurate in his judgment. When subjects fail and are praised, the appraiser has been grossly inaccurate in his estimates. It may be said, then, that *evaluation accuracy* plays an important role in our feelings toward someone who has appraised us. We may appreciate an accurate evaluator for several reasons. For one thing, he typically gives us information about ourselves that we can utilize. If we feel he is inaccurate in his estimates of us, he is irrelevant to our concern with developing a realistic and useful picture of self. Secondly, the credibility of the appraiser suffers when he is inaccurate. The inaccurate appraiser seems untrustworthy and possibly stupid. In addition, we are more likely to see the inaccurate appraiser as lacking in personalism. He may seem less attuned to us as persons and possibly influenced by ulterior motives. For a male to tell a female she is 'beautiful' when she is feeling particularly unattractive may raise considerable suspicion about his motives.

But we have yet to deal with the major paradox. What do we feel toward a person who evaluates us much more positively than we typically evaluate ourselves? On the one hand, the more positive the other's evaluation, the more gratifying to our needs for esteem. On the other hand, the greater the difference between self-evaluation and the other's evaluation of self, the less the perceived accuracy. In effect, these two processes tend to work against each other. The one predicts greater attraction as the other's evaluation becomes more positive (an esteem-enhancement effect), while the other predicts less attraction (an accuracy effect). Are we destined to accept the flatterer or sychophant who feeds our needs for esteem? Or must we forsake personal happiness in order to reject false praise? How is this conflict resolved?

It seems wise not to search for a universal answer to this question, that is, for a solution holding under all conditions. Rather, the specific conditions of a relationship may be all important. Certain conditions or factors may cause self-enhancement effects to predominate; other conditions may cause accuracy effects to hold sway. Five factors may be particularly important.

Characteristics of the evaluator   As we pointed out, part of the reason for disliking an inaccurate evaluator is that his inaccuracy reflects on his character. In particular, he may seem 'stupid', 'impersonal', or 'driven by ulterior motives'. It thus follows that any factors reinforcing such characterizations should enhance accuracy effects (reducing attraction) and offset the positive effects of esteem gratification.

An experiment by Dickoff (1961) nicely demonstrates this point. Undergraduate women participated in an interview procedure in which they were to be evaluated by a graduate student. One group of subjects found that the graduate student-evaluator (an experimental accomplice) agreed with their own evaluations of self very closely, while a second group found that the evaluator's appraisals of them were considerably more positive than their own self-ratings. Half the subjects in each of these groups were further told that it was the evaluator's task to be as honest as possible in her appraisals. The remaining half, however, were told that the graduate student wanted them to volunteer for an additional experiment—in other words, her motives for evaluating the subject were made to appear suspect. After the procedure subjects were asked to rate the evaluator. The results were clear: when the evaluator's motives seemed honest (that is, she could be trusted), subjects liked her much more when she had a high (but inflated) view of them. In contrast, when the evaluator's motives were suspect, there was no increase in attraction as she became more flattering. In fact, there was a tendency for her to be liked less when she was flattering than when her appraisals corresponded to the subject's own self-estimates.

Characteristics of the evaluation: *Conditional versus unconditional*   Evaluations received from others vary in a number of ways. Of particular importance is distinction between conditional versus unconditional appraisals. Conditional evaluations are tied to specific characteristics or behaviour. As we explained earlier, the person is evaluated positively or liked because of specific things that he does or is capable of doing. By implication he would not be acceptable if he did not do these things. Grading systems consist of conditional evaluations and, unfortunately, so do many love or friendship relations. Unconditional approval is effusive and expresses generalized good-will, a positive feeling that exists without regard to the person's specific behaviour. The simple expression of friendship is unconditional; the positive feelings do not depend on a series of activities that the person might be called on to perform.

Both conditional and unconditional evaluations may enhance one's self-esteem. Receiving hugs and kisses after winning a race may be as gratifying as receiving an unsolicited expression of warmth. However, our orientations are not the same for both; we do not look to both for the same thing. With conditional evaluations, a higher premium is placed on accuracy. Such evaluations inform us that we have performed well or poorly and knowledge of the success of performance may be useful on future occasions. In matters of friendship, companionship, or love, however, unconditional evaluations are usually more relevant. Here we may not wish the other's evaluations to depend on our performance at the moment. In such instances, attraction to the other should increase as he is more positive toward us. Accuracy should be a minor concern.

Characteristics of the situation: The demand for accuracy   Certain situations place a strong premium on being accurate about oneself. It would be unprofitable to enter a beauty contest without others' honest evaluations of one's talents and appearance or to set out to save a drowning man without an accurate estimate of one's own ability to swim. When rewards and punishments are contingent on accuracy, the person should be less attracted to inaccurate appraisals from others. As Pepitone (1967) has suggested, this set toward accuracy may account for the Deutsch and Solomon results discussed above. The task on which subjects were caused to succeed or fail involved their abilities to form accurate impressions. The situation emphasized the importance of being accurate; therefore, subjects may have been especially inclined to reject inaccurate appraisals of themselves by others.

The need for self-esteem   People clearly differ in the extent to which they fulfill their need for self-esteem. Although social approval is readily available to some persons, others may be chronically impoverished. Success or failure may also affect our esteem needs at any moment. If we fail, our esteem is temporarily lowered and our need is greater. When one's esteem needs are unfulfilled, the approval of others becomes particularly valuable. It is the person most deficient in self-esteem who most exerts himself to obtain it. Most touching is the individual so lacking the love or affection of others that his grasping demands stifle precisely those who might be able to fulfill his needs.

One's need for self-esteem has a direct bearing on one's reaction to others' evaluations. The person who is deprived of support, either chronically or at one particular time, should be most gratified by a positive evaluation. For him, evaluation accuracy should have little importance. When his esteem is high, he should be less attracted to one who evaluates him positively and unrealistically.

Support for this position is found in an engaging study carried out by Walster (1965). In this experiment Stanford coeds filled out a battery of personality questionnaires. While each subject waited for the next phase of the experiment, a handsome male student (an experimental accomplice) 'happened in'. He struck up a conversation and after 15 minutes asked the subject out for a date. After he left, the experimenter gave the subject an evaluation of certain aspects of her personality. At random, half the subjects were told they were deficient in a number of respects (for example, immature) —in effect, their need for self-esteem was temporarily increased. The other half were told they were vastly superior to others taking the same tests. Their esteem needs were presumably lowered as a result. As part of a separate study the subject was then asked to evaluate her parents, friends, and, most important, the male visitor.

Attraction to the flattering male differed significantly for subjects in the two conditions. Those who had experienced a temporary deficit in self-esteem reacted much more positively; failure on the test made them more vulnerable to the male's attention. Those who had been praised were quite neutral in their feelings about him. To lack self-regard causes one to be much more appreciative of regard from others, whether they are sincere or not.[1]

[1] This argument is further expanded in Berscheid and Walster (1969), pp. 60-61.

D

Functional value of relevant concepts   Concepts differ in their functional value to the person. Holding the concept of himself as 'intelligent' may render a person less vulnerable to others' attacks and allow him to engage in social relations without anxiety. Other concepts, such as 'great grandson' may be less generally important; these are used less often in achieving goals. It seems quite likely that for concepts of great functional value, self-enhancement is pre-eminent. When it is important for a person to see himself in a certain way, receiving strong support (even if inaccurate) for this self-view may well yield attraction. On the other hand, if the aspect of self has little value to the person, praise is less gratifying and accuracy considerations may have greater weight. This reasoning leads to the conclusion that the more important a particular self-view is to the person, the more susceptible he is to the inflated and flattering remarks of others. But empirical evidence to support this is needed.

Power, influence, and the self

People vary greatly in their capacity to influence or control the behaviour of those about them. In large organizations such as industry or government, one's power is largely determined by one's formal position within the hierarchy. In most interpersonal relationships, however, the extent to which one individual determines the destiny of his associates is highly reliant on his personal characteristics. What type of person, by virtue of training or basic temperament, will be motivated to influence others? What type of person is more apt to be influenced? Although such questions cannot be answered simply, we can begin by considering *self-conception*.

First, how is it that some persons have such great influence over their peers? Many studies suggest that an individual's esteem for himself is strongly related to the amount of pressure he exerts on others. In an early study by Thomas and Burdick (1954), individuals with generally high esteem, as indicated on a self-assessment measure, were paired together and asked to reach a joint conclusion in diagnosing several case histories. Other two-man groups were composed of persons low in self-esteem. In ratings made after the discussions, members of high-esteem groups rated each other as attempting to influence them more often than members of low-esteem groups did. Cohen (1956) reached similar conclusions, and also found that high self-esteem persons rated themselves higher in attempted influence as well.

The fascinating work of Hastorf, Bavelas, Gross, and Kite (see Hastorf, 1970) is also relevant to the point at hand. Subjects participated in discussions in groups of six persons. Before each subject was placed a signal light that only he could see. The signal was controlled by trained observers behind a one-way mirror, and it indicated to the subject when he should feel free to speak and when he should refrain from doing so. During the first part of this research, subjects were all given a 'go' signal for 15 minutes. During this period it could be determined which subject was quietest or least motivated to lead the group discussion. Then, all subjects were signalled to refrain from speaking except this one. The result was dramatic. During the next 15 minutes signs of timidity began to vanish, and the chosen individual came to dominate the group discussion. During a third 15-minute segment, all participants were again given the 'go' signal. The esteem-boosting effects of speaking out while the others attentively listened seemed to have lasting effects on the speaker. Not only did the originally timid member become one of the group's most dominant contributors, but team members later rated him as one of the most influential members of the group. High self-esteem, then, seems strongly related to an individual's social power.

Many studies demonstrate that low self-esteem is closely related to one's tendency to accept the influence attempts of others. Although most of this research has been conducted with adolescent or adult samples, a study by Lesser and Abelson (1959) is especially interesting because it suggests that susceptibility to influence may be learned at an early age. Grammar school children were first tested for generalized self-esteem . . . (and) . . . were divided into two groups, those with low and those with high self-esteem.

In order to test the extent to which each group would yield to social influence, the experimenter presented 14 pairs of pictures to each of the 56 subjects. The experimenter indicated which of the two pictures she preferred (predetermined on a random basis) and then asked the subject to name a preference. The amount of influence was measured by the number of times the subject agreed with the experimenter. For those whose self-esteem was low, the mean number of agreements with the experimenter was over twelve. In contrast, high self-esteem children agreed with the experimenter on the average of only eight out of fourteen trials, barely exceeding chance.[2]

We have now seen that there is strong support for the proposition that high self-esteem persons tend to be more powerful in social relationships; they attempt more to influence others and they are less susceptible to others' attempts to influence them. As yet, however, research has not answered the question precisely why this is so. A number of factors may be determinant. First, we have already seen that low-esteem persons are generally more anxious to have others' acceptance and support. Attempts to influence others involves a great risk of alienating them and might thus be avoided by this group, while accepting others' opinions and yielding to their desires may often gain their acceptance. Second, low-esteem persons may be less confident in their opinions and judgments. Typically, such persons have not benefited from the praise of others and may feel unsure about the validity of their views. They should thus

[2] It should be further noted that this effect was most striking when preliminary experience with the experimenter had been positive. This is, when the experimenter's praise was available the low self-esteem children were most conforming. When her approval was not available, high and low-esteem children differed little in their conformity. This finding is especially pertinent to understanding the dynamics underlying the relationship between self-esteem and persuasibility.

be reticent in drawing others to their position and more accepting of what they feel to be authoritative opinions.

Cohen (1959) has also argued that high and low esteem is accompanied by different psychological defences. When a person is high in esteem and satisfied with himself and his world-view, he may wish to remain invulnerable. He therefore tries to bring others to his position and to avoid whatever might threaten him with change. In contrast, the low-esteem individual has little to lose by change and may even long to be remoulded for the better. From this viewpoint, the incessant joiner of social groups, or 'true believer' as Eric Hoffer has labelled him, may be one who is not so much dissatisfied with the state of the world as he is with himself. But again, further research will be needed to clarify many of these issues.[3] We may now turn to a third way in which self-conception affects our behaviour.

Self-conception and personal aspirations

We have already seen that aspirations may bias self-conception. Wanting to be something can influence one to see oneself as one wishes to be. Yet, one's conception of self can also affect one's aspirations—what one chooses to do and how much effort one expends in doing it. The primary reason is that people aspire to do that which will yield success and shun activities which may lead to failure. Self-conception is central to this process in two ways.

The first is implicit in our earlier discussions of esteem needs. 'Success' in the above formulation usually involves gaining social approval, either real or implied, and thus feeling enhanced esteem for self.

Second, in order to gauge the probability of succeeding at a given activity we must have some idea of our own capacities. Whether we play bridge with experts depends on how we appraise our sophistication at the game, and whether we choose to attend college depends in part on how we estimate our mental capacities. Our aspirations thus depend on our estimates of self.

Let us examine data from two studies related to these arguments. In the first, Backman and Secord (1968) studied the preferences of undergraduate females for certain marital roles. Earlier research had isolated three major types of roles: the traditional *wife-and-mother role*, in which the woman is expected to bear and rear children, care for the home, and maintain a dependent economic and social status; the *companion role*, in which she shares a variety of pleasures and activities with her husband, strives to be attractive, intellectually challenging, and stimulating, and cultivates social contacts; and the *partner role*, in

---

[3] These arguments must be qualified in one important way. Almost all the research reporting a positive relationship between self-esteem and persuasibility has used male subjects; the relationship between the two variables may be different for females. Both Cox and Bauer (1964) and Gergen and Bauer (1967) have found that low self-esteem females reject influence attempts in the same way that high-esteem females do. With women, medium-esteem females seem to be most conforming.

which she has equal authority in making family decisions, mantains an independent career and does not provide domestic services. These roles were described in greater detail to the students,and they were asked to order their preference for each. On a separate occasion they were asked to judge themselves in relation to a variety of traits such as 'absent-minded', 'ambitious', 'bossy', and 'cautious'. A group of independent raters then judged each of the role models on the same series of traits. (For example, the partner role might be rated high on 'ambition' while the wife-and-mother role would receive a low rating on this trait.)

Armed with these data the investigators asked whether the students' judgments of self would predict their preferences for roles as adults. The answer to this question was highly affirmative. The findings showed that the closer the subject's self-descriptions were to the characteristics of a given role, the greater the preference for the role. Students seeing themselves as 'ambitious', then, would prefer the role of partner to the role of wife-and-mother, while girls rating themselves as 'cautious' were less likely to prefer the partner role.

Although this research documents the close relationship between self-conception and aspirations for the future, it does not demonstrate that self-conception affects actual behaviour. Can we move from the level of what one plans to do to what he actually does. A laboratory experiment by Diggory, Klein, and Cohen (1964) not only shows the close tie between self-conception and behaviour but, in addition, highlights the close dependency of this process on the individual's momentary experience of success and failure. In this experiment, naval personnel worked on a difficult symbol-sorting task. Each subject was exposed to a series of cards, on each was printed one of ten different symbols. For each symbol there was a corresponding number displayed nearby. When a symbol card was presented it was the subjects' task to look up or try to remember the corresponding number and to tap out this number on a telegraph key placed by his right hand. There were to be ten one-minute trials, and it was the subject's task to reach a performance level of 40 correct responses per trial.

Since the experimenter was in a position to announce the subject's score at the end of each trial, he could also control his success and failure at will. All subjects were informed that they were continually improving. However, as the trials progressed, half the subjects (success condition) found that if their rate of improvement continued they might reach the desired criterion. The other half (failure condition) saw that their rate of improvement could not possibly yield success.

The dependent variables in the study were two in number: first, the subject's written estimate after every trial of the probability that he could finally succeed (a self-estimate of capability); and second, a measure of muscle tension or work performance. The latter measure was obtained by attaching electrodes to the right arm of the subject and recording electronically the moment-to-moment state of the muscles. Two measures of muscular activity were obtained: the state of the muscles while actually performing the task and muscle tension when the subject was at rest or waiting to perform the task.

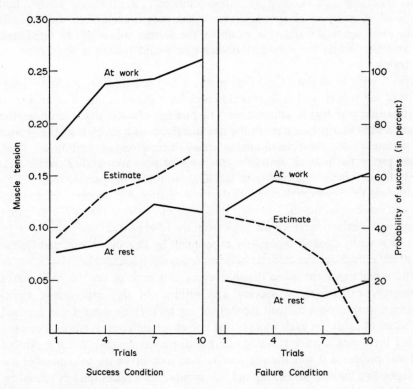

Figure 1 Probability of success and muscle tension as a function of task success versus failure

In Figure 1 are plotted the results for these various measures. We can first examine the subjects' estimates of whether they felt they could succeed. As might be expected, the difference between these ratings in the success as opposed to the failure condition is dramatic. In the former, subjects increasingly feel they are capable of succeeding, while in the latter there is a continuous drop in these estimates. Estimates of one's capacities is highly dependent, then, on the moment-to-moment feedback provided by the environment. But what happens to actual performance of work? As we can see, muscle activity is also affected as the subject sees himself more or less capable of achieving his goal. Not only under working conditions do the success subjects show greater muscle tension, but also under conditions of rest. In essence, they remain tense and involved when they feel they are capable of succeeding. When it appears they will fail, subjects diminish their effort.[4] Not to believe that you are capable of success may actually guarantee your failure.

The presentation of self

We are indebted to Erving Goffman for directing attention to the following account of Preedy, an Englishman who is making his first appearance on the beach at a summer vacation spot:

But in any case he took care to avoid catching anyone's eye. First of all, he had to make it clear to those potential companions of his holiday that they were of no concern to him whatsoever. He stared through them, round them, over them—eyes lost in space. The beach might have been empty. If by chance a ball was thrown his way, he looked surprised ; then let a smile of amusement lighten his face (Kindly Preedy), looked around dazed to see that there *were* people on the beach, tossed it back with a smile to himself and not a smile at the people, and then resumed carelessly his nonchalant survey of space.

But it was time to institute a little parade, the parade of the Ideal Preedy. By devious handlings he gave any who wanted a chance to see the title of his book—a Spanish translation of Homer, classic thus, but not daring, cosmopolitan too—and then gathered together his beach-wrap and bag into a neat sand-resistant pile (Methodical and Sensible Preedy), rose slowly to stretch his huge frame (Big-Cat Preedy), and tossed aside his sandals (Carefree Preedy, after all). [Sansom, 1956, pp. 230–31].

Undoubtedly, all of us can recognize a bit of Preedy in ourselves, as distasteful as the image may be. But we are all faced with the important task of providing others with an idea of who we are, for until others can identify us they cannot know how to behave toward us. To be a 'foreigner' or 'mentally ill', for instance, is of crucial significance for others in determining their actions. By the same token, the definition we present to others influences our level of reward or punishment in the relationship. To present oneself as 'gruff' and 'ill-tempered' is usually to reduce the pleasure we receive at the hands of others. Finally, by defining ourselves to others we can better predict their behaviour. We know that to be perceived as 'rich' yields certain responses; to be seen as 'poor' yields different ones. Through self-presentation, the environment moves from a random state to one of order.

Self-conception has obvious implications for the way we publicly present ourselves to others. It would be very handy, of course, if there were a one-to-one relationship between people's private and public definitions of self. We could then be sure of the other's behaviour and where we stood with respect to him. Indeed, Western culture generally condemns those whose public face differs from their private conception of self. We find this view reflected in Shakespeare's 'To thine own self be true'. However, a wide number of factors

[4] A delightful study by Kiesler and Baral (1970) extends the implications of this finding. These investigators found that male college students whose self-esteem was temporarily increased were more likely to seek out an attractive girl for a date than an unattractive one. In contrast, if self-esteem was temporarily lowered, their aspirations were lowered and an unattractive girl was more likely to be approached than an attractive one.

cause the person to shift his public identity as an actor in ancient times might have changed masks from one scene to the next.

What are the primary factors that produce such chameleon-like activity? Essentially, the major sources of influence fall into three main categories: the *other*, the *interaction environment*, and *motivation*.

The other

The identity of the other person and his behaviour towards us can be central in determining the self-image that we present. If you have ever moved rapidly from one group to another or from one friend to another, you have undoubtedly noticed this fact in yourself. You may be energetic and happy-go-lucky with friends but appear serious and conscientious when conferring with a banker, and the 'ideal' characteristics of self you present in a romantic relationship may jar with your identity as viewed by a brother or sister. As William James has said, a man has 'as many different social selves as there are distinct groups of persons about whose opinion he cares' (1892).

Those round us may affect our 'social selves' in three ways, two of which are familiar to us. First, others are continuously teaching us who we are. Others have varying images of us and depending on these images they treat us as a particular kind of person. Weinstein (1967) has called this process *altercasting*. We are cast into specific roles or identities by those around us. At the same time we are being cast into a particular identity, each of us harbours a multitude of self-concepts in various stages of development. Thus, the cues that others give to us about ourselves serve to reinforce certain of these concepts and reduce the salience of others. Continuous learning about self thus takes place.

A second reason that we shift public identities is related to the first As pointed out earlier, we develop over time certain ways of viewing ourselves in the presence of particular people. With Fred we may have learned to see ourselves as 'intense' and 'philosophical', whereas Susan has always made us realize that we are 'superficially frivolous'. According to principles of association learning, the sheer presence of these persons should thereafter serve to elicit these differential views of self. We react with the 'self' learned in the presence of the other. To spot Susan on the street may cause our face to blossom in smile, while our reaction to Fred's appearance may be an anguished grimace and eyes turned upward toward the heavens.

Of course, both of these processes are 'honest' ones; that is, the person may be fully convinced of the accuracy of his overt presentation at the moment. A third process, however, borders on a more selfish side of everyday relations. We are all interested in maximizing our benefits in social relations. We seek rewards and do our best to avoid punishment. The characteristics of others and their behaviour toward us serve as cues for effective maximization. They aid us in performing optimally, often without regard to our sincerity.

While Goffman (1959, 1961) has discussed numerous ways in which this maximization takes place, an experiment by Gergen and Wishnov (1965) presents empirical evidence. The special interest of the study was in people's reactions to others who differ in self-esteem—from the flamboyant egotist to the diffident 'poor mouth'. It was reasoned that people who are extreme in their self-praise or their self-condemnation raise particular tactical problems for those who interact with them.

The egotist creates a power problem. By accentuating his virtues he implies that others are not equal to him. His manner bespeaks his assumption that he deserves status, a greater share of whatever rewards are available, and the right to lead in decision making. Skillful self-presentation may be helpful in dealing with this kind of person; in particular, we might well react in kind, accentuating our assets and hiding our shortcomings. The self-derogator presents a far different type of problem. We may wish to nurture or aid him out of commiseration and at the same time wish to avoid further dealings with him because he seems so weak and dependent. Thus, we might be inclined to admit that we have shortcomings but not wish to identify ourselves as being on the same level as the other.

As a means of observing such strategies in action, undergraduate females were asked during a class period to rate themselves on a series of positive and negative characteristics (for example, 'I am generally attractive to others', 'I am often nervous and anxious'). Approximately one month later they participated in an experiment in which they were to exchange a set of written communications with another coed whose identity was unknown to them. These communications would 'allow them to get acquainted' more rapidly. During this exchange, each subject received a set of self-ratings supposedly filled out by her partner. By design, one group received a set of ratings in which the partner described herself in most glowing terms. She enjoyed her work, her dating life, her home and saw herself as having no faults, but many virtues (egotism condition). A second experimental group received a self-description from the supposed partner that was quite opposite in character. She felt distinct lacks in all aspects of her life and saw numerous faults in herself with no redeeming virtues (humility condition). It was then the subject's turn to respond, and in part this response took the form of self-ratings of the same variety she had made a month earlier. The major interest of the study was to see the way she would change these ratings in reaction to the partner's rating.

Self-rating change on both positive and negative characteristics is found. Both egotism and humility have strikingly different effects on the way subjects identify themselves. The egotist causes them to become much more positive about themselves—boosting their positive characteristics and de-emphasizing their negative ones—in an apparent attempt to offset the power balance. Humility, in contrast, causes subjects to portray themselves as being much more fault-ridden in terms of their characterizations on negative traits. However, they are not willing to give up their claim to positive qualities. When faced with another's humiliation, the reaction seems to be one of commiserating by showing faults but retaining independence through the maintenance of positive characteristics.

The interaction environment

In determining the self that we present, the environment in which the encounter takes place is as important as others' identities. We are not likely to identify ourselves in the same way at a formal dance as we do in a pool hall, regardless of who is present. Situations bring about shifts in identity primarily because they offer cues for maximization of reward. For example, we know from past experience what patterns of behaviour are expected in varying circumstances. We know that we are expected to be polite and reserved in a religious setting, and, therefore, to avoid censure we may create the impression (however mistaken) of being a 'perfect gentleman'. Likewise, immediate situations themselves have ways of creating exigent behaviours. In team sports, cooperation is the keynote, in debating, rationality and rhetoric are necessary to achieve success. As Goffman (1961) has shown, even patients entering a mental institution must learn how to become as 'proper' psychotics.

Environmental cues are demonstrated in a study by Gergen and Taylor (1969). Junior and senior ROTC students were to work together in pairs on one of two types of tasks. Half the subject pairs were to work on a task that demanded great productivity—manoeuvring a mock submarine out of danger in a complex situation. The other half of the subjects were given a task for which social compatibility was most important—being understanding and tolerant in working out a set of ship manoeuvres. Before work began each subject was to describe himself to his partner (who was either higher or lower than himself in ROTC rank) in order that they could be 'better acquainted'. The results showed that regardless of rank subjects in the productivity setting became more positive about themselves. They represented themselves as having many more positive qualities than they had professed a month earlier on a similar measure. Exactly the reverse took place when compatibility was at stake. In an apparent attempt to make themselves seem more 'human' and less defensive, subjects de-emphasized their virtues and were more willing to admit shortcomings. On the job, people seem bent on displaying virtues; in social settings they are more likely to underestimate themselves.

Personal motivation

The individual's presentation of self may be determined also by his motives in a relationship. If a person wishes to be treated with deference, his demeanour may be marked by superiority; if he wishes to be trusted, he may ensure that his behaviour is always consistent. Research on the effects of motivation on self-presentation has primarily concentrated on approval seeking. How do people manage their public identity in order to acquire the liking and acceptance of others? Unsurprisingly, the results of such studies (see Jones, Gergen,

& Davis, 1962) show that in order to gain approval people typically emphasize their positive characteristics and withhold their personal failings from public view.

One exception to the general rule has been found (Jones, Gergen, & Jones, 1963). In this study it was discovered that in order to gain favour among their subordinates, senior members of an organization presented themselves less positively on characteristics that were not relevant to their position of command. As Blau (1964) has reasoned, the senior person is seen by his juniors as remote, aloof, and threatening. By suggesting that he, too, has shortcomings, the senior member makes himself more accessible. Of course, he does it in such a way as not to undermine his position of seniority—the boss may admit he is a terrible golfer to facilitate interaction, but he is much less likely to admit that he sometimes makes poor professional decisions.

This discussion of self-presentation has emphasized the fact that people will often forgo their true conceptions of self for purposes of social gain. However, before responding indignantly to the charade that surrounds us, we must take note of people's experience as they play the game. In a number of studies just discussed, subjects have been asked about their experiences—how honest did they feel they could be, how sincere did they feel, to what extent did the other person or situation make a difference to their behaviour, and so forth. Responses to such questions typically reveal that people do *not* generally feel insincere when they alter their social identity. They may describe themselves in one way at one moment and the reverse the next, and feel equally honest and sincere at both times. This finding is quite consistent with our earlier discussions of self-concept learning and role playing. As we pointed out, a person may harbour a variety of concepts of himself which differ in salience from moment to moment. When a particular role is used in a particular situation, the salience of certain concepts may increase and others may be lost from awareness. Thus, self-presentation may convince a person for the moment that he is indeed what he says he is. To be sure, not all presentation is accompanied by feelings of 'true self'. Highly learned concepts of self may be continuously salient and nag when one violates them. However, there is a strong tendency in social relations for the person to become the mask.

References

Backman, C. W. and Secord, P. F., 1968. The self and role selection. In C. Gordon and K. J. Gergen (eds), *The Self in Social Interaction*. Vol. 1. New York: Wiley.

Berscheid, E., and Walster, E. H., 1969. *Interpersonal Attraction*. Reading, Mass: Addison-Wesley.

Blau, P. M., 1964. *Exchange and Power in Social Life*. New York: Wiley.

Cohen, A. R., 1956. Experimental effects of ego-defense preference on interpersonal relations. *Journal of Abnormal and Social Psychology*, [52], 19-27.

Cohen, A. R., 1959. Some implications of self-esteem for social influence. In C. I. Hovland and I. L. Janis (eds), *Personality and Persuasibility*. New Haven, Conn.: Yale University Press.

Cox, D. B., and Bauer, R. A., 1964. Self-confidence and persuasibility in women. *Public Opinion Quarterly*, [28], 453-466.

Deutsch, M., and Solomon, L., 1959. Reactions to evaluations by others as influenced by self evaluations. *Sociometry*, [22], 93-112.

Dickoff, H., 1961. Reactions to evaluations by another person as a function of self evaluation and the interaction context. Unpublished doctoral dissertation, Duke University.

Diggory, J. C., Klein, S. J., and Cohen, N. M., 1964. Muscle-action potentials and estimated probability of success. *Journal of Experimental Psychology*, [68], 448-456.

Fromm, E., 1939. Selfishness and self love. *Psychiatry*, [2], 507-523. (Also reprinted in Gordon & Gergen.)

Gergen, K. J., Perception of others and the self. In K. Back (ed.), *Basic Issues in Social Psychology*. New York: Wiley, in press.

Gergen, K. J., and Bauer, R. A., 1967. The interactive effects of self-esteem and task difficulty on social conformity. *Journal of Personality and Social Psychology*, [6], 16-22.

Gergen, K. J., and Taylor, M. G., 1969. Social expectancy and self-presentation in a status hierarchy. *Journal of Experimental Social Psychology*, [5], 79-92.

Gergen, K. J., and Wishnov, B., 1965. Others' self evaluations and interaction anticipation as determinants of self presentation. *Journal of Personality and Social Psychology*, [2], 348-358.

Goffman, E., 1959. *The Presentation of Self in Everyday Life*. New York: Doubleday.

Goffman, E., 1961. *Asylums*. New York: Doubleday.

Hastorf, A., 1970. The creation of group leaders. In K. J. Gergen and D. Marlowe (eds), *Personality and Social Behavior*, Reading, Mass.: Addison Wesley.

James, W., 1892. *Principles of Psychology*. New York: Holt.

Jones, E. E., Gergen, K. J., and Davis, K., 1962. Some reactions to being approved or disapproved as a person. *Psychological Monographs*, [76] (whole no. 521).

Jones, E. E., Gergen, K. J., and Jones, R. G., 1963. Tactics of ingratiation among leaders and subordinates in a status hierarchy. *Psychological Monographs*, [77] (whole no. 566).

Kiesler, S. B., and Baral, R. L., 1970. The search for a romantic partner: the effects of self-esteem and physical attractiveness on romantic behavior. In K. J. Gergen, and D. Marlowe (eds), *Personality and Social Behavior*. Reading, Mass.: Addison-Wesley.

Lesser, G., and Abelson, R., 1959. Correlates of persuasibility of children. In C. I. Hovland and I. L. Janis (eds), *Personality and Persuasibility*. New Haven: Yale University Press.

Pepitone, A., 1967. Some conceptual and empirical problems of consistency models. In S. Feldman (ed.), *Cognitive Consistency*. New York: Academic Press.

Rogers, C., 1959. Therapy, personality, and interpersonal relationships. In S. Koch (ed.), *Psychology: A Study of a Science*. Vol. III. New York: McGraw-Hill. (Outstanding statement of relationship between self-regard and mental disorder.)

Sansom, E., 1956. *The Perfect Gentleman*. London: Heath.

Thomas, R., and Burdick, R., 1954. Self-esteem and inter-personal influence. *Journal of Personality and Social Psychology*, [51], 419-426.

Walster, E., 1965. The effect of self-esteem on romantic liking. *Journal of Experimental Social Psychology*, [1], 184-197.

Weinstein, A., 1967. Altercasting and interpersonal relations. In P. Secord and C. Backman (eds), *Readings in Social Psychology*. Englewood Cliffs, N.J.: Prentice-Hall.

Part two

Social Contexts
and
Individual Action

Part Two

Social Contexts
and
Individual Action

Robert D. Hess
School of Education, Stanford University

Virginia C. Shipman
Educational Testing Service, Princeton

Early experience and the socialization of cognitive modes in children[1]

R. D. Hess and Virginia C. Shipman, Early experience and the socialization of cognitive modes in children, published in *Child Development,* 1965, [36], 869-886.

This is an edited version of the original article. D.F.

The problem

One of the questions arising from the contemporary concern with the education of culturally disadvantaged children is how we should conceptualize the effects of such deprivation upon the cognitive faculties of the child. The outcome is well known: children from deprived backgrounds score well below middle-class children on standard individual and group measures of intelligence (a gap that increases with age); they come to school without the skills necessary for coping with first grade curricula; their language development, both written and spoken, is relatively poor; auditory and visual discrimination skills are not well developed; in scholastic achievement they are retarded an average of 2 years by grade 6 and almost 3 years by grade 8; they are more likely to drop out of school before completing a secondary education; and even when they have adequate ability are less likely to go to college (Deutsch, 1963; Deutsch & Brown, 1964; Eells, *et al.*, 1951; John, 1963; Kennedy, Van de Riet, & White, 1963; Lesser, 1964).

In this paper we will argue that the structure of the social system and the structure of the family shape communication and language and that language shapes thought and cognitive styles of problem-solving. In the deprived-family context this means that the nature of the control system which relates parent to child restricts the number and kind of alternatives for action and thought that are opened to the child; such constriction precludes a tendency for the

1 This research is supported by the Research Division of the Children's Bureau, Social Security Administration; Department of Health, Education, and Welfare; Ford Foundation for the Advancement of Learning; and grants-in-aid from the Social Science Research Committee of the Division of Social Sciences, University of Chicago. Project staff members who made specific contributions to the analysis of data are Jere Brophy, Dina Feitelson, Roberta Meyer, and Ellis Olim. Hess's address: Committee on Human Development, University of Chicago, Chicago, Ill. 60637.

child to reflect, to consider and choose among alternatives for speech and action. It develops modes for dealing with stimuli and with problems which are impulsive rather than reflective, which deal with the immediate rather than the future, and which are disconnected rather than sequential.

This position draws from the work of Basil Bernstein (1961) of the University of London. In his view, language structures and conditions what the child learns and how he learns, setting limits within which future learning may take place. He identifies two forms of communication codes or styles of verbal behaviour: *restricted* and *elaborated*. Restricted codes are stereotyped, limited, and condensed, lacking in specificity and the exactness needed for precise conceptualization and differentiation. Sentences are short, simple, often unfinished; there is little use of subordinate clauses for elaborating the content of the sentence; it is a language of implicit meaning, easily understood and commonly shared. It is the language form often used in impersonal situations when the intent is to promote solidarity or reduce tension. Restricted codes are nonspecific clichés, statements, or observations about events made in general terms that will be readily understood. The basic quality of this mode is to limit the range and detail of concept and information involved.

Elaborated codes, however, are those in which communication is individualized and the message is specific to a particular situation, topic, and person. It is more particular, more differentiated, and more precise. It permits expression of a wider and more complex range of thought, tending toward discrimination among cognitive and affective content.

The effects of early experience with these codes are not only upon the communication modes and cognitive structure—they also establish potential patterns of relation with the external world. It is one of the dynamic features of Bernstein's work that he views language as social behaviour. As such, language is used by participants of a social network to elaborate and express social and other interpersonal relations and, in turn, is shaped and determined by these relations.

The interlacing of social interaction and language is illustrated by the distinction between two types of family control. One is oriented toward control by *status* appeal or ascribed role norms. The second is oriented toward *persons*. Families differ in the degree to which they utilize each of these types of regulatory appeal. In status- (position-) oriented families, behaviour tends to be regulated in terms of role expectations. There is little opportunity for the unique characteristics of the child to influence the decision-making process or the interaction between parent and child. In these families, the internal or personal states of the children are not influential as a basis for decision. Norms of behaviour are stressed with such imperatives as, 'You must do this because I say so', or 'Girls don't act like that', or other statements which rely on the status of the participants or a behaviour norm for justification (Bernstein, 1964).

In the family, as in other social structures, control is exercised in part through status appeals. The feature that distinguishes among families is the extent to which the status-based control manoeuvres are modified by orientation toward persons. In a person-oriented appeal system, the unique characteristics of the child modify status demands and are taken into account in interaction. The decisions of this type of family are individualized and less frequently related to status or role ascriptions. Behaviour is justified in terms of feelings, preference, personal and unique reactions, and subjective states. This philosophy not only permits but demands an elaborated linguistic code and a wide range of linguistic and behavioural alternatives in interpersonal interaction. Status-oriented families may be regulated by less individuated commands, messages, and responses. Indeed, by its nature, the status-oriented family will rely more heavily on a restricted code. The verbal exchange is inherent in the structure—regulates it and is regulated by it.

These distinctions may be clarified by two examples of mother-child communication using these two types of codes. Assume that the emotional climate of two homes is approximately the same; the significant difference between them is in style of communication employed. A child is playing noisily in the kitchen with an assortment of pots and pans when the telephone rings. In one home the mother says, 'Be quiet', or 'Shut up', or issues any one of several other short, peremptory commands. In the other home the mother says, 'Would you keep quiet a minute? I want to talk on the phone'. The question our study poses is this: what inner response is elicited in the child, what is the effect upon his developing cognitive network of concepts and meaning in each of these two situations? In one instance the child is asked for a simple mental response. He is asked to attend to an uncomplicated message and to make a conditioned response (to comply); he is not called upon to reflect or to make mental discriminations. In the other example the child is required to follow two or three ideas. He is asked to relate his behaviour to a time dimension; he must think of his behaviour in relation to its effect upon another person. He must perform a more complicated task to follow the communication of his mother in that his relationship to her is mediated in part through concepts and shared ideas; his mind is stimulated or exercised (in an elementary fashion) by a more elaborate and complex verbal communication initiated by the mother. As objects of these two divergent communication styles, repeated in various ways, in similar situations and circumstances during the preschool years, these two imaginary children would be expected to develop significantly different verbal facility and cognitive equipment by the time they enter the public-school system.

A person-oriented family allows the child to achieve the behaviour rules (role requirements) by presenting them in a specific context for the child and by emphasizing the consequences of alternative actions. Status-oriented families present the rules in an assigned manner, where compliance is the *only* rule-following possibility. In these situations the role of power in the interaction is more obvious, and indeed, coercion and defiance are likely interactional possibilities. From another perspective, status-oriented families use a more rigid learning and teaching model in which compliance, rather than rationale, is stressed.

A central dimension through which we look at maternal behaviour is to inquire what responses are elicited and permitted by styles of communication and interaction. There are two axes of the child's behaviour in which we have a particular interest. One of these is represented by an *assertive, initiatory* approach to learning, as contrasted with a *passive, compliant* mode of engagement; the other deals with the tendency to reach solutions impulsively or hastily as distinguished from a tendency to *reflect*, to compare alternatives, and to choose among available options.

These styles of cognitive behaviour are related, in our hypotheses, to the dimensions of maternal linguistic codes and types of family control systems. A status-oriented statement, for example, tends to offer a set of regulations and rules for conduct and interaction that is based on arbitrary decisions rather than upon logical consequences which result from selection of one or another alternatives. Elaborated and person-oriented statements lend themselves more easily to styles of cognitive approach that involve reflection and reflective comparision. Status-oriented statements tend to be restrictive of thought. Take our simple example of the two children and the telephone. The verbal categoric command to 'Be quiet' cuts off thought and offers little opportunity to relate the information conveyed in the command to the context in which it occurred. The more elaborated message, 'Would you be quiet a minute? I want to talk on the phone' gives the child a rationale for relating his behaviour to a wider set of considerations. In effect, he has been given a *why* for his mother's request and, by this example, possibly becomes more likely to *ask* why in another situation. It may be through this type of verbal interaction that the child learns to look for action sequences in his own and others' behaviour. Perhaps through these more intent-oriented statements the child comes to see the world as others see it and learns to take the role of others in viewing himself and his actions. The child comes to see the world as a set of possibilities from which he can make a personal selection. He learns to role play with an element of personal flexibility, not by role-conforming rigidity.

Research plan

For our project a research group of 163 Negro mothers and their 4-year-old children was selected from four different social status levels: Group A came from college-educated professional, executive, and managerial occupational levels: Group B came from skilled blue-collar occupational levels, with not more than high-school education; Group C came from unskilled or semiskilled occupational levels, with predominantly elementary-school education. Group D from unskilled or semiskilled occupational levels, with fathers absent and families supported by public assistance.

These mothers were interviewed twice in their homes and brought to the university for testing and for an interaction session between mother and child in which the mother was taught three simple tasks by the staff member and then asked to teach these tasks to the child.

One of these tasks was to sort or group a number of plastic toys by colour and by function; a second task was to sort eight blocks by two characteristics simultaneously; the third task required the mother and child to work together to copy five designs on a toy called an Etch-a-Sketch. A description of various aspects of the project and some preliminary results have been presented in several papers (Brophy, Hess, & Shipman, 1965; Jackson, Hess, & Shipman, 1965; Meyer, Shipman, & Hess, 1964; Olim, Hess & Shipman, 1965; Shipman & Hess, 1965).

Results

The data in this paper are organized to show social-status differences among the four groups in the dimensions of behaviour described above to indicate something of the maternal teaching styles that are emerging and to offer examples of relations between maternal and child behaviour that are congruent with the general lines of argument we have laid out.

Social-status differences

Verbal codes: restricted versus elaborated One of the most striking and obvious differences between the environments provided by the mothers of the research group was in their patterns of language use. In our testing sessions, the most obvious social-class variations were in the total amount of verbal output in response to questions and tasks asking for verbal response. Mothers from the middle-class gave protocols that were consistently longer in language productivity than did mothers from the other three groups.

Taking three different types of questions that called for free response on the part of the mothers and counting the number of lines of typescript of the protocols, the tally for middle-class mothers was approximately 82 contrasted with an average of roughly 49 for mothers from the three other groups.

These differences in verbal products indicate the extent to which the maternal environments of children in different social-class groups tend to be mediated by verbal cue and thus offer (or fail to offer) opportunities for labelling, for identifying objects and feelings and adult models who can demonstrate the usefulness of language as a tool for dealing with interpersonal interaction and for ordering stimuli in the environment.

In addition to this gross disparity in verbal output there were differences in the quality of language used by mothers in the various status groups. One approach to the analysis of language used by these mothers was an examination of their responses to the following task: they were shown the Lion Card of the Children's Apperception Test and asked to tell their child a story relating to the card. This card is a picture of a lion sitting on a chair holding a pipe in his hand. Beside him is a cane. In the corner is a mouse peering out of a hole. The lion appears to be deep in thought. These protocols were the source of language samples which were summarized in nine scales, two of which we wish to describe here.

The first scale dealt with the mother's tendency to use abstract words. The index derived was a proportion of abstract noun and verb types to total number of noun and verb types. Words were defined as abstract when the name of the object is thought of apart from the cases in which it is actually realized. For example, in the sentence, 'The lion is an *animal*,' 'animal' is an abstract word. However, in the sentence, 'This animal in the picture is sitting on his throne,' 'animal' is not an abstract noun.

In our research group, middle-class mothers achieved an abstraction score of 5.6; the score for skilled work levels was 4.9; the score for the unskilled group was 3.7; for recipients of Aid to Dependent Children (ADC), 1.8.

The second scale dealt with the mother's tendency to use complex syntactic structures such as coordinate and subordinate clauses, unusual infinite phrases (e.g., 'To drive well, you must be alert'), infinitive clauses (e.g., 'What to do next was the lion's problem'), and participial phrases (e.g., 'Continuing the story, the lion . . .'). The index of structural elaboration derived was a proportion of these complex syntactic structures, weighted in accordance with their complexity and with the degree to which they are strung together to form still more complicated structures (e.g., clauses within clauses), to the total number of sentences.

In the research group, mothers from the middle class had a structure elaboration index of 8.89; the score for ADC mothers was 6.46. The use of complex grammatical forms and elaboration of these forms into complex clauses and sentences provides a highly elaborated code with which to manipulate the environment symbolically. This type of code encourages the child to recognize the possibilities and subtleties inherent in language not only for communication but also for carrying on high-level cognitive procedures.

Control systems: person versus status orientation   Our data on the mothers' use of status- as contrasted with person-oriented statements comes from maternal responses to questions inquiring what the mother would do in order to deal with several different hypothetical situations at school in which the child had broken the rules of the school, had failed to achieve, or had been wronged by a teacher or classmate. The results of this tally are shown in Table 1.

As is clear from these means, the greatest differences between status groups is in the tendency to utilize person-oriented statements. These differences are even greater if seen as a ratio of person-to-status type responses.

The orientation of the mothers to these different types of control is seen not only in prohibitive or reparative situations but in their instructions to their children in preparing them for new experiences. The data on this point come from answers to the question: 'Suppose your child were starting to school tomorrow for the first time. What would you tell him? How would you prepare him for school?'

Table 1 Person-oriented and status-oriented units on school situation protocols (mothers)

A Mean number

Social class	Person-oriented		Status-oriented		P/S ratio	N
Upper middle	9.52	(1–19)	7.50	(0–19)	1.27	40
Upper lower	6.20	(0–20)	7.32	(2–17)	0.85	40
Lower lower	4.66	(0–15)	7.34	(2–17)	0.63	35
ADC	3.59	(0–16)	8.15	(3–29)	0.44	34

B Mean per cent

Social class	Person-oriented	Status-oriented	N
Upper middle	36.92	27.78	40
Upper lower	31.65	36.92	40
Lower lower	26.43	40.69	35
ADC	20.85	51.09	34

One mother, who was person-oriented and used elaborated verbal codes, replied as follows:

'First of all, I would remind her that she was going to school to learn, that her teacher would take my place, and that she would be expected to follow instructions. Also that her time was to be spent mostly in the classroom with other children, and that any questions or any problems that she might have she could consult with her teacher for assistance.'

'Anything else?'

'No, anything else would probably be confusing for her at her particular age.'

In terms of promoting educability, what did this mother do in her response? First, she was informative; she presented the school situation as comparable to one already familiar to the child; second, she offered reassurance and support to help the child deal with anxiety; third, she described the school situation as one that involves a personal relationship between the child and the teacher; and, fourth, she presented the classroom situation as one in which the child was to learn.

A second mother responded as follows to this question:

'Well, John, it's time to go to school now. You must know how to behave.

The first day at school you should be a good boy and should do just what the teacher tells you to do.'

In contrast to the first mother, what did this mother do? First, she defined the role of the child as passive and compliant; second, the central issues she presented were those dealing with authority and the institution, rather than with learning; third, the relationship and roles she portrayed were sketched in terms of status and role expectations rather than in personal terms; and, fourth, her message was general, restricted, and vague, lacking information about how to deal with the problems of school except by passive compliance.

Status differences in concept utilization   One of the measures of cognitive style used with both mothers and children in the research group was the S's mode of classificatory behavior. For the adult version, (Kagan, Moss & Sigel, 1963) S is required to make 12 consecutive sorts of MAPS figures placed in a prearranged random order on a large cardboard. After each sort she was asked to give her reason for putting certain figures together. This task was intended to reveal her typical or preferred manner of grouping stimuli and the level of abstraction that she uses in perceiving and ordering objects in the environment. Responses fell into four categories: descriptive part-whole, descriptive global, relational-contextual, and categorical-inferential. A descriptive response is a direct reference to physical attributes present in the stimuli, such as size, shape, or posture. Examples: 'They're all children', or 'They are all lying down', or 'They are all men'. The subject may also choose to use only a part of the figure—'They both have hats on.' In a relational-contextual response, any one stimulus gets its meaning from a relation with other stimuli. Examples: 'Doctor and nurse', or 'Wife is cooking dinner for her husband', or 'This guy looks like he shot this other guy'. In categorical-inferential responses, sorts are based on nonobservable characteristics of the stimulus for which each stimulus is an independent representative of the total class. Examples: 'All of these people work for a living' or 'These are all handicapped people'.

Table 2 Mean responses to adult Sigel Sorting task (Maps)

	Social status			
Category	Upper middle $N = 40$	Upper lower $N = 42$	Lower lower $N = 39$	ADC $N = 41$
Total descriptive	3.18	2.19	2.18	2.59
Descriptive part-whole	1.65	1.33	1.31	1.49
Descriptive global	1.52	0.86	0.87	1.10
Relational-contextual	5.52	6.79	7.38	6.73
Categorical-inferential	3.30	3.00	3.23	2.66

As may be seen in Table 2, relational responses were most frequently offered; categorical-inferential were next most common, and descriptive most infrequent. The distribution of responses of our status groups showed that the middle-class group was higher on descriptive and categorical; low-status groups were higher on relational. The greater use of relational categories by the working-class mothers is especially significant. Response times for relational sorts are usually shorter, indicating less reflection and evaluating of alternative hypotheses. Such responses also indicate relatively low attention to external stimuli details (Kagan, 1964). Relational responses are often subjective, reflecting a tendency to relate objects to personal concerns in contrast with the descriptive and categorical responses which tend to be objective and detached, more general, and more abstract. Categorical responses, in particular represent thought processes that are more orderly and complex in organizing stimuli, suggesting more efficient strategies of information processing.

The most striking finding from the data obtained from the children's Sigel Sorting Task was the decreasing use of the cognitive style dimensions and increasing nonverbal responses with decrease in social-status level. Although most upper middle-class children and a majority of the upper lower-class children use relational and descriptive global responses, there is no extensive use of any of the other cognitive style dimensions by the two lower lower-class groups. In looking at particular categories one may note the relative absence of descriptive part-whole responses for other than the middle-class group and the large rise in nonverbal responses below the middle-class level. These results would seem to reflect the relatively undeveloped verbal and conceptual ability of children from homes with restricted range of verbal and conceptual content.

Relational and descriptive global responses have been considered the most immature and would be hypothesized to occur most frequently in pre-school children. Relational responses are often subjective, using idiosyncratic and irrelevant cues; descriptive global responses, often referring to sex and occupational roles, are somewhat more dependent upon experience. On the other hand, descriptive part-whole responses have been shown to increase with age and would be expected to be used less frequently. However, these descriptive part-whole responses which are correlated with favourable prognostic signs for educability (such as attentiveness, control and learning ability), were almost totally absent from all but the upper middle-class group. Kagan (1964) has described two fundamental cognitive dispositions involved in producing such analytic concepts: the tendency to reflect over alternative solutions that are simultaneously available and the tendency to analyse a visual stimulus into component parts. Both behaviours require a delayed discrimination response. One may describe the impairment noted for culturally disadvantaged children as arising from differences in opportunities for developing these reflective attitudes.

The mother's use of relational responses was significantly correlated with their children's use of nonscorable and nonverbal responses on the Sigel task and with poor performance on the 8-Block and Etch-a-Sketch tasks. The mothers' inability or disinclination to take an abstract attitude on the Sigel task was correlated with ineffectual teaching on the 8-Block task and inability to plan and control the Etch-a-Sketch situation. Since relational responses have been found (Kagan, Moss, & Sigel, 1963) to be correlated with impulsivity, tendencies for nonverbal rather than verbal teaching, mother-domination, and limited sequencing and discrimination might be expected and would be predicted to result in limited categorizing ability and impaired verbal skills in the child.

Analysis of maternal teaching styles

These differences among the status groups and among mothers within the groups appear in slightly different form in the teaching sessions in which the mothers and children engaged. There were large differences among the status groups in the ability of the mothers to teach and the children to learn. This is illustrated by the performance scores on the sorting tasks.

Let us describe the interaction between the mother and child in one of the structured teaching situations. The wide range of individual differences in linguistic and interactional styles of these mothers may be illustrated by excerpts from recordings. The task of the mother is to teach the child how to group or sort a small number of toys.

The first mother outlines the task for the child, gives sufficient help and explanation to permit the child to proceed on her own. She says:

'All right, Susan, this board is the place where we put the little toys; first of all you're supposed to learn how to place them according to colour. Can you do that? The things that are all the same colour you put in one section; in the second section you put another group of colours, and in the third section you put the last group of colours. Can you do that? Or would you like to see me do it first?'

Child: 'I want to do it'.

This mother has given explicit information about the task and what is expected of the child; she has offered support and help of various kinds; and she has made it clear that she impelled the child to perform.

A second mother's style offers less clarity and precision. She says in introducing the same task:

'Now, I'll take them all off the board; now you put them all back on the board. What are these?'

Child. 'A truck.'

'All right, just put them right here; put the other one right here; all right put the other one there.'

This mother must rely more on nonverbal communication in her commands; she does not define the task for the child; the child is not provided with ideas or information that she can grasp in attempting to solve the problem; neither is she told what to expect or what the task is, even in general terms.

A third mother is even less explicit. She introduces the task as follows:
'I've got some chairs and cars, do you want to play the game?' Child does
not respond. Mother continues: 'O.K. What's this?'

Child: 'A wagon?'

Mother: 'Hm?'

Child: 'A wagon?'

Mother: 'This is not a wagon. What's this?'

The conversation continues with this sort of exchange for several pages.
Here again, the child is not provided with the essential information he needs
to solve or to understand the problem. There is clearly some impelling on the
part of the mother for the child to perform, but the child has not been told
what he is to do. There were marked social-class differences in the ability of
the children to learn from their mothers in the teaching sessions.

Each teaching session was concluded with an assessment by a staff member
of the extent to which the child had learned the concepts taught by the mother.
His achievement was scored in two ways: first, the ability correctly to place
or sort the objects and, second, the ability to verbalize the principle on which
the sorting or grouping was made.

Children from middle-class homes were well above children from working-
class homes in performance on these sorting tasks, particularly in offering
verbal explanations as to the basis for making the sort. Over 60 per cent of
middle-class children placed the objects correctly on all tasks; the performance
of working-class children ranged as low as 29 per cent correct. Approximately
40 per cent of these middle-class children who were successful were able to
verbalize the sorting principle; working-class children were less able to explain
the sorting principle, ranging downward from the middle-class level to one
task on which no child was able to verbalize correctly the basis of his sorting
behaviour. These differences clearly paralleled the relative abilities and teaching skills of the mothers from differing social-status groups.

The difference among the four status levels was apparent not only on these
sorting and verbal skills but also in the mother's ability to regulate her own
behaviour and her child's in performing tasks which require planning or care
rather than verbal or conceptual skill. These differences were revealed by the
mother-child performance on the Etch-a-Sketch task. An Etch-a-Sketch toy
is a small, flat box with a screen on which lines can be drawn by a device
within the box. The marker is controlled by two knobs : one for horizontal
movement, one for vertical. The mother is assigned one knob, the child the
other. The mother is shown several designs which are to be reproduced.
Together they attempt to copy the design models. The mother decides when
their product is a satisfactory copy of the original. The products are scored
by measuring deviations from the original designs.

These sessions were recorded, and the nonverbal interaction was described
by an observer. Some of the most relevant results were these: middle-class
mothers and children performed better on the task (14.6 points) than mother

and children from other groups (9.2; 8.3; 9.5). Mothers of the three lower-status groups were relatively persistent, rejecting more complete figures than the middle-class mothers; mothers from the middle class praised the child's efforts more than did other mothers but gave just as much criticism; the child's cooperation as rated by the observer was as good or better in low-status groups as in middle-class pairs, there was little difference between the groups in affect expressed to the child by the mother (Brophy *et al.*, 1965).

In these data, as in other not presented here, the mothers of the four status groups differed relatively little, on the average, in the affective elements of their interaction with their children.The gross differences appeared in the verbal and cognitive environments that they presented.

Against this background I would like to return for a moment to the problem of the meaning, or, perhaps more correctly, the lack of meaning in cultural deprivation. One of the features of the behaviour of the working-class mothers and children is a tendency to act without taking sufficient time for reflection and planning. In a sense one might call this impulsive behaviour—not by acting out unconscious or forbidden impulses, but in a type of activity in which a particular act seems not to be related to the act that preceded it or to its consequences. In this sense it lacks meaning; it is not sufficiently related to the context in which it occurs, to the motivations of the participants, or to the goals of the task. This behaviour may be verbal or motor; it shows itself in several ways. On the Etch-a-Sketch task, for example, the mother may silently watch a child make an error and then punish him. Another mother will anticipate the error, will warn the child that he is about to reach a decision point; she will prepare him by verbal and nonverbal cues to be careful, to look ahead, and to avoid the mistake. He is encouraged to reflect, to anticipate the consequences of his action, and in this way to avoid error. A problem-solving approach requires reflection and the ability to weigh decisions, to choose among alternatives. The effect of restricted speech and of status orientation is to foreclose the need for reflective weighing of alternatives and consequences; the use of an elaborated code, with its orientation to persons and to consequences (including future), tends to produce cognitive styles more easily adapted to problem-solving and reflection.

The objective of our study is to discover how teaching styles of the mothers induce and shape learning styles and information-processing strategies in the children. The picture that is beginning to emerge is that the meaning of deprivation is a deprivation of meaning—a cognitive environment in which behaviour is controlled by status rules rather than by attention to the individual characteristics of a specific situation and one in which behaviour is not mediated by verbal cues or by teaching that relates events to one another and the present to the future. This environment produces a child who relates to authority rather than to rationale, who, although often compliant, is not reflective in his behaviour, and for whom the consequences of an act are largely considered in terms of immediate punishment or reward rather than future effects and long-range goals.

When the data are more complete, a more detailed analysis of the findings will enable us to examine the effect of maternal cognitive environments in terms of individual mother-child transactions, rather than in the gross categories of social class. This analysis will not only help us to understand how social-class environment is mediated through the interaction between mother and child but will give more precise information about the effects of individual maternal environments on the cognitive growth of the young child.

References

Bernstein B., 1961. Social class and linguistic development: a theory of social learning. In A. H. Halsey, Jean Floud, & C. A. Anderson (eds), *Education, Economy, and Society*. Glencoe, Ill.: Free Pr.

Bernstein, B., 1964. Family role systems, communication, and socialization. Paper presented at Conf. on Develpm. of Cross-National Res. on the Education of Children and Adolescents, Univer. of Chicago, February.

Brohy, J., Hess, R. D., & Shipman, Virginia, 1965. Effects of social class and level of aspiration on performance in a structured mother-child interaction. Paper presented at Biennial Meeting of Soc. Res. Child Develpm., Minneapolis, Minn., March.

Deutsch, M., 1963. The disadvantaged child and the learning process. In A. H. Passow (ed.), *Education in depressed areas*. New York: Columbia Univer. T.C. Pp. 163-180.

Deutsch, M., & Brown, B., 1964. Social influences in Negro-white intelligence differences. *J. soc. Issues,* [20] (2), 24-35.

Eells, K., Davis, Allison, Havighurst, R. J., Herrick, V. E., & Tyler, R. W., 1951. *Intelligence and cultural differences*. Chicago: Univer. of Chicago Pr.

Hess, R. D., 1964. Educability and rehabilitation: the future of the welfare class. *Marr. fam. Lvg,* [26], 422-429.

Jackson, J. D., Hess, R. D. & Shipman, Virginia, 1965. Communication styles in teachers: an experiment. Paper presented at Amer. Educ. and Res. Ass., Chicago, February.

John, Vera, 1963. The intellectual development of slum children: some preliminary findings. *Amer J. Orthopsychiat.,* [33], 813-822.

Kagan, J., Moss, H. A., & Sigel, I. E., 1963. Psychological significance of styles of conceptualization. *Monogr. Soc. Res. Child Develpm.,* [28], No. 2.

Kagan, J., 1964. Information processing in the child: significance of analytic and reflective attitudes. *Psychol. Monogr.,* [78], No. 1 (whole no. 578).

Kennedy, W. A., Van de Riet, V., & White, J. C., Jr., 1963. A normative sample of intelligence and achievement of Negro elementary school children in the southeastern United States. *Monogr. Soc. Res. Child Develpm.,* [28], No. 6.

Lesser, G., 1964. Mental abilities of children in different social and cultural groups. New York: Cooperative Research Project No. 1635.

Meyer, Roberta, Shipman, Virginia, & Hess, R. D., 1964. Family structure and social class in the socialization of curiosity in urban preschool children. Paper presented at APA meeting in Los Angeles, Calif. September.

Olim, E. G., Hess, R. D., & Shipman, Virginia, 1965. Relationship between mothers' language styles and cognitive styles of urban preschool children. Paper presented at Biennial Meeting of Soc. Res. Child Develpm., Minneapolis, Minn., March.

Shipman, Virginia, & Hess, R. D., 1965. Social class and sex differences in the utilization of language and the consequences for cognitive development. Paper presented at Midwest. Psychol. Ass., Chicago, April.

Julienne Ford
Department of Sociology, Enfield College of Technology
Douglas Young
Department of Sociology, West Ham College of Technology
Steven Box
Department of Sociology, University of Kent at Canterbury

Functional autonomy, role distance, and social class

From *British Journal of Sociology*, 1967, [18], pp. 370-381.
Reproduced by permission from Routledge and Kegan Paul Ltd., and Dr. Ford.
This is an edited version of the original article. D.F.

An observation commonly made about working class[1] childhoods is that they are characterized by long periods in which parental control is virtually absent.[2] At the earliest opportunity children are allowed to go out to play in the streets, local parks, playgrounds and building-sites, or to go alone to the local cinema. One might assume from this that working class children grow up with a highly developed sense of independence and an ability to cope with ambiguity. Yet our knowledge of the adult working class indicates the opposite. Their lives have a routinized collective quality in which notions of the traditional are standards for 'the proper'. The lives of adults are governed by what we may call 'rulefulness' whereas those of children seem to be anarchic.

In this paper we intend to explain this paradox by exploring the implications of differential relationship to social structure for individual dramaturgical skill. We argue that the show of role distance[3] is a mode of role-playing normally available only to the middle class, while working class behaviour is more typically an expression of rulefulness. Thus we consider that interpretation of society in dramaturgical terms[4] is not wholly useful to an understanding of working class behaviour; for the latter 'receive' rather than 'interpret' social structure.[5]

[1] Throughout this paper a conception of social class in terms of two simple ideal types will be employed. We are, of course, aware that the detailed picture is more complex than this. However we consider that the literature on the 'new' class structure suggests that certain core features of 'middle' and 'working' class subcultures remain distinct. There is a vast literature which could be cited to support our usage; two of the most recent overviews are: M. Kahan, D. Butler and D. Stokes (1966), and D. Lockwood (1966).

[2] See for examples of this J. Klein (1965); W. B. Miller (1958); J. B. Mays (1954).

[3] On this see E. Goffman (1961). For a recent discussion of the concept see R. L. Coser, (1966).

[4] For examples, see E. Goffman (1959); P. Berger (1963), esp. ch. 6; G. J. McCall and J. L. Simmons (1966). For summaries of the main tenets of this school of thought see A. M. Rose (1962: 3-19); and B. J. Biddle and B. J. Thomas (1966: 3-4).

[5] It has been suggested that man is differentiated from the animals in that the latter can only receive meanings whereas he can create them; see R. A. Schermerhorn (1963). We believe however that the equation of the human with the voluntary is misleading, and that this differentiation also obtains *between* men.

Where social structure is 'received' emphasis is on the imperative nature of mores without reference to a legitimating rationale. The only possible answer to the question 'Why?' is 'Because it is right'. This 'emphasis on the binding power of the mores and folkways . . . on the blind adherence to custom corresponds with a society populated by people playing roles principally as sets of expectations with which they must comply'.[6] Where structure is 'interpreted', on the other hand, custom is seen as defining *ranges* of tolerable variation rather than the precise content of behaviour. The individual thus interprets concrete social events in the light of abstract principles—he has a 'theory' of social structure. In this case ideas of what is situationally appropriate rather than what is 'right' provide parameters for behaviour. The discretionary element in role behaviour thus affords the options not only of playing but also of *playing at*[7] roles.

Examples of this can be found in the different meanings which persons from different social class backgrounds impute to a similar form of address. Both middle and working class persons may call a policeman, 'Officer', but the former may do so with an awareness that to play out his citizen role in a deferential manner may be situationally advantageous to him, while the latter may do so because he sees it as the 'proper' thing to do.

Far from being at odds with differential childhood behaviours, we argue that these adult social class differences in role playing actually derive from certain differences in childhood experience. For we hope to show that it is only in a condition of functional autonomy (Gouldner, 1959) that the option of role distance is created for the actor. We argue that working class patterns of elementary behaviour[8] are productive of functional dependence, while those of the middle class tend to generate independence, or functional autonomy. Intervening in these processes are the distinctive concepts of *justice, friendship* and *privacy* which characterize the social classes.

We shall first describe these ideal types of social exchange behaviour in terms of class conceptions of justice, friendship and privacy. Then we shall discuss the interrelations of the concepts of *social exchange, functional autonomy* and *role distance* on a higher level of abstraction. Finally we shall suggest some implications of our observations for the Interactionist conception of society.

Class notions of justice, friendship and privacy

An individual's conception of justice is centrally related to his basic

6 R. Turner (1962) p. 38. Turner is not talking, as we are, about two distinct modes of role-taking. He sees what we call 'received' and 'interpreted' structures as alternative modes of explanation of role-taking in general. Other students have isolated some aspects of received culture in their relationship to childhood socialization. See, for example, M. L. Kohn (1959a) and (1959b).

7 This is Goffman's (1961) distinction, *op. cit.*, p. 99.

8 For an explanation of the use of this term, see G. C. Homans (1961).

notions about the difference between individuals and will hence affect his approach to social exchange. If we accept the premise that the child's earliest idea of justice is based on parity of distribution (Piaget, 1932) we can trace the way in which this notion is modified for both social classes, and draw out the implications of this for differential dramaturgical perception.

In a cultural-historical sense, the working class family setting can be seen as one of chronic scarcity of material resources; in these circumstances distribution within the household is governed by rationing. This rationing must be effected in order both to ensure physical survival and to minimize conflict within the family. Both these imperatives favour a distribution according to the ascribed statuses of age, sex and familial function. For example where distribution of food is concerned physiological necessity dictates that the working males shall be favoured. Allocation on the bases of such highly visible criteria as age and sex also provides an overtly just rationale for distribution, and in this manner rationing is effected with minimum threat to group cohesion.

The necessity to avoid conflict within the group also explains why the sanctions maintaining these principles of distribution tend to be characterized by appeals to self-evidence. Since the mother not only lacks material resources but also the time for any complicated explanations these appeals will be backed ultimately by recourse to physical or verbal coercion. Thus the child learns a model of justice as a self-evident order, as something which is 'right and proper'; while parity remains the underlying principle he modifies this in consideration of a growing number of overt status distinctions.

Congruent with this conception of justice is the working class concept of friendship as a dense area of reciprocal rights and duties based on parity. The child has learned from his experiences in the family to categorize people in terms of simple ascribed status distinctions. Since this is the only mode of differentiation between individuals of which he is aware, status equivalence (in terms of age and sex) becomes the sole criterion of eligibility for friendship. Friends emerge, from the undifferentiated category of individuals of similar status, as children become willing to accept a greater degree of interaction with one another on a 'share and share alike' principle. Hence inter-personal approach behaviours will be concerned with demonstrations of willingness to share; this may be in swopping, lending, or even passing the ball in a game. Thus friendship can be seen to grow out of behavioural rather than verbal demonstration, and confirmation of reciprocal social exchange.

Working class friendships can therefore be expected to be high on both scope and pervasiveness for as the demands for reciprocity intensify, both the number of friends it is possible to have and the frequency of extra-friend interaction will be restricted.[9] Thus working class friendships are multi-

9 There is surprisingly little evidence available on social class differentials in number, intensity and duration of friendships. For findings tending to support our hypothesis see F. Dotson (1951); W. A. Anderson (1946). For more direct evidence of the relationship between social class and gregariousness, see E. Katz and P. F. Lazarsfeld (1964).

functional rather than segmentary, a situation which may lead to a lack of differentiation between friends and self and a minimization of unique behaviours. For as Simmel[10] has pointed out, the more the group becomes differentiated from non-members the less the members can be differentiated from each other: the distinct group is the homogeneous group.

The mode of friendship described here, with its age-specific and unindividuated activities, will clearly not provide the child with experience of social exchange which is cumulative and transferable. Participation in the initiation and termination of working class friendships does not lead to the learning of generalizable interpersonal techniques. On the one hand the initial approach behaviours are geared to subculturally peculiar activities and do not engender any learning of universally valid principles of exploration. Friendship formation is therefore a one-time activity, or at least one which is seldom repeated. On the other hand the termination of such friendships is also a rare event, since the restricting elements in the procedures defend them from intrusion. For relationships based on behavioural demonstration are particularly fragile: whereas verbal expressions of withdrawal and reparation can be subject to later reinterpretation, behavioural indiscretions are undeniably disruptive and hence usually final. Fear of the certain consequence of negative behaviours on the part of any member leads to an institutionalized caution in in-group relations. So in a double sense the working class friendship pattern precludes experimentation in role-playing techniques.

The homogeneous long-enduring working class friendship group is thus characterized by reciprocal social exchange on the basis of intrinsic rather than extrinsic reward: for the powerful affective bond becomes of primary importance. The friendship is therefore in the very fullest sense unindividuated, for it is characterized by an extreme lack of segmental participation; indeed the role segmentation involved in it may be even less than that involved in the love relationship for, as Simmel has said, 'This entering of the whole undivided ego into the relationship may be more plausible in friendship than in love for the reason that friendship lacks the specific concentration on one element which love derives from its sensuousness. . . . It may therefore be more apt than love to connect a whole person with another in its entirety.' Such a situation has little use for the concept of privacy and the verbal planning procedures or 'tact' that go with it.

In contrast with the above the middle class child can be seen as developing a theory of justice which takes account of individual differences. He is aware not only of status distinctions but of individual circumstances, of special local attributes; thus for example he would recognize 'being miserable' as a circumstance mitigating reciprocal duty, indeed as a special need entailing certain rights.

Congruent with his theory of justice is his approach to friendship formation. For him there are a range of characteristics to be considered in differentiating

---

10 G. Simmel (1965: 110). See also D. N. Levine (1959: 15).

the eligible from the ineligible in the process of choosing friends. He scans others for points of similarity, for willingness to be explored. Whereas the working class child takes interests for granted as being largely identical and confronts his peers totally, 'on the other hand, unique individuals can engage one another only at odd points or at rare intervals. Like meshed gears they can touch only at limited segments of their perimeters' (Wolff, 1959; 315). The confrontation is activity-specific; the child may ask, 'I like fishing. How about you?' Hence the resultant friendship is itself activity specific rather than total.[11] These friendships are based on the extrinsic benefits to be gained from reciprocal exchange. For this reason these scanning procedures may provide cumulative experience, in effect apprenticeship, in the instrumental use of expressive behaviours which is central to much adult middle class role playing.

The distinctive nature of middle class ideas of privacy is understandable in the light of the above. The concept which Simmel discusses under the head of 'discretion' is really only applicable to the middle class interpersonal relationship. Discretion, which 'consists . . . in staying away from knowledge of all that the other does not expressly reveal to us', (Simmel, 1965: 321) can only apply where social exchange is extrinsic rather than intrinsic, segmented rather than total. The notion of 'safeguard distance', (Head, 1961) which applies in the working class only outside friendship boundaries, is present in all middle class interpersonal behaviour.

Thus far we have argued that the different conceptions of justice, friendship and privacy which characterize the social classes produce differences in the degree to which children gain cumulative experience of manipulation of social exchange processes which will be relevant to adult role-playing. We consider that these differences, which will be analysed below as differences in the condition of functional autonomy, derive from the differential relationship to social structure of the social classes. We have indicated that the characteristic working class conception of justice may have derived historically from scarcity of material resources; this pattern may have assumed cultural autonomy which accounts for its persistence even in the absence of such scarcity. One can less readily 'explain' the pattern of justice and the derivative conceptions of friendship and privacy for the middle class. Clearly the conditions described for working class families are absent; there is no shortage of goods or of maternal time. It might, however, also be suggested, following Blau, (1964. Ch. 4) that their relative resources place them in an advantageous position in the processes of social exchange in which they engage.

Social exchange, functional autonomy and role distance

In the above discussion we have been concerned to argue that, only where an individual's social exchange transactions place him in a position of functional

[11] The activity-specific nature of the typical middle class friendship is illuminated by Elizabeth Bott (1964: 779).

autonomy, does he acquire role-playing techniques which enable him to exploit the interaction situation to his benefit. It is now time to turn our attention to consideration of the interrelations of the concepts of social exchange, functional autonomy and role distance on a more abstract level.

The notion that most social behaviour is of a reciprocal or exchange nature is by now widely accepted. Ego's actions are clearly affected by his expectations of alter's reciprocal, though not necessarily complementary, reactions. Of course it would be tautologous to discuss all interaction in exchange terms, for, as Gouldner (1962) cautions, the notion of reciprocity must be supplemented by that of force. Yet the 'elementary' behaviour with which we are here concerned certainly falls into the category which it is useful to discuss in these terms.

If we consider the individual actor as a system part, then the relevance of Gouldner's discussion of functional autonomy for the analysis of interpersonal relations becomes clear. The various system parts can be seen as offering and requiring different goods and services; their very heterogeneity makes them interdependent. Yet because exchange does not occur in isolated dyadic relations, the needs of one individual structure may be 'spread' such that they are satisfied by a large number of others. It is in this way that functional autonomy or independence is attained; for the individual structure is not dependent on any one structure for all its needs. (Gouldner, 1959).

Varying degrees of functional autonomy can be explained initially with reference to Blau's categorization of alternatives to compliance (dependence). Where a structure A has a particular need which can only be fulfilled by one particular other structure, B, then A is potentially dependent on B. However, if A can *either* supply inducements to B, *or* force B to benefit it without reciprocation (or, of course if A can, in some way, do without the gratification in question), then A can avoid dependence on B. However, as indicated above, a dyadic exchange relation does not occur in isolation but in the context of a complete system of exchanges. Thus it must be emphasized that A's ability to avoid dependence on B will be determined by A's relative independence in respect to all its other relations of exchange. For, clearly, not only the ability to supply inducements, but also the ability to use force, will depend on resources external to the particular exchange relation in question.

Blau's fourfold choice schema is thus ultimately reducible to the single issue of the extent to which a structure is able to 'spread its risks', derive different benefits from different structures, and hence attain functional autonomy.

The claim has been made above that, for the individual actor, the situation of functional autonomy can be seen as a prerequisite for the enactment of role distance behaviours. We shall now turn to a closer examination of this.

Goffman sees his formlation of role distance as providing 'a sociological means of dealing with one type of divergence between obligation and actual performance' (Goffman, 1961: 115). Role distance behaviours, then, are those which 'constitute a wedge between the individual and his role, between his

E

doing and being' (Goffman, 1961: 108). What the actor is doing when he expresses role distance is to deny the 'virtual self', or 'ready-made me' implied by the role; but he does not deny that he is playing the role. Whether this is done by extreme casualness—insinuation that the role can be played without effort—or by deliberate 'overplaying',[12] the effect is the same: the actor is claiming that he is not defined by his role, it is only a segment of his whole being. Role distance is thus a situational expression of role segmentation, a signal to others of the existence of exchange transactions external to the current relationship.

Now role segmentation is ultimately dependent on audience segregation. For, only when the role-others figuring in one of an individual's role sets do not figure in others, can the individual avoid dependence on one role relationship[13] for full definition of his identity. On the other hand, when an individual plays out most of his roles in front of the same audience, he becomes entirely dependent on them: because they alone can define him. It is only where roles are played to a variety of different audiences that the actor can say to one group of role-others, 'I am not only what you think I am. I am also something else.' Thus where the various roles which constitute the whole self are played before several different audiences, that is to say where there is functional autonomy in social exchange, then role distance techniques are always possible as means of retreat from one self to another.

Now, for an actor to take advantage of the options available to him in a situation of functional autonomy, it is necessary for him to have a dramaturgical perspective on society. Instead of a vision of society as a prison in which behaviour or views; where the questions used are open-ended the answers flexible enough to withstand many variant interpretations.[14]

Summary and discussion

We have argued above that working class culture is of a 'received' type, and that the conditions surrounding the transmission and reception of this culture are likely to produce behaviour which is best described as 'ruleful'. By contrast the middle class can be understood as 'interpreting' rather than 'receiving' a culture. They come to learn the broad range of behaviours which are tolerable in a given situation, the rationales for these behaviours, and the consequences likely to follow from the various different strategies.[15]

12 For one example of application of the technique of 'underplaying' and 'overplaying', see T. Burns and G. M. Stalker (1959: 215-16).

13 Southall (1959), distinguishes between role and role relationship. A teacher has one role and as many role relationships as pupils, a father who has his son as partner in his business has one role relationship and two roles.

14 These opposing perspectives are discussed by Berger (1963) chs. 4 and 6.

15 For reasons of brevity we have not developed a further elaboration of this distinction by including in our discussion the obviously related concepts of 'sociological ambivalence', 'cognitive dissonance' and 'intolerance of ambiguity'. See, on these respectively, R. K. Merton and E. Barber (1963); L. Festinger (1957); E. Frenkel-Brunswick (1949-50).

The theme of this paper can now be summarized briefly. The particular notions of justice to which working class children are introduced can be seen as giving rise to conceptualizations of friendship based on 'total' affective relations. Thus early social exchange transactions take place in a situation of functional dependence, rather than autonomy. Such associations preclude the development of notions of privacy outside of those involved in crude in-group/out-group distinctions. In these circumstances they do not gain experience of universally valid interpersonal behaviour techniques such as role distance.

As a result of these childhood experiences adult working class persons, when they are afforded functional autonomy (such as that which is involved in the physical separation of work and home life), are unable to take up the dramaturgical option. They are able only to *play* but not to *play at* roles.

Thus it seems to us that a serious limitation is imposed upon the sociological view of society as drama. The suggestion that man attempts consciously to control his presentation of self, and to maximize his gratification from the identity options available to him, entails a misleading assumption of voluntarism. Berger (1963: 142) suggests that if men, reflecting on why they obey institutional imperatives, say, 'I have no choice', they are deceiving themselves. Even where there is no choice within a particular role, he argues 'nevertheless the individual has the choice of stepping outside the role'. Similarly Sartre (1943) maintains that to act only within the requirements of a role is to act in 'bad faith', and he sees 'bad faith' as a dishonest rejection of freedom.

Yet we have attempted to show that, for those who are not in a situation of functional autonomy, and for those who have not acquired the relevant skills to exploit such a situation, the option of role distance is not available.

If the above interpretation is correct then, in addition to imposing limitations on the utility of the Interactionist perspective, it has crucial implications for certain research procedures and also for educational policy. If we have given a true description of the way in which the working class individual is related to social structure then limits are set upon the validity of his reportage of structure. Often respondents are required to give 'reasons' for behaviour or views; where the questions used are open-ended the answers may look like rationales. However these responses may, in fact, be merely 'received' ideas: they may represent no more than the respondents' perceptions of what is the proper answer to give.[16] In some cases, however, the working class respondent may find a question requiring a reason for actions or attitudes so meaningless that he does not even have a 'received' notion of what answer to give. Bernstein and Young (1967) in a study of social class differences in conceptions about the uses of toys, gave a closed schedule in which mothers were required to rank six 'ideas about what toys are for' in order of importance. They found a tendency for working class mothers to rank in a purely

---

[16] They appeal, in other words, to an acceptable 'vocabulary of motives'. See H. Gerth and C. W. Mills (1953).

E*

random manner while middle class respondents showed a clear pattern of preference. Thus the idea of 'received' structure indicates critical problems for questionnaire design and the interpretation of data.

The above discussion also suggests certain practical imperatives in the field of the sociology of education. For, if one of the major handicaps which the working class child suffers is deficiency in role-playing ability, then the relevant remedial measures are those directed towards impregnating the child with a dramaturgical awareness. Only the individual who has this dramatic skill will be able to *create* structure : Only he can experience the freedom which can come from exploitation of a functionally autonomous situation.

References

Anderson, W. A., 1946. Family social participation and social status self-rating. *American Sociological Review*, [11], 253-58.

Berger, P., 1963. *Invitation to Sociology*. New York: Anchor.

Bernstein, B., and Young, D., 1967. Social class differences in conceptions of the uses of toys. *Sociology*, [1], 131-40.

Biddle, B. J., and Thomas, B. J., 1966. *Role Theory: Concepts and Research*. New York: Wiley.

Blau, P. M., 1964. *Exchange and Power in Social Life*. New York: Wiley.

Bott, E., 1964. *Family and Social Network*. London: Tavistock.

Burns, T., and Stalker, G. M., 1959. *The Management of Innovation*. London: Tavistock.

Coser, R. L., 1966. Role distance, ambivalence and transition status. *American Journal of Sociology*, [72], 173-87.

Dotson, F., 1951. Patterns of voluntary association among urban working class families. *American Sociological Review*, [16], 687-93.

Festinger, L., 1957. *A Theory of Cognitive Dissonance*. Evanston: Row, Peterson.

Frenkel-Brunswick, E. 1949-50. Intolerance of ambiguity as an emotional and perceptual personality variable. *Journal of Personality*, [18], 109-43.

Gerth, H., and Mills, C. W., 1953. *Character and Social Structure*. London: Routledge.

Goffman, E., 1959. *Presentation of Self in Everyday Life*. New York: Anchor.

Goffman, E., 1961. Role Distance. In *Encounters*. Indianapolis: Bobbs Merrill. Pp. 83-152.

Gouldner, A. W., 1959. Reciprocity and autonomy in functional theory. In L. Gross (ed.), *Symposium on Sociological Theory*, New York: Harper and Row.

Gouldner, A. W., 1962. The norm of reciprocity. *American Sociological Review*, [27], 31-41.

Head, W. G., 1961. Adaptive sociology. *British Journal of Sociology*, [12], 23-40.

Homans, G. C., 1961. *Human Behaviour: its Elementary Forms*. London: Routledge.

Kahan, M., Butler, D., and Stokes, D., 1966. On the analytical division of social class. *British Journal of Sociology*, [17], 122-32.

Katz, E., and Lazarsfeld, P. F., 1964. *Personal Influence*. New York: Free Press.

Klein, J., 1965. *Samples from English Cultures*, Vol. 1. London: Routledge.

Kohn, M. L., 1959a. Social class and parental values, *American Journal of Sociology* [64], 337-51.

Kohn, M. L., 1959b. Social class and the exercise of parental authority. *American Sociological Review*, [24], 352-66.

Levine, D. N. 1959. The structure of Simmel's social thought. In K. H. Wolff (ed.), *Essays on Sociology, Philosophy, and Aesthetics*, New York: Harper.

Lockwood, D., 1966. Sources of variation in working class images of society. *Sociological Review*, [14], 249-67.

McCall, G. J., and Simmons, J. L., 1966. *Identities and Interactions*. New York: Free Press.

Mays, J. B., 1954. *Growing Up in the City*. Liverpool University Press.

Merton, R. K., and Barber, E., 1963. Sociological ambivalence. In E. A. Tiryakian (ed.), *Sociological Theory, Values and Sociocultural Change*. New York: Free Press.

Miller, W. B., 1958. Lower class culture as a generating milieu for gang delinquency, *Journal of Social Issues*, [14], 5-9.

Piaget, J., 1932. *The Moral Judgement of the Child*. London: Kegan Paul.

Rose, A. M., (ed.), 1962. *Human Behaviour and Social Processes*. London: Routledge.

Sartre, J. P., 1943. *L'être et le Néant*. Paris: Gallimard.

Schermerhorn, R. A., 1963. Man the unfinished. *Sociological Quarterly*, [4], 5-17.

Simmel, G., 1965. *The Sociology of Georg Simmel*, translated and edited by K. H. Wolff. Glencoe: Free Press.

Southall, A., 1959. An operational theory of role. *Human Relations*, [12], 17-34.

Turner, R., 1962. Role taking: process versus conformity. In A. Rose (ed.), *Human Behaviour and Social Processes*. London: Routledge.

Wolff, K. H., (ed.), 1959. *Essays on Sociology, Philosophy, and Aesthetics*. New York: Harper.

Rosabeth Moss Kanter
Department of Sociology, Brandeis University

Commitment and social organization: a study of commitment mechanisms in utopian communities*

Reprinted from *American Sociological Review,* 1968, Vol. 33, pp. 499-517, copyright by the American Sociological Association, and reproduced by permission of the Association and the Author.

This is an edited version of the original article. D.F.

The material in this article is further elaborated in Rosabeth Moss Kanter, *Commitment and Community*: *Communes and Utopias in Sociological Perspective, Cambridge, Mass*: *Harvard University Press,* 1972. D.F.

Commitment is a consideration which arises at the intersection of organizational requisites and personal experience. On the one hand, social systems organize to meet systemic 'needs'; and on the other hand, people orient themselves positively and negatively, emotionally and intellectually, to situations. Since social orders are supported by people, one problem of collectivities is to meet organizational requisites in such a way that participants at the same time become positively involved with the system—loyal, loving, dedicated, and obedient. This requires solutions to organizational or systemic problems that are simultaneously mechanisms for ensuring commitment through their effects on individuals—their experience and orientations. Commitment, then, refers to the willingness of social actors to give their energy and loyalty to social systems, the attachment of personality systems to social relations which are seen as self-expressive. As such, the concept is of major theoretical importance, since it promises to join structural-functional considerations with phenomenology. At the same time, it has practical importance in a society in which many social problems are seen as stemming from lack of commitment. Yet, according to Becker (1960: 32), 'there has been little formal analysis of the concept of commitment and little attempt to integrate it explicitly with current sociological theory'. (And, I may add, little attempt to utilize it in organizational

*Funds for the research described here were provided by a National Institute of Mental Health Pre-Doctoral Research Fellowship and the Center for Research on Social Organization, University of Michigan, under the direction of Albert J. Reiss, Jr. Earlier versions of this paper were read at the 1967 Meetings of the American Sociological Association and at a Department of Social Relations Colloquium, Harvard University. It includes portions of a doctoral dissertation submitted to the Department of Sociology, University of Michigan. Helpful comments were made by William A. Gamson, Leon H. Mayhew, Daniel Katz, Naphtali Golomb, Lewis A. Coser, and Stuart A. Kanter.

research, even though it is central to the understanding of both human motivation and system maintenance.) Such an integration and utilization is attempted here. By focusing on a kind of organization for which the securing of commitment is crucial to success, this paper will describe a number of structural arrangements and organizational strategies which promote and sustain commitment.

Theoretical considerations

Commitment may be defined as the process through which individual interests become attached to the carrying out of socially organized patterns of behaviour which are seen as fulfilling those interests, as expressing the nature and needs of the person. This definition bears some conceptual similarities to Parsons' notion of 'institutionalization': 'the integration of the expectations of actors in a relevant interactive system of roles with a shared normative pattern of values.' (Parsons and Shils, 1962: 20). What is added here, however, is a broader conception of commitment, in which actors become committed not only to norms but also to other aspects of a social system.

We may distinguish three major social system problems involving the commitment of actors: social control, group cohesiveness,[1] and continuation as an action system (retaining participants).[2] Continuance, cohesion, and control are three analytically distinct problems, with potentially independent solutions. An actor may be committed to continuing his system membership but be continually deviant within the system, uncommitted to its control. For example, a rebellious teenager may reject his parents' control but be unwilling to withdraw from the family system. Futhermore, an actor may be very solidary with a group in a social system but be uncommitted to continued participation in the system, because of other circumstances. An office worker, for example, may take a better job even though her best friends work in her former office. The inmate of a prison may form close ties with fellow prisoners

[1] In very complex systems it might seem likely that group cohesiveness would be limited to peer groups. However, if cohesiveness is defined not in terms of sociability and mutual attraction but rather in terms of the ability to withstand disruptive forces and threats from outside the group ('sticking together') it would apply to systems of any degree of complexity. This improved meaning of cohesiveness has been proposed by Gross and Martin (1952).

[2] While *recruitment* of actors would seem at first glance to be as important for continuation of a system as *retention* of actors, recruitment and retention are two analytically distinct problems, solved by different kinds of organizational strategies. I would argue that recruitment does not particularly require commitment but may be accomplished in many other ways, with non-committed actors; e.g., birth, accident, and external organizational phenomena may serve to recruit uncommitted individuals. However, once a person has performed any single act within a system, the problem arises of committing him to further and future participation. Thus, the *commitment* necessary for continuation deals with retaining participants. Recruiting them is not a commitment problem (although, of course, the ways in which they are recruited has implications for commitment).

and even with guards, yet certainly wish to leave the system at the earliest opportunity. In specific social systems, one or another of these commitment problems may be of paramount importance; e.g,. a business organization may concentrate on solving problems of continuance rather than cohesion. In other cases the three may be causally related; in fact, solutions to all three problems may be mutually reinforcing and multiply determined. But it is analytically possible to distinguish *continuance, cohesion* and *control* as the social system axes of commitment.

It is proposed here that commitment of actors to participating in the system, remaining members, (*continuance commitment*) involves primarily their *cognitive* orientations. When profits and costs are considered, participants find that the cost of leaving the system would be greater than the cost of remaining: 'profit' compels continued participation. (Considerations of cognitive consistency enter here.) Continuance commitment, in a more general sense, can be conceptualized as commitment to a social system role. Commitment of actors to group solidarity, to a set of social relationships, (*cohesion commitment*) involves primarily their forming positive *cathectic* orientations; affective ties bind members to the community, and gratifications stem from involvement with all the members of the group. Solidarity is high: 'infighting' and jealousy low. A cohesive system can withstand threats to its existence; members 'stick together'. Commitment of actors to uphold norms and obey the authority of the group (*control commitment*) involves primarily their forming positive *evaluative* orientations. Demands made by the system are evaluated as right, as moral, as just, as expressing one's own values, so that obedience to these demands is a normative necessity, and sanctioning by the system is regarded as appropriate.[3]

The three kinds of commitment proposed here can be seen to cover the major aspects of the linking of the individual, as a personality system, to a social system,[4] and as such, articulate with other formulations concerning a person's willingness to carry out socially organized lines of behaviour. Cognitive-continuance commitment is commitment to social *roles*, or to positions in social systems, with no affectivity or evaluation attached to the role; the role merely has a positive valence. This is on a similar level to what Kelman (1958) has termed 'compliance', acting in terms of rewards and punishments, profits and costs. Cathectic-cohesion commitment is attachment to social *relationships*, which absorb the individuals' fund of affectivity, but again do not have internal moral imperatives attached to them. This resembles Kelman's

[3] Social control is possible without control commitments by participants, of course, i.e., without their positive evaluative or normative orientations, but it should not be as efficient or effective.

[4] There is one additional aspect of commitment, concerning cognitive orientations, which should be mentioned, although it is not central to the present analysis. Commitment can also link the personality system to the cultural system, creating a cognitive-cultural commitment in which the individual comes to internalize group symbols and to see things as the group sees them. (This idea was suggested by Leon H. Mayhew.)

'identification'. Finally, evaluative-control commitment is commitment to *norms*, the values and inner convictions which morally obligate the individual. This resembles Kelman's third type, 'internalization', in which the individual accepts influence which appears congruent with and even necessitated by his inner core of beliefs. The three kinds of commitment can also be seen to form a scale similar to that which may be proposed for the development of morality in children: the child first obeys social system demands because of rewards and punishments, then because of emotional attachment to others, and finally in terms of an internalized moral code.[5]

What the present formulation emphasizes that others do not, however, are the implications of the types of commitment not merely for the individual but for the social system. First, it is to different areas of the social system that the three personal orientations are attached, so that different consequences stem from different kinds of commitment. Groups in which members have formed cognitive-continuance commitments should manage to hold their members. Groups in which members have formed cathectic-cohesion commitments should be able to withstand threats to their existence, should have more 'stick-together-ness'. Groups in which members have formed evaluative-control commitments should have less deviance, challenge to authority, or ideological controversy—of course ignoring for the moment all the other diverse sources of influence on group life. Systems with all three kinds of commitment, with total commitment, should be more successful in their maintenance than those without.

At the same time, the reasons for gaining this commitment exist on the social system level—in the way the system is organized, in the implications of social arrangements for whether or not actors *do* tend to positively cognize, cathect, and evaluate the system. Since the social order is the *object* of commitment, differences in social organization should affect commitment. Thus, a criterion for the success of a social system in gaining commitment is whether or not it implements a program of social arrangements which tend to involve and bind participants' orientations. Such programs represent one kind of 'social management of experience', a perspective taking into account both social-structural and phenomenological variables. When people are committed to social orders, structure and phenomenology are mutually re-inforcing, and maintenance of the social system is intimately linked with maintenance of the self.

The proposition follows, then, that groups whose existence is dependent on the commitment of their participants should be more successfully maintained if they utilize social arrangement which promote commitment of all three types. Such commitment mechanisms can be proposed and their efficacy tested.

[5] This becomes apparent when one attempts to integrate the many findings on moral development embodying diverse points of view. It is suggested, for example, by the juxtaposition of studies reviewed by Roger Brown (1960: 381-417).

The empirical setting and research design

Utopian communities provide an interesting universe of organizations in which to study commitment mechanisms because in them certain problems are highlighted. Since they represent attempts to establish ideal social orders, but exist within a larger society, they, especially, must vie with the outside for members' loyalties. They must ensure high member involvement despite external competition without sacrificing their distinctiveness or ideals. They must often contravene earlier socialization in securing obedience to new demands. They must calm internal dissension in order to present a united front to the world. The problem of securing total commitment, i.e., in all three organizational areas, is central.

In addition, historical material permits a direct comparison of communities of relatively long duration (which we may term 'successful')[6] with those of relatively short duration (which we may term 'unsuccessful') under a fairly similar set of external social conditions. (Thus we can, in a sense, hold external variables constant while we examine differences in internal organization.) About a hundred utopian communities were born and died in the nineteenth century America, most founded before 1850. Some of these lasted as long as 180 years (the Shaker Villages),[7] while others were in existence only six months (Yellow Springs, Ohio). The population of utopias chosen for examination, then, were those founded in the United States between the Revolutionary and the Civil Wars (roughly 1780 to 1860). This population, although experiencing similar external conditions, varied in type as well as in longevity. Some were more or less sectarian, some primarily secular; some were celibate, others favoured free love. Some utopias derived from immigrant groups and spoke a foreign language. There was a Catholic community, Owenite communes, Fourierite phalanxes (phalansteries), and even one community derived from a literary utopia (Icaria, after Etienne Cabet's *Voyage en Icarie*). While many of the 19th century American utopian communities shared general values, they often implemented them in different ways. This variation in organizational characteristics, then, affords the opportunity for testing comparative hypotheses. Finally, these communities share an advantage of historical rather than contemporary research in that their ultimate historical fate is known: their entire life-span is accessible to the analyst.

A list of 91 utopian communities, representing a population of American utopias founded between 1780 and 1860, was generated from historical sources. A single instance of a community, a unit utopia, was defined using the following criterion: identity of organizational structure with some centralized control

6 'Success' as used here is measured solely by longevity, although it is of course recognized that there may be other criteria for successful maintenance. With respect to utopian communities, however, it is possible to make a case for the argument that one of their primary aims is the creation of an enduring social world.
7 In fact, the Shakers today have a very tenuous hold on life; the remnants of two Shaker villages still exist, but populated by a few old women.

over successive or simultaneous locations. Thus, the Shakers, for example, are considered one case, even though they had at various times 22 villages in different locations. This list was divided into 'successful' and 'unsuccessful' cases and a sample of each drawn. Success was measured by length of time in existence: a system had to exist as a utopian community for at least 25 years in order to be considered successful (a sociological definition of a generation). A case was considered a utopian community as long as all relevant relations among members were centrally controlled by a single organization. Thus, for example, Oneida was considered to be finished as a utopian community when it shifted to formal organization as an economic system and gave up jurisdiction over members' social and marital relations. Its duration as a utopian community was 33 years, even though as some kind of social system it has persisted 119 years. The utility of the 25-year criterion was tested on the whole population, and it was found that only one successful utopia lasted less than 33 years, and no unsuccessful case lasted more than 16 years. The population was found to include 11 successful utopias, 79 unsuccessful ones, and one case that proved to be unclassifiable (Icaria).

The sample consisted of 9 successful and 21 unsuccessful cases, communities for which there were available at least two independent sources of information.[8]

Availability of data was not the only criteria used for selection of the 21 unsuccessful cases . . . All major types and time periods are included. Those of relatively longer duration were over-represented. This was . . . deliberately designed to increase the meaningfulness and validity of the comparison between successful and unsuccessful cases. Social organization does not usually arise suddenly and in toto; it often requires slow periods of getting organized. To include only 3 communities of less than two full years' duration and 14 of at least three full years tends to ensure that the differences between successful and unsuccessful cases will not be wholly due to differences in their stage of organizational development but rather to differences in the kinds of organization they do establish.

Data were collected from sources representing four categories of informants: central members, such as leaders; peripheral members, such as deviants and apostates; visitors and first-hand observers; and historians. In addition, a number of documents, such as constitutions and financial records, were examined.

[8] The sample consisted of the following communities, listed in order of longevity: *Successful*: Shakers (180 years), Harmony (100), Amana (90), Zoar (81), Snowhill (70), St. Nazianz (42), Bethel and Aurora (36), Jerusalem (33), and Oneida (33); *Unsuccessful*: Hopedale (15), Modern Times (15), Bishop Hill (14), North American Phalanx (13), Communia (8), Oberlin (8), Brook Farm (6), Wisconsin Phalanx (6), Northampton (4), Utopia (4), Kendal (3), Nashoba (3), First Mormon United Order (3), Skaneateles (3), Iowa Pioneer Phalanx (2), Jasper (2), New Harmony (2), Preparation (2), Blue Spring (1), Fruitlands (8 months), and Yellow Springs (6 months).

For each kind of commitment defined earlier, cognitive-continuance, cathectic-cohesion, and evaluative-control, two processes were conceptualized —one a dissociative process, which would operate to free the personality system from other commitments, and one an associative process, operating to attach the personality to the current object of commitment. Commitment mechanisms were derived in terms of these processes and a series of hypotheses tested by comparing successful and unsuccessul utopias in their use of the mechanisms. The data were then analysed, with certain underlying assumptions. Since for individual commitment processes there are a number of functional alternatives, it was considered inappropriate to compute tests of statistical significance on individual indicators. It was predicted only that a *class* of mechanisms must be utilized and that groups may use any combination of strategies from a pool of possibilities, so that the presence or absence of a *single* indicator was not considered definitive evidence. Furthermore, the mechanisms themselves are not analytically pure.[9] Accordingly the data on single measures were analysed in the form of raw and percentaged frequencies. At the same time, however, the extent to which systems implement *programmes* of commitment-producing arrangements can be tested. Thus, summary scores which compare the utilization of entire classes of mechanisms by successful and unsuccessful communities were derived, and tests of significance employed.

Continuance commitment mechanisms

Commitment to continued participation involves securing a person's positive *cognitive* orientations, inducing the individual to cognize participation in the organization as profitable when considered in terms of rewards and costs. Cognitive orientations are those which view objects and attach positive or negative valences to them, merely perceiving the properties of the objects; in a purely cognitive judgment there is no notion of emotional gratification (cathexis) or of morality (evaluation) attached to the object. For positive cognition to become attached to a social system, then, the system must be organized in such a way that it is viewed as rewarding. The individual who makes a cognitive-continuance commitment finds that what is profitable to him is bound up with his position in the organization, is contingent on his participating in the system—he commits himself to a role. For the actor there is a 'profit' associated with continued participation and a 'cost' associated

9 This has several implications for the understanding of the indicators and the description of commitment mechanisms to follow. The indicators conceptualized here are, first of all, only particular concrete possibilities; groups may concretely implement the *general* kinds of processes that produce commitment in radically different ways. So in some sense the indicators used in this study are certainly not exhaustive; they are representatives of a larger population of commitment strategies serving the same functions. In addition, the concrete practices themselves often serve more than one function at the same time, overlapping my conceptual categories. For this reason I have tended to place them in categories according to my conception of their primary function.

with leaving. Thus sacrifice (negative) and investment (positive) are among the components of cognitive-continuance commitments. Sacrifice involves the giving up of something considered valuable or pleasurable in order to belong to the organization; this stresses the importance of role of member to the individual. Sacrifice means that membership becomes more costly and is therefore not lightly regarded or likely to be given up easily.[10] Investment is a process whereby the individual gains a stake in the organization, commits current and future profits to it so that he must continue to participate if he is going to realize them. Investment generally involves the tying of a person's present and potential resources to the organization, future gain to be received from present behaviour. Organizational strategies which promote cognitive-continuance commitments work through sacrifice and investment, and the use of such mechanisms should distinguish between successful and unsuccessful utopian communities.

Sacrifice.

The process of sacrifice asks members to give up something as a price of membership; once members agree to make the 'sacrifices', their motivation to remain participants should increase. Membership should become more 'sacred', more valuable and meaningful.[11] (The issue here is not how the organization induces the original concessions or manages to recruit people willing to make them; rather, it is proposed that those systems exacting sacrifices will survive longer because sacrifice is functional for their maintenance.) Sacrifice operates on the basis of a simple principle from cognitive consistency theories: the more it 'costs' a person to do something, the more 'valuable' he will have to consider it, in order to justify the psychic 'expense' and remain internally consistent. Thus, it has been demonstrated in a laboratory setting that when people work for very small rewards they must justify their doing so on the basis of belief or commitment, and they come to believe strongly in what they are doing (Festinger and Carlsmith, 1959). To continue to do it would thus justify the sacrifice involved. In many religions, finally, sacrifice has been conceptualized as an act of consecration, bringing one closer to and more worthy of the deity. A vow of poverty, for example, may aid commitment. In the eyes of the group and in the mind of the individual, sacrifice for a cause indeed makes it sacred and inviolable. It is also a gesture of trust in the group, indicating the importance of membership. Sacrifice symbolizes to the group the lengths to which members are willing to go in order to belong—how positively cognized membership is.

Organizational arrangements involving abstinence and austerity support sacrifice. The following were considered indicators of a utopian community's

[10] Sacrifice is considered functional for *continuance;* it has, of course, different and possibly dysfunctional implications for recruitment.
[11] This is similar to an idea formulated by Jerome P. Boime.

use of sacrifice to secure cognitive-continuance commitment: abstention from any oral gratification (tobacco, alcohol, meat, etc.); abstention from personal adornment or indulgence (e.g., dancing, reading); celibacy, or sexual abstinence; and, as a measure of austerity, that the community had to build its own buildings, indicating primitive or rudimentary beginnings. Such sacrifices should aid commitment and hence success.

These arrangements were found more often in successful than in unsuccessful utopias. In general, a larger proportion of successful than unsuccessful groups tended to use these strategies at some time in their history. On a more stringent summary measure of the sample's use of sacrifice mechanisms, sacrifice was also found to be related to success. An overall index was computed in which each community received a score based on the number of mechanisms used, in how strong a form, and whether they were present throughout the community's history or only for part of its history. In the use of sacrifice a total score of nine was possible, if a community had all the mechanisms in their more stringent forms throughout its history. Table 1 indicates that successful communities tended to score higher on this index than unsuccessful ones, with the difference significant at the 0.10 level.

Table 1 Use of sacrifice mechanisms

Mean of successful cases	6.4	
(N = 9)		Standard deviation of difference 2.4
Mean of unsuccessful cases	3.2	
(N = 20)*		
t = 1.3 (d.f. = 27)	(p < .10)	(one-tailed test)

* One community was eliminated from the analysis because of missing data on 2 of the 4 indicators comprising this measure.

Investment.

The process of investment provides the individual with a stake in the fate of the organization; he commits his 'profit' to the organization, so that leaving it would be costly. Investment allows a person future gain from present involvement. It can be a simple economic process involving tangible resources or it can involve intangibles like time and energy. If an organization desires a set of committed members, it should require them to devote their time and energy to the system, to commit their present as well as potential profits, and to derive gain only from the system because of this commitment. Utopian communities thus should not have non-resident members, people who can share in organizational benefits without active participation; active involvement of time and energy should be a requirement in order to gain anything at all from belonging to the system.

Through investment individuals become integrated with the system, since their time and resources have become part of its economy. They have, in effect, purchased a share in the proceeds of the organization and now have a stake in its continued good operation. Often, in fact, organizations themselves can *give* members the basis for this kind of commitment, by providing them with a share in the benefits of success. In addition, when individuals invest their resources in one system rather than in other potential paths, they tie their rewards and the future usefulness of their resources, in effect, to the success of this system, burning other bridges, cutting themselves off from other ways to allocate resources. Here Becker's (1960) concept of commitment is relevant. Becker describes the unanticipated involvement of other sources of reward or other aspects of a person once a line of action is chosen. One's reputation, for example, or the utility of one's skills, become involved in any social pathway, making it difficult to disengage oneself from the 'career' and turn to others on the same terms as before the commitment. Becker is talking primarily of continuance—the conditions under which an individual will continue a line of action once undertaken; he attributes this to the making of 'side bets', the unanticipated investment of other, often intangible, resources once a person is a member of a system. The 'side bet' is that the line of action chosen will be satisfactory or rewarding. Thus investment aids commitment; for a person to realize his gains, to reap his rewards, he must continue to support the system.

Table 2 Use of investment mechanisms

Mean of successful cases	10.3	
(N = 7)*		Standard deviation of difference 4.45
Mean of unsuccessful cases	4.8	
(N = 17)*		
t = 1.25 (d.f. = 22)	(p < .15)	(one-tailed test)

* Six communities were eliminated from the analysis because of missing data on 5 of the 9 indicators comprising this measure.

Investment is made tangible by such requirements as financial donations by new members, assigning of recruits' property to the community, and giving over of any money or property received while in the community. It can be further reinforced by emphasizing its irreversibility, that investment in a utopia, committing oneself to it, is for all time. A variety of strategies can indicate irreversibility: no records kept of contributions of property or capital; or an official policy of no refunds to defectors for their original contributions or for their service to and labour in the community, along with a history of no refunds in actual practice. It is proposed that commitment should be stronger and utopias more successful if investment and its irreversibility are emphasized.

In general, this proposition is warranted: a higher proportion of successful than unsuccessful groups tends to employ these investment strategies. On an overall index of the use of investment, using summary scores computed in a similar way to those for sacrifice, with a total possible score of 18, successful communities tended to score higher than unsuccessful ones, the difference being significant at the 0.15 level. This is shown in Table 2.

Cohesion commitment mechanisms

Cohesion commitment involves the attaching of an individual's fund of affectivity and emotion to the group; emotional gratification stems from participation in and from identification with all the members of a close-knit group. Cathectic-cohesion commitment is commitment to a set of social relationships. The individual cathects each member of the group, and his loyalty and allegiance are thus to the group as a whole. Hence, if members form such attachments, the ties that bind the group should be strong enough to withstand threats to group existence, to maintain the brotherhood even in the face of adverse circumstances.

This kind of commitment requires, first, that members relinquish any attachments which might compete with their emotional involvement with the entire group. Second, it requires that members be brought into meaningful contact with a collective whole, that they experience the fact of one-ness with the group. Two general processes work towards these ends: renunciation (of other ties) and communion (with the group as a whole). The use of mechanisms supporting renunciation and communion should thus distinguish successful and unsuccessful utopian communities.

Renunciation

Renunciation involves the relinquishing of any relationships potentially disruptive to group cohesion, thereby heightening the relationship of individual to group. Seeking renunciation, an organization discourages relationships with certain categories of others, with conflicting collectivities, in order to provide maximum internal cohesiveness. Behavioural rules specify relationships members of the community may and may not have; no loyalties which might conflict with members' obligations to the group should be permitted. According to Bittner (1963), it is functional for radical groups in general to require that all traditional extra-group ties be suspended; Coser (1954, 1967) has made a similar point with respect to sex. Structural arrangements which ensure that the individual give up relationships outside the group and with any number less than the total group concentrate not only his loyalties and allegiances but also his emotional attachments and gratifications within the social system. Thus, under such arrangements a great fund of affectivity and involvement should bind members, increasing their collective strength and ability to withstand threats to group existence. Mechanisms which promote renunciation of extra-group ties are thus functional for cathectic-cohesion commitment and hence for the success of a utopian community. Renunciation may centre around relationships in three categories: with the outside world, in the dyad, and in the family.

Renunciation of the outside world can be promoted by the development of a set of insulating boundaries—rules and structural arrangements which minimize contact with the outside, place clear-cut barriers between members and the outside, and 'reduce the influence of the outside when contact necessarily occurs'. (Wilson, 1959: 11). Insulation may take the form of geographical isolation, 'the ecological segregation of group life,' (Stinchcombe, 1965: 186) as measured by the community's distance from neighbours and accessibility to transportation such as waterways and railroads. Stinchcombe's (1965) concept of 'institutional completeness' is another arrangement involving insulation, as measured by a community's provision of medical services. A special term for the outside world, a negative attitude toward the outsider, the failure to read outside newspapers or to celebrate national patriotic holidays, a distinctive language, and distinctive styles of dress also promote insulation. Control of movements across community boundaries so that these do not threaten the group's insulation or permit attachments outside the group serves as a correlate of insulation. In communities with such control, ordinary members should leave the group infrequently, e.g., less than yearly, with control strategies such as confession required for those who leave and return, and rules should be provided restricting and controlling members' interaction with visitors. In Oneida, for example, the problem of renouncing the outside was complicated by the large number of outsiders visiting the community; various practices were accordingly instituted to reinforce renunciation. Thus, after daily visitors left, those members most exposed to contact with them were required to submit to mutual criticism, so as to be 'freed from contamination by worldly influences', (Estlake, 1900: 11). Furthermore, the whole group joined together for a ritualistic 'bee', to 'purify' the community.

Dyadic renunciation[12] can take the form of free love or celibacy, experientially opposite but functionally alternative organizational arrangements which forbid individualistic ties. With free love, each member is expected to have intimate relations with *all* others; celibacy permits *no* member to have relations with *any* other. In both cases, individual ties are structurally minimized and the ties of the actor to the total group are thereby emphasized. Successful groups should require either of these practices or, at the very least, encourage or prefer them and reward their adoption. Furthermore, they should regulate both practices so as to prevent dyadic attachments. Free love at Oneida, for example, was not really free; the group controlled both the quantity of sexual relations and who could have relations with whom. *Fidelity* was negatively sanctioned.

[12] Slater (1963) states very well the problem of 'dyadic withdrawal' for larger collectivities and points out the importance of giving up intimate dyadic ties for the welfare of collectivities.

Renunciation of the family, finally involves family ties both inside and out-side of the community, competing loyalties which must be erased. A Shaker hymn (Andrews, 1962: 20) portrays this renunciation:

Of all the relations that ever I see
My old fleshly kindred are furthest from me
So bad and so ugly, so hateful they feel
To see them and hate them increases my zeal
   O how ugly they look!
   How ugly they look!
   How nasty they feel!

That the purpose of this requirement is to increase in-group cohesiveness is indicated elsewhere in the same hymn:

My *gospel relations* are dearer to me
Than all the flesh kindred that ever I see . . .
   O how pretty they look! . . .

It is proposed, then, that successful communities should not permit families to share a dwelling unit and should separate children from parents.

In general, a larger proportion of successful than unsuccessful groups tended to make use of these renunciation strategies to promote cohesion com-mitment. On an overall index of the sample's use of renunciation, with a total score of 35 possible if all indicators were present in their more stringent forms, successful communities tended to score higher than unsuccessful ones, with the different significant at the 0.10 level. (See Table 3).

Table 3 Use of renunciation mechanisms

Mean of successful cases	17.4	
($N = 7$)*		Standard deviation of difference 6.9
Mean of unsuccessful cases	6.7	
(N = 18)*		
$t = 1.6$ (d.f. $= 23$)	(p $< .10$)	(one-tailed test)

* Five communities were eliminated from the analysis because of missing data on 7 of the 23 indicators comprising this measure.

Communion

The process of communion may be defined as becoming part of a whole, the mingling of self with the group, and relinquishing separateness in order to identify with all the members of the collective whole. Communion generates what various writers have termed 'we-feeling' or 'we-sentiment'. Blumer (1953: 199), in fact, has defined the membership of a social movement as a collectivity of individuals characterized by a 'we-consciousness'. Infield (1944: 136-152) has included 'we-sentiment' among 'associative elements', i.e., integrating elements, in the Kibbutz. The function such communion processes serve for group cohesion is well stated by Turner and Killian (1957 : 422):

A social movement must weld [members] into a group with a strong in-group sense and enthusiasm for the 'fellowship' or 'comradeship' of the movement and give them determination to continue in the face of obstacles.

Accordingly, the emphasis in communion mechanisms is on group participation, with members as homogeneous, equal parts of a whole, rather than as differentiated individuals. The need for members' equality, fellowship, group consciousness, and group dependence may be supported by various kinds of structural arrangements. These arrangements include homogeneity of religious, class, and ethnic background, as well as prior acquaintance; communistic sharing, in which the individual relinquishes both control over his own goods and private symbols of identity, in favour of group control and ownership; communistic labour, which emphasizes joint effort, with all members performing all tasks for equal reward, including communal work efforts like 'bees'; and regularized group contact, via communal dwellings and dining halls, limited opportunity for privacy, and frequent group meetings, which ensure participation and involvement. Group ritual, which involves collective participation in ceremonies or recurring events of symbolic importance, also enhances communion. Ritual provides symbols under which 'the group loyalty is commonly raised to the level of the universal and abiding', (Boisen, 1939; Blumer, 1953). Community songs and group singing may be used as measures of ritual, as well as celebration of special community occasions or important community dates. Finally, an experience of persecution welds the group together in the face of a common threat and 'heightens the symbolic intensity of a group's values' (Turner and Killian, 1957: 399). The persecution experience can serve as a kind of 'social vaccination', in which the group's defences are built and strengthened, and the group becomes immune to more extreme future attacks, whether in the form of natural disasters or out-group discrimination. Facing collective problems then, aids communion.[13]

The use of social arrangements involving communion distinguishes rather strongly between successful and unsuccessful utopias. When various forms of communion were further operationalized and their presence in the sample communities noted, it was found that in general a larger proportion of successful than unsuccessful groups had them at some time in their history. On an overall index of the sample's use of communion, with a total score of 51 possible if all indicators were present in their more stringent forms, successful communities tended to score higher than unsuccessful, with the difference significant at the 0.05 level. (See Table 4).

[13] The common threat or shared fate as a builder of cohesiveness is widely documented. See, for example, Simmel (1964); Coser (1964); Blumer (1953); Freud (1962: 61). A field experiment by the Sherifs demonstrates the phenomenon rather dramatically. (See Sherif and Sherif, 1953).

Table 4 Use of communion mechanisms

Mean of successful cases	36	
(N = 7)*		Standard deviation of difference 7.8
Mean of unsuccessful cases	20	
(N = 17)*		
t = 2.06 (d.f. = 22)	(p < .05)	(one-tailed test)

* Five communities were eliminated from the analysis because of missing data on 9 of the 29 indicators comprising this measure.

Control commitment mechanisms

Commitment to social control, or commitment to norms, involves securing a person's positive *evaluative* orientations, redefining his symbolic environment so that the system's demands are considered right in terms of his self-identity, and obedience to authority becomes a moral necessity. An individual whose personality system is attached to the norms of a social system should see himself as carrying out the dictates of a higher-order system, a system which orders and gives meaning to his life. This kind of commitment requires that the individual see himself as humble and hapless without the group, that he reformulate his identity in terms of meeting the ideal conditions set by the system. And, at the same time, he must experience the great power represented by the organization, so that he will attach the meaning of his life to the carrying out of the demands of this power. Thus, mortification (a negative process) and surrender (a positive process) are among the components of evaluative-control commitments. Mortification involves the submission of private states to social control, the exchanging of a private identity for one provided by the organization, one subject to its control. Surrender is a process whereby an individual attaches his decision-making prerogative, jurisdiction over even private domains, to a greater power. Organizational strategies which aid the processes of mortification and surrender promote evaluative-control commitment, and these strategies should distinguish successful and unsuccessful utopian communities.

Mortification

Mortification processes emphasize the individual's smallness before the greatness of the organization; they reduce his sense of autonomous identity, so that he can have no self-esteem unless he commits himself to the norms of the group, evaluating its demands as just and morally necessary. These processes attempt to convince him that he is of little worth without the guidance and meaning provided by the organization, that he must instead open his self-concept to direction by the group. In order to be totally committed to the group, an individual may reserve no private areas of himself, no domains not subject to the group's awareness, at the very least, if not its jurisdiction. Mortification processes provide a new set of criteria for evaluating the self, and they transmit the message that the self is adequate, whole, and fulfilled only when it conforms to the model offered by the collectivity. In more or less extreme forms these kinds of processes have been noted in the military (Dornbusch, 1954; Vidich and Stein, 1960), in concentration camps (Abel, 1951; Cohen, 1954), in religious communities (Hulme, 1956; Stunkard, 1951), and in general in total institutions (Goffman, 1961), organizations which demand total involvement and submission to social control. One intended consequence of mortification processes in these settings is to strip away aspects of an individual's identity, making him dependent on authority for direction, and place him in a position of uncertainty with respect to appropriate behaviour. Goffman (1961), in particular, describes in detail 'mortification of the self', which operates by removing the individual's sense of self-determination and making him acutely aware of the presence of others.

In less extreme and less coercive forms of mortification, religious groups often attempt to erase the 'sin of pride', the sin of being too independent or self-sufficient, substituting instead a self which is subject to the influence of the collectivity. Hoffer (1963: 66) calls this 'the effacement of individual separateness'. In noncoercive groups, such as sensitivity training groups, mortification can be a sign of trust in the group, a willingness to share weaknesses, failings, doubts, problems, and one's innermost secrets with others. At the same time, its use is also a sign that the group cares about the individual, about his thoughts and feelings, about the content of his inner world. It thus facilitates commitment of the evaluative-control type and generates loyalty, binding the evaluative components of the personality system to the norm of the social system, through the system's invasion of phenomenological privacy.

Many kinds of mortification strategy may be proposed. Confession, self-criticism, and mutual criticism all promote mortification; in these sessions the individual 'bares his soul' to the social control of the group, which is present either actually or symbolically. The functions served by such events are attested to in a pamphlet published by Oneida, in which the experiences of members undergoing mutual criticism were recounted; in Bethel and Aurora, as another example, confession was deliberately and consciously used to ensure humility. (Bek, 1909: 276). Confession and mutual criticism may be supported by some kind of surveillance of the behaviour of members, either by the members themselves or by leaders. Stratification can also promote mortification, if it takes a form such as 'spiritual differentiation', which recognizes achievement in the spiritual or moral domain and rewards it. An absence of stratification based on skill, intelligence or expertise is also important, for mortification requires that only achievements relevant to group identification and humility be recognized. Spiritual differentiation is supported by certain kinds of socialization practice: instruction in esoteric community doctrines, revealing the recruit's ignorance;

provision of rules or information which recruits must master; segregation of new members from old; and a formal probationary period.

Mortifying sanctions may also be employed, including public denouncement, removal of some privilege of membership, not allowing a deviant to participate in a valued community activity, and punishment within the group rather than expulsion. Finally, a variety of de-individuating mechanisms may be present, which anchor a person's identity in things which are collective or communal rather than individual, including a uniform style of dress, communal dwellings and dining halls, and little opportunity or place for privacy.

The use of some mortification processes was found in a higher proportion of successful than unsuccessful utopias, although other measures fail to distinguish between the two groups. Often there was a great deal of missing data; in the case of mortifying sanctions, in particular, there were few recorded instances of deviance in the data gathered; this made it impossible to determine the use of various kinds of sanctions. However, on an overall index of the sample's use of mortification, with a total score of 33 possible if all the indicators were present in their more stringent form, successful communities still tended to score higher than unsuccessful ones, as Table 5 demonstrates.

Table 5 Use of mortification mechanisms

Mean of successful cases	13.2	
(N = 9)		Standard deviation of difference 7.3
Mean of unsuccessful cases	7.3	
(N = 18)*		
t = 1.08 (d.f. = 25)	(p < .15)	(one-tailed test)

* Three communities were eliminated from the analysis because of missing data on 10 of the 20 indicators comprising this measure.

Surrender

Surrender involves the attaching of a person's decision-making prerogative to a greater power, total involvement with a larger system of authority which gives both meaning and direction to an individual's life. In surrender, personal identity is fused with the social entity, so that the carrying out of system demands becomes a moral necessity for the maintenance of the self. For surrender to occur, the individual must first experience great power and meaning residing in the organization. Weber has proposed that this experience is transmitted through the quality of charisma, a felt connection with some central and meaningful feature of existence, generally related to the presence of charismatic leaders. But for surrender to result in more or less permanent commitments, persisting over long periods of time and independent of the presence or existence of any one person, charisma diffused throughout the corporate group is required. I call charisma in this form 'institutionalized awe', a characteristic of an on-going, formalized social system which imbues the system with power and meaning. Shils (1965: 200) also reformulates the meaning of charisma in this way, as a possible property of a social system, its 'awe-arousing centrality'.

Institutionalized awe consists of ideological systems and structural arrangements which order and give meaning to the individual's life and attach this order and meaning to the social system. These not only satisfy the individual's 'need for meaning', (Cantril, 1941: 141) but also provide a sense of rightness, certainty, and conviction (Hartmann, 1952: 588) that promotes a moral-evaluative commitment and surrender to collective authority. Such arrangements should also elevate the group to the level of the sacred, setting it apart as something wonderful, remarkable, and awful, and, at the same time, indicate the system's mastery of or control over human existence. This can involve, for example, a pervasive philosophy on the one hand and minute regulation of behaviour on the other. All of this enhances and makes tangible and meaningful surrender to the collective will.

Ideology can contribute to institutionalized awe in a variety of ways. Ideologies which include any of the following characteristics should be related to this property of a system: explanations of human nature, of the essential character of man; a comprehensive elaborate philosophical system; provision for the investing of power in persons with particular awe-inspiring qualities, e.g., wisdom, age, spiritualness, inspiration;[14] legitimation of demands made on members by reference to a higher order principle, e.g. justice, the will of nature, the will of God;[15] imputation of special or magical powers to members by virtue of their belonging; taking as evidence of good standing in the group the possession of magical or special powers; and linking the system to great figures of historical importance. If ideologies with these features are actually to serve surrender functions, they should be a potent part of the life of the organization, a factor both in decisions and in day-to-day operations.

Institutionalized awe may be structurally reinforced in several ways. One means is to increase the distance and mystery of the decision-making process for ordinary members, to enhance the sense of 'tremendous mystery' surrounding the organization, so that obedience and moral conviction must be absolute. Distance and mystery may be promoted by several mechanisms: an authority hierarchy, insulated from members; physical separation of leaders from members; special leadership prerogatives (special privileges or immunities); and an irrational basis for decisions (inspiration, intuition, or magic as opposed to logic, scientific reasoning, pragmatism, or democratic consent).

[14] Amana, for example, was officially called 'The Society of True Inspiration'. The particular quality that its ideology defined as necessary for authority in the group was 'inspiration', or the ability to receive directly divine messages and guidance.
[15] Shils (1965:207) has proposed that a charismatic social order must also seem to be connected with a transcendent moral order.

Insulation of an authority hierarchy may occur through choosing leaders not directly by democratic means but by other criteria, e.g., they founded the organization, were named by their predecessors, or groomed for leadership by them; and providing no impeachment or recall privileges over leaders.

In addition to institutionalized awe, surrender may also be promoted by programming (provision of a specific programme of behavioural rules); by requiring ideological conversion for membership; and by the existence of tradition. The existence of programming is indicated by a more or less fixed daily routine, detailed specification of the daily routine, and personal conduct and deportment rules for members. All of these reinforce the role of the organization as an order-creating power which is responsible for and gives shape to every aspect of a member's life. Shaker programming, for example, extended even to such minor activities as dressing and getting out of bed. At the first 'trump' (bell) everyone arose according to the following programme:

Put your right foot out of bed first. Place your right knee where your foot
first touched the floor in kneeling to pray. Do not speak, but if absolutely
necessary whisper to the room leader.
(Webber, 1959:67).

Requiring ideological conversion, which can be measured in a variety of ways ensures that members share a faith that gives meaning and legitimacy to the organization. Tradition, finally, imbues group demands with what Weber called 'the authority of the external yesterday'. This can be utilized by a utopian community if it derives from a prior organization or organized group, and one of relatively long duration.

The use of these surrender mechanisms was generally found in a higher proportion of successful than unsuccessful utopias—even those organizational arrangements like a daily routine that would appear to be minimal requirements for organizational functioning. Finally, on an overall index of the sample's use of surrender, with a total score of 49 possible if all the indicators were present in their more stringent forms, successful communities tended to score higher than unsuccessful ones, with the difference significant at the 0.05 level. (See Table 6).

Table 6 Use of surrender mechanisms*

Mean of successful cases	33.6	
(N = 9)		Standard deviation of difference 11.7
Mean of unsuccessful cases	13.1	
(N = 21)		
t = 1.75 (d.f. = 28)	(p < .05)	(one-tailed test)

* Indicators of programming were eliminated from the analysis for all communities in view of a large amount of missing data on these measures.

Conclusion

This article has presented a discussion of commitment as a process binding actors into social systems. Commitment has been conceptualized as involving the areas of continuance, cohesion, and control, each being supported by a dissociative and an associative process, and operationalized in terms of specific mechanisms—organizational practices and arrangements—which distinguish successful from unsuccessful commitment-requiring organizations.

The results help explain why it is that members of some groups are highly committed while members of others are not; it locates this problem in the structure of the groups and in the phenomenological impact of their organizational arrangements. Systems which employ the kinds of mechanisms enumerated here, whether in the specific forms described or in others which serve the same functions, should find their participants dedicated, obedient, loyal, and involved. It is possible, furthermore, that alienation is related to arrangements in which the commitment processes proposed here are absent or negated.

The commitment-producing strategies discussed here are applicable to commitment on many levels and to many diverse kinds of system. The conceptual framework is potentially useful in analysing any organization which seeks to establish strong ties with its members, maintain control over behaviour, and, in general, integrate individuals into social systems. The mechanisms apply, for example, to small groups such as sensitivity-training groups, to resocialization institutions such as professional schools or brain-washing camps, to business organizations such as sales companies, to residential communities such as the urban negro ghetto, to political parties, and to nations. This paper is a further step toward the understanding of human loyalty and involvement in social groupings.

References

Abel, Theodore M., 1951. The sociology of concentration camps. *Social Forces,* [30], (December), 150-155.

Andrews, Edward Deming, 1962. *The Gift to be Simple: Songs, Dances, and Rituals of the American Shakers.* New York: Dover.

Becker, Howard, S., 1960. Notes on the concept of commitment. *American Journal of Sociology,* [66], (July), 32-40.

Bek, William, G., 1909. The community at Bethel, Missouri, and its offspring at Aurora, Oregon. *German American Annals* n.s., [7]) (September), 257-276, 306-328.

Bittner, Egon, 1963. Radicalism and the organization of radical movements. *American Sociological Review,* [28], (December), 928-940.

Blumer, Herbert, 1953. Collective behavior. In A. M. Lee (ed.), *Principles of Sociology.* New York: Barnes and Noble. Pp. 167-222.

Boime, Jerome, P., 1967. Personal communication.

Boisen, Anton, T., 1939. Economic distress and religious experience: a study of the Holy Rollers. *Psychiatry,* [2], (May), 185-194.

Brown, Roger, 1960. *Social Psychology.* New York: The Free Press.

Cantril, Hadley, 1941. *The Psychology of Social Movements.* New York: Wiley.

Cohen, Elie, 1954. *Human Behavior in the Concentration Camp.* London: Jonathan Cape.

Coser, Lewis A., 1954. Sects and sectarians. *Dissent,* [1] (Autumn), 360-369.

Coser, Lewis A., 1964. *The Functions of Social Conflict.* New York: The Free Press.

Coser, Lewis A., 1967. Greedy organizations. *European Journal of Sociology,* [8], (October), 196-215.

Dornbusch, Sanford, 1954. The military academy as an assimilating institution. *Social Forces,* [33], (May), 316-321.

Estlake, Allan, 1900. *The Oneida Community.* London: George Redway.

Festinger, Leon and Carlsmith, J., 1959. Cognitive consequences of forced compliance. *Journal of Abnormal and Social Psychology,* [58], (March), 203-210.

Freud, Sigmund, 1962. *Civilization and Its Discontents.* Translated by James Strachey. New York: Norton.

Goffman, Erving, 1961. *Asylums.* Garden City, New York: Doubleday Anchor.

Gross, Neal and Martin, William E., 1952. On group cohesiveness. *American Journal of Sociology,* [57], (December), 535-546.

Hartman, George W., 1952. The psychology of American socialism. In Donald Drew Egbert and Stow Persons (eds), *Socialism and American Life.* Princeton: Princeton University Press. Pp. 557-597.

Hoffer, Eric, 1963. *The True Believer: Thoughts on the Nature of Mass Movements.* New York: Time, Inc.

Hulme, Kathryn, 1956. *The Nun's Story.* Boston: Little, Brown.

Infield, Henrik F., 1944. *Cooperative Living in Palestine.* New York: The Dryden Press.

Kelman, Herbert C., 1958. Compliance, identification and internalization, three processes of attitude change. *Journal of Conflict Resolution,* [2], (March), 51-60.

Mayhew, Leon H., 1967. Personal communication.

Parsons, Talcott and Shils, Edward A., (eds), 1962. *Towards a General Theory of Action.* New York: Harper and Row.

Sherif, Muzafer and Sherif, Carolyn, 1953. *Groups in Harmony and Tension.* New York: Harper and Row.

Shils, Edward A., 1965. Charisma, order, and status. *American Sociological Review,* [30], (April), 199-213.

Simmel, Georg, 1964. *Conflict.* Translated by Kurt H. Wolff, New York: The Free Press.

Slater, Philip E., 1963. On social regression. *American Sociological Review* [28], (June), 339-364.

Stinchcombe, Arthur, 1965. Social structure and organizations. In James G. March (ed.), *Handbook of Organizations.* Chicago: Rand McNally. Pp. 142-191.

Stunkard, A., 1951. Some interpersonal aspects of an Oriental religion. *Psychiatry,* [14], (November), 419-431.

Turner, Ralph H. and Killian, Lewis M., 1957. *Collective Behavior.* Englewood Cliffs, New Jersey: Prentice-Hall.

Vidich, Arthur J. and Stein, Maurice R., 1960. The dissolved identity in military life. In Maurice R. Stein et al. (eds), *Identity and Anxiety.* Glencoe, Illinois: Free Press. Pp. 493-505.

Webber, Everett, 1959. *Escape to Utopia: The Communal Movement in America.* New York: Hastings House.

Wilson, Bryan R., 1959. An analysis of sect development. *American Sociological Review,* [24], (February), 1-15.

Barney G. Glaser   Anselm L. Strauss
Department of Sociology, University of California, San Francisco

Time, structural process, and status passage: the case of dying

Reprinted from Barney G. Glaser and Anselm L. Strauss, *Time for dying* (Chicago:
Aldine Publishing Company, 1968); copyright © 1968 by Barney G. Glaser and Anselm
L. Strauss. Reprinted by permission of the authors and Aldine-Atherton, Inc.

This is an edited version of pp. 1-13 and pp. 238-47. D.F.

Temporal features of terminal care

Any study of dying—not merely of death, the end of dying—must take into
consideration the fact that dying takes time. In hospitals where death is a
common occurrence, the staff's work is organized in accordance with expectation that dying will take a longer or shorter time. Sometimes the organization
of hospital work fits an individual patient's -course of dying—his 'dying
trajectory'—but at other times the work pattern is, at least in some respects,
out of step with the dying process. Much of the behaviour of people toward the
dying may be viewed as *work*. This is as true when a person dies at home as
when he dies in the hospital. Usually during the course of his dying he is unable
to fulfil all his physiological and psychological needs by himself. He may need
to be fed, bathed, taken to the toilet, given drugs, brought desired objects when
too feeble to get them himself, and near the end of his life, even be 'cared for'
totally. Whether persons in attendance on him enjoy or suffer these tasks, they
are undeniably work. Wealthier families sometimes hire private nurses to do all
or some of this work. In the hospital, there is no question that terminal care,
whether regarded as distasteful or as satisfying, is viewed as work.

This work has important temporal features. For instance, there are prescribed schedules governing when the patient must be fed, bathed, turned in
bed, given drugs. There are times when tests must be administered. There are
crucial periods when the patient must be closely observed or when crucial
treatments must be given or actions taken to prevent immediate deterioration
—even immediate death. Since there is a division of labour, it must be organized
in terms of time. For instance, the nurse must have the patient awake in time
for the laboratory technician to administer tests, and the physician's visit must
not coincide with the patient's bath or with the visiting hours of relatives.
When the patient's illness grows worse, the pace and tempo of the staff's work
shift accordingly: meals may be skipped and tests may be less frequent, but
the administration of drugs and the reading of vital signs may be more

frequent. During all this work, calculated organizational timing must consider turnover among staff members or their absence on vacations or because of illness.

With rare exceptions, medical services always include both recovering and dying patients. Even on intensive care units or on cancer services, not all patients are expected to, or do, die. On any given service, the temporal organization of work with dying patients is greatly influenced by the relative numbers of recovering and dying patients and by the types of recovering patients. For instance, on services for premature babies, babies who die usually do so within 48 hours after birth; after that, most are relatively safe. The 'good preemie' does not stay very long on the service, but moves along to the normal babies' service. Hence the pace and the kind of work in the case of a premature baby vary in accordance with the number of days since birth, and when a baby begins to 'turn bad' a few days after birth—usually unexpectedly—the pace and the kind of work are greatly affected.

The temporal ordering of work on each service is also related to the predominant types of death in relation to the normal types of recovery. As an example, we may look at intensive care units: some patients there are expected to die quickly, if they are to die at all; others need close attention for several days because death is a touch-and-go matter; while others are not likely to die but do need temporary round-the-clock nursing. Most who die here are either so heavily drugged as to be temporarily comatose or are actually past consciousness. Consequently, nurses or physicians do not need to converse with these patients. When a patient nears death he may sometimes unwittingly compete with other patients for nurses' or physicians' attention, several of whom may give care to the critically ill patient. When the emergency is over, or the patient dies, then the nurses, for instance, return to less immediately critical patients, reading their vital signs, managing treatments, and carrying out other important tasks.

Each type of service tends to have a characteristic incidence of death, which also affects the staff's organization of work. Closely allied with these incidences are the tempos of dying that are characteristic of each ward. On emergency services, for example, patients tend to die quickly (they are accident cases, victims of violence, or people stricken suddenly and acutely). The staff on emergency services, therefore, is geared to perform urgent, critical functions. Many emergency services, especially in large city hospitals, are also organized for frequent deaths, especially on weekends. At such times, recovering (or non-sick) patients sometimes tend to receive scant attention, unless the service is organized flexibly to handle both types of patients.

The already complex organization of professional activity for terminal care is made even more so by several other matters involving temporality. For one, what may be conveniently termed the 'experiential careers' of patients, families, and staff members are highly relevant to the action around dying patients. Some patients are familiar with their diseases, but others are encountering their symptoms for the first time. The patient's knowledge of the course of his disease, based on his previous experience with it, has an important bearing on what happens as he lies dying in the hospital. Similarly, some personnel are well acquainted with the predominant disease patterns found on their particular wards; but some, although possibly familiar with other illnesses, may be newcomers to these diseases. They may be unprepared for sudden changes of symptoms and vital signs; taken by surprise at crucial junctures, they may make bad errors in timing their actions. More experienced personnel are more likely to be able to take immediate appropriate action at any turn in the illness.

Experiential careers also include the differing experiences that people have had with hospitals. Some patients return repeatedly to the same hospital ward. When a familiar face appears, the staff may be shocked at the patient's deterioration, thinking 'Now he is going to die', and may therefore react differently than they would to someone new to the ward. Likewise, the extent of the patient's familiarity with the ways of hospitals or of a particular hospital influence his reactions during the course of dying. In short, both the illness careers and the hospital careers of all parties in the dying situation may be of considerable importance, affecting both the interaction around the dying patient and the organization of his terminal care.

One other type of experience is highly relevant: the differing 'personal careers' of the interactants in the dying situation—the more personal aspects of the interaction. We shall later discuss instances where the reactions of young nurses and physicians indicated 'involvment' in the deaths of young terminal patients—much more so, generally, than in the deaths of elderly patients. Similarly, if an older woman patient reminds a young nurse of her own deceased mother, the nurse's actions towards her may be affected.

Another aspect of the effect of personal career on the dying situation is in the conception of time. Recognizing his approaching death, an elderly patient who has had a long and satisfying life may welcome it. He may also wish to review that life publicly. His wife or nurse, however, may refuse to listen, telling him that he should not give up hope of living, or even cautioning him against being 'so morbid'. On the other hand, other patients may throw the staff into turmoil because they will not accept their dying. Nonacceptance sometimes signifies a patient's protest against destiny for making him leave 'unfinished work'. These various time conceptions of different patients in the dying situation may run counter not only to each other, but also to the staff's work time concepts; as, for instance, when a patient's personal conception prevents the nurse from completing scheduled actions.

One further class of events attending the course of dying is of crucial importance for the action around the dying patient. These events are the characteristic work required by medical and hospital organization which occurs at critical junctures of the dying process. That the person is actually dying must be recognized if he is to be treated like a dying person. At some point, everyone may recognize that there 'is nothing more to do'. As dying approaches its conclusion, a death watch usually takes place. When death has ended the process, there must be a formal pronouncement, and then an announcement to the family. At each point in time, the staff's interrelated actions must be properly organized.

Taken all together, then the total organization of activity—which we call 'work'—during the course of dying is profoundly affected by temporal considerations. Some are evident to almost everyone, some are not. The entire web of temporal interrelationships we shall refer to as the *temporal order*. It includes the continual readjustment and coordination of staff effort, which we term the *organization of work*.

Dying trajectories

The dying trajectory of each patient has at least two outstanding properties. First, it takes place over time: it has *duration*. Specific trajectories can vary greatly in duration. Second, a trajectory has *shape*: it can be graphed. It plunges straight down; it moves slowly but steadily downward; it vacillates slowly, moving slightly up and down before diving downward radically; it moves slowly down at first, then hits a long plateau, then plunges abruptly to death.

Neither duration nor shape is a purely objective physiological property. They are both perceived properties; their dimensions depend on when the perceiver initially *defines* someone as dying and on his *expectations* of how that dying will proceed. Dying trajectories themselves, then, are perceived courses of dying rather than the actual courses. This distinction is readily evident in the type of trajectory that involves a short reprieve from death. This reprieve represents an unexpected deferment of death. On the other hand, in a lingering death bystanders may expect faster dying than actually occurs.

Since dying patients enter hospitals at varying distances from death, and are defined in terms of when and how they will die, various types of trajectories are commonly recognized by the hospital personnel. For instance, there is the abrupt, surprise trajectory: a patient who is expected to recover suddenly dies. A trajectory frequently found on emergency wards is the expected swift death: many patients are brought in because of fatal accidents, and nothing can be done to prevent their deaths. Expected lingering while dying is another type of trajectory; it is characteristic, for example, of cancer. Besides the short-term reprieve, there may also be the suspended-sentence trajectory: the patient is actually sent home and may live for several years thereafter. Another commonly recognized pattern is entry-reentry: the patient, slowly going downhill, returns home several times between stays at the hospital. All these generalized types of trajectories rest upon the perceivers' expectations of duration and shape.

Regardless of the particular attributes of a specific patient's trajectory, ordinarily there are certain events—we shall term them 'critical junctures'— that appear along the dying trajectory and are directly handled by the temporal organization of hospital work. These occur in either full or truncated form: (1) The patient is defined as dying. (2) Staff and family then make preparations for his death, as he may do himself if he knows he is dying. (3) At some point, there seems to be 'nothing more to do' to prevent death. (4) The final descent may take weeks, or days, or merely hours, ending in (5) the 'last hours', (6) the death watch, and (7) the death itself. Sometimes along the course of dying, there may be announcements that the patient is dying, or that he is entering or leaving a phase. After death, death itself must be legally pronounced and then publicly announced.

When these critical junctures occur as expected, on schedule, then all participants—sometimes including the patient—are prepared for them. The work involved is provided for and integrated by the temporal order of the hospital. For instance, the nurses are ready for a death watch if they can anticipate approximately when the patient will be very near death. When, however, critical junctures occur unexpectedly or off schedule, staff members and family alike are at least somewhat unprepared. The point we wish to emphasize here is that expectations are crucial to the way critical junctures are handled by all involved. For that reason we turn next to a discussion of dying expectations.

Expectations of death[1]

When a person enters a hospital, one of the most important initial questions is 'What's the diagnosis?' This question is no less important if the patient is fated to die soon, unless death is so imminent that diagnosis is pointless. What is done to and for most patients depends mainly on the answers to the diagnostic questions and its allied prognoses. Modern hospitals are organized to ensure relatively speedy answers. If initial diagnosis is uncertain, then additional soundings are usually made; the course of the illness itself during the next few days may prompt more accurate answers.

From a sociological perspective, the important thing about any diagnosis, whether correctly established or not, is that it involves questions of definition. Even with a known terminal patient, however, another important question— how fast will he die?—must still be answered. Many a hospital patient poses for the staff both questions simultaneously: Is this patient going to die here, and if so, when? The first of these questions refers to 'uncertainty of death', the second to 'time of death'. Even more specifically, let us say that relative *certainty* of death means the degree to which the defining person (physician,

1 The material in this section is adapted from Glaser and Strauss (1965a) Chapter 2.

nurse, or even the patient himself) is convinced that the patient will die. Let us say that *time* of death means the expectation of either (a) when the certain death will occur, or (b) when the uncertainty about death will be resolved. Units of time can range from minutes to months, varying with the nature of the illness and the patient's location in the hospital. For example, on emergency wards only a few minutes may pass before it is known for certain a patient will live. With premature babies, nurses usually think of death in terms of hours or a few days at most. For cancer patients, the time unit may be months.

In combination, *certainty* and *time* yield four types of 'death expectations': (1) certain death at a known time, (2) certain death at an unknown time, (3) uncertain death but a known time when certainty will be established, and (4) uncertain death and an unknown time when the question will be resolved. As we shall show, these expectations have varying effects on ·the interaction of participants in the dying situations.

Anyone may read the medical signs and draw his own conclusions, the terminal patient included. But in American hospitals the attending physician is the only one who can legitimately define the patient's condition, because of his professional expertise and the professional mandate that he be medically responsible for the patient. Ordinarily, only he may tell patients that they are dying. Under extraordinary conditions, nurses tell patients or relatives directly, but this is not the usual practice.

However, nurses still must correctly assess whether the patient is dying and when he will die. To make those assessments is often no easy matter. In forming their expectations, the nurses may rely on their own reading of cues—how the patient looks and acts, what his charts report about him—as well as on cues given, perhaps unwittingly or obliquely, by the doctor. Sometimes they also receive direct information from the doctor; typically, they trust this source more than their own individual or collective reading of cues, although the reverse may be true if they are experienced nurses and the doctor seems inexperienced, incompetent, or not well acquainted with the case. Sometimes the cues are so obvious that the physician needs to say little or nothing. So, although the most legitimate source for forming and expressing death expectations is the physician, the nurses also observe cues constantly.

Two principal types of cues that nurses can read are the patient's physical condition and the temporal references made either by themselves or the medical staff. Physical cues, ranging from those that spell hope to those that indicate immediate death, generally establish the certainty of death expectations. Temporal cues, however, have many reference points. A major one is the typical progression of the disease, against which the patient's actual movement is measured (he is 'going fast' or 'lingering'). Another is the doctor's expectation about how long the patient will remain in the hospital. For instance, one patient's hospitalization was 'lasting longer' than the short stay anticipated by the physician. Work schedules also provide a temporal reference: nurses adjust their expectations according to whether the patient can continue to be bathed, turned, fed, and given sedation regularly. All such references pertain to the temporal aspect of dying—to how long the patient is expected to live.

Because physical cues are generally easier to read, and help to establish some degree of certainty about dying, temporal cues are rather indeterminate without them. The patient may die 'sometime' or 'at any time.' As both types of cues accumulate, they may support each other; for example, as a patient's condition becomes more grave, his hospitalization grows longer. But physical and temporal cues can also cancel each other: thus, an unduly long hospitalization can be balanced or even negated by increasingly hopeful physical cues. When cues cancel each other, nurses can use the more hopeful one ('he is going home sooner than expected') to balance or deny the less hopeful ('he looks bad'). As physical and temporal cues accumulate faster and become more severe, they become harder to deny, and the expectation of death is gradually more firmly established.

Nurses' definitions of the patient's illness status—that is, their expectations —affect their behaviour toward him. Therefore, the particular moment when their expectations change is significant. For example, even when the physician's cues imply that the patient is doomed, as when he stops blood transfusions, the nurses may still not be absolutely sure that the implied prediction is accurate. They may not lower their levels of alertness or reduce their efforts to save the patient. They may say, as one nurse did, 'If he comes out of it, we'll work on him. He only has to give us the slightest cue.' Since the doctor has said nothing official, even nurses who believe the patient is dying can still give him an out-side chance and stand ready to save him. They remain constantly alert to counter-cues. 'Everybody is simply waiting', said one nurse. If the doctor had indicated that the patient would die within the day, nurses would have ceased their constant watch for counter-cues and reduced their efforts to save him, concentrating instead on giving comfort to the last, with no undue prolonging of life.

These changing expectations of nurses and physicians actually map out the patient's changes of status. Many patterns of 'status passage', with typical rates of movement, are well known. A classical pattern is the lingering patient: he is certain to die, but when he will do so is unknown, and he does not die for some while. On one cancer ward we studied, an all-too-typical sequence of expectations for the lingering patient ran the gamut of various stages of determinancy: from original prognosis of certain death but uncertain time, through the weeks when the patient began obviously to decline, to the time when his precise time of death finally became relatively certain. Before the final decline takes place, such patients may alternate between hospital visits and periods at home. Often the nurses feel that a lingering patient is taking more time than is 'proper', because there is really no hope for him. (In this sense, even an unknown time period has limits.)

The two extremes toward which patients move are 'getting well' or 'certain to die at a specific time', but nurses and physicians may have other, intermediate expectations for a given patient who leaves the hospital. He may have arrived with uncertain prognosis, but is being sent home diagnosed as cancerous: certain to die, but with the 'when' quite unknown. The prognoses of more puzzling cases may be uncertain on both counts.

The staff may be surprised by unexpected changes in the expected passage of patients toward death. Among the most surprising changes are the sudden death, or onset of death, of a patient for whom the previous prognoses had been doubtful as to certainty and time. Of course, the surprise is greatest when there has been no death expectation whatever, as when seemingly healthy or recovering patients die. When such patients die on the operating table, the impact is tremendous. Death is too sudden: there is no time to prepare for it. In one instance, a surgeon much admired by his nursing staff shocked them with an unexpected loss on the operating table. Rumours of negligence were rife, until autopsy showed that the man had died of unanticipated natural causes. In less traumatic instances, when, although expectations are revised as the patient moves toward death, his progress turns out to be unusual, personnel may experience a disquieting feeling of having missed certain steps.

Time

In general, sociological writing about groups, organizations and institutions tends to leave their temporal features unanalysed.[2] When they are handled explicitly, the focus is on such matters as deadlines, scheduling, rates, pacing, turnover, and concepts of time which may vary by organizational, institutional or group position. The principal weakness of such analyses stems from an unexamined assumption that the temporal properties worth studying involve only the work of organizations and their members. For instance, the work time of personnel must be properly articulated—hence deadlines and schedules. Breakdowns in this temporal articulation occur not only through accident and poor planning, but also through differential valuation of time by various echelons, personnel and clientele. But from our analysis the temporal order of the organization appears to require much wider range of temporal dimensions. We have assumed (here) that, for instance, people bring to an organization their own temporal concerns and that their actions there are profoundly affected by those concerns.[3] Thus, woven into our analysis were experiential careers (hospital, illness, and personal), as well as the patients' and the families' concepts of time. In our analysis, we have attempted to show how temporal order in the hospital refers to a total, delicate, continuously changing articulation of

[2] The following pages are adapted or quoted from the introduction to *George Herbert Mead on Social Psychology* (Strauss 1964: xiii-xiv).
[3] This kind of view is implicit in the writings of G. H. Mead. Herbert Blumer has attempted to make the view more explicit in his writing about Mead and in various papers about symbolic interactionism. *Cf.*, Blumer (1962).

these various temporal considerations. Such articulation, of course, includes easily recognizable organizational mechanisms but also less visible ones, including 'arrangements' negotiated by various relevant persons.

The kind of analysis required when studying temporal order brings our discussion to the two other topics of this chapter—structural process and status passage. Such a conception of how to study temporal order emphasizes the continual interplay of structure and process. Critics who incline toward a processual view of society have frequently criticized—and in our judgment effectively—the over-determinism of structuralists. But that critique need not necessitate an abandonment of the tremendously useful mode of thinking which is called 'structural'. That analytic mode need only be combined systematically with an allied concern with process. The study of dying trajectories within hospital organizations happens to have led easily to *thinking generally* about 'structural process' and 'status passage'. Let us consider each in turn.

Structural process

One of the central issues in sociological theory is the relationship of structure to process. If one considers dying as a process extending over time, then the hospital's structure can be seen as continually changing to handle different phases in that process. Its structure, then, is in process; which phenomenon we call 'structural process'. We have seen how a person may be brought into one section of the hospital and then moved to another, as his trajectory is re-defined or as he reaches certain critical junctures in an anticipated or defined trajectory. Even when a dying patient remains on one ward, he can be moved around within that ward so that different aspects of its 'structure' can be brought into play. If he is never moved, the ward's or hospital's varying resources of manpower, skill, drugs or machinery may be brought into play as his trajectory proceeds. What is true for the staff's relationships with a patient is also true for its relationships with his family.

Sociological analysis ordinarily does not join structure and process so tightly as our notion of 'structural process' does. Structure tends to be treated as relatively fixed—because it is what it is, then certain processes can occur. Or inversely, because the major goals involve certain processes, as in a factory or in a governmental agency, the structure is made as nearly consonant with the processes as possible. New processes are conceived as leading to new structural arrangements; while innovations in structure similarly lead to associated processual changes. A major implication of our book is that structure and process are related more complexly (and more interestingly) than is commonly conceived.

We have, for instance, remarked how during a given phase of a trajectory a ward may be quite a different place than before. For instance, when the sentimental order has been profoundly disrupted, the structural elements that can be called on are not quite the same as before; some elements no longer exist and may never again exist. If afterward an 'equilibrium' is reached, it is a moving equilibrium with the ward calmed down but forever at least a somewhat different place.

So, rather than seeing a relatively inflexible structure, with a limited and determinable list of structural properties, we have to conceive of a ward, hospital, or any other institution as a structure in process. It therefore has a potential range of properties far greater than the outsider (the sociologist) can possibly imagine unless he watches the insiders at work. He can be surprised at the ways in which staff, family or patients can call on diverse properties of the hospital or local community, for bringing in resources that he never dreamed existed but which became permanently or temporarily part of the structural processes of the ward.

Perhaps we need especially to emphasize that the clients of an institution— patients or family members—are also structural features of it. Thus, a Japanese mother who cares for her dying son at a hospital becomes part of the hospital's structure. If the family gathers around during a patient's last days, then the hospital's structure is amplified. If families are banished or voluntarily 'pull out' during certain phases of dying, then they do not loom large as structural possibilities for the staff to call on or to handle.[4]

Structural process relates to the various participants' awareness. They will vary, of course, in their awareness of which structural properties are operating, or can be brought to operate, during various phases of the dying process. Misperceptions are involved as well as awareness; a doctor, for instance, may assume that he can call on some structural resource (e.g. an oxygen tank) when it no longer exists. He may discover its 'disappearance' too late; or he may never discover his error, if it is not very consequential. Others, such as the nurses, may or may not be aware of the absence or presence of his knowledge. The relationships of these 'awareness contexts' to structural processes are neither accidental nor unpredictable, as staff and patients sometimes believe.

Perhaps the point that most requires underlining, however, is that structural process has consequences which themselves enter into the emergence of a *new* structural process. For the sociologist, this fact implies an important directive: part of his job is to trace those consequences that significantly affect the un-rolling course of events called 'structural process'—not for particular cases, but for *types* of cases. Sociologists, for instance, are not interested in a dying person, but in *types* of dying persons and the patterned events relevant to their dying. When focusing on the consequences of structure and process, it is all too easy to settle for lists of consequences for, say, various personnel or for the repetitive functioning of an organization or institution. But the explicit directive given by the concept of structural process is that the sociologist cannot rest until he has analytically related the interactional consequences to

4 Herbert Simon makes the point that clients are as much part of an organization as its personnel, but he makes the point statically. See Simon (1948).

the next phases in interaction—or, in our terms, present structural processes to later structural processes.

The dying trajectory as a status passage

It is not necessary to review our substantive theory of dying trajectories, except to remind readers of several points: dying must be defined in order to be reacted to as dying; defining occurs not only at the beginning but throughout the courses of the various trajectories; hospitals are organized for handling various trajectories, including the establishment of specialized locales for handling different types of trajectories; work at those locales is organized in terms of a range of expected trajectories; a principal feature of these trajectories is the attempts by various parties to shape them; this shaping is affected by various cross-cutting variables (such as social loss, experiential careers and awareness); the various parties may differentially perceive the trajectories; the juggling of tasks, people and relationships during the course of anyone's dying opens possibilities for a considerable misalignment of actions that are usually quite well aligned. Our analyses have established that ascertainable structural conditions are related to the above items, and that their important consequences are also explainable—even somewhat predictable, provided one has advance knowledge of the relevant variables.

This substantive theory of dying trajectories has two especially valuable features. First, it is *dense:* it consists of a great number of propositions, so many indeed that the total theory is not easily summarized. Second, the theory is *integrated:* the numerous propositions are related systematically to each other throughout our total discussion, and in complex fashion—and yet, we trust, with sufficient clarity to indicate the varying levels of abstractness at which they are formulated.

These two features—density and integration—contribute to the theory's *generality.* By this term, we mean that the theory is applicable to the multitude of diverse situations of dying trajectories. We remarked on this in our earlier book, *Awareness of Dying.*[5]

> Through the level of generality of our concepts we have tried to make the theory flexible enough to make a wide variety of changing situations understandable, and also flexible enough to be readily reformulated, virtually on the spot, when necessary, that is, when the theory does not work. The person who applies our theory will, we believe, be able to bend, adjust, or quickly reformulate . . . theory as he applies it in trying to keep up with and manage the situational realities that he wishes to improve.
> (Glaser and Strauss, 1965a:265).

This implies that the density, integration, and generality of the substantive

---

[5] For a general discussion of generality, density and integration see our *Discovery of Grounded Theory* (Glaser and Strauss, 1967).

F

theory increase the control that the user can obtain over various contingencies that may arise during the course of dying. To quote again:

To give this kind of control, the theory must provide a sufficient number of general concepts and their plausible interrelations; and these concepts must provide him with understanding, with situational controls, and with access to the situation in order to exert the controls.
(Glaser and Strauss, 1965a:268).

It scarcely seems necessary to emphasize that such control also stems from the 'grounded' origins of the substantive theory: that is, the theory was not conceived prior to the research but evolved during it.

After a substantive theory is formulated, it is useful, when possible, to scrutinize its relationship to an existing formal theory. The aim is twofold: The scrutiny can lead to further formulation of the substantive theory; it can also lead to discovery and development of gaps in the formal theory. A dying trajectory, as we have suggested, can be usefully thought of as a type of *status passage:* the dying person is passing—through 'transitional' statuses—between the statuses of being alive and being dead; various other participants are correspondingly involved with and implicated in his passage. (cf. Glaser and Strauss, 1965b.)

The phenomena of status passages were enduringly called to the attention of sociologists and anthropologists by Van Gennep's *Rites du Passage*. In that book, the French scholar remarked on various types of passages between what, in modern vocabulary, are termed 'statuses'. Mainly, he analysed such passages as those which occur between age-linked statuses such as adolescence and adulthood, and between being unmarried and being married. Those kinds of passages have, of course, been very thoroughly studied since Van Gennep's day. Sociologists have also expended considerable effort in studying passages that occur within occupations ('socialization', for instance) and within organizations ('mobility', for instance). A principal characteristic of most of those passages is that they are governed by rather clear rules, bearing on when the passage should or can be made and by whom (scheduled); the sequences of steps that the person must go through to have completed the passage (prescribed steps); and what actions must be carried out by various participants so that the passage will actually be accomplished (regularized actions). These dimensions are so integral in numerous status passages that anthropologists and sociologists usually have focused on descriptions of the rituals—extremely scheduled, prescribed sequences of regulated actions—that tend to accompany at least certain phases of those passages.

Scheduling, regularization, and prescription are important dimensions of many, but not all, status passages. Each dimension can be absent, or present only to a degree. Furthermore, certain other relevant dimensions may characterize a type of passage. Thus, the passage may be considered (by the person making the passage or by other relevant parties) as in some measure *desirable* or undesirable. The passage may or may not be *inevitable*. It may be *reversible* and, if so, it may even be *repeatable*. The person undergoing the passage may do so *alone*, or *collectively* with any number of other persons of whose passages he may or may not be *aware*. Also, *clarity* of the signs of passage as seen by various people may be very great or very slight. The person making the passage may do so *voluntarily* or have no choice in the matter, have degrees of choice about varying aspects of it. Another dimension is the degree of *control* that various agents, including the central figure, have over various aspects, and during various phases, of the passage. One final dimension is especially noteworthy: the passage may require special *legitimation* by one or more agents.

Our research has shown the importance of distinguishing clearly among such structural dimensions of passage, and among their various possible permutations. When studying particular types of passage, the analyst could focus, according to their relevance, on several characteristic dimensions. Thus, Julius Roth (1963) has, without explicitly recognizing that recovery from severe TB can be conceptualized as a status passage, quite correctly emphasized the indeterminant pace of recovery, the ambiguity of signs of recovery as the patient sees them, and the patient's manipulations in getting his condition defined 'upward' by the legitimating physician. Similarly, when writing of degradation ceremonies, Harold Garfinkel (1956) almost inevitably emphasized legitimacy: the degrading agent must manage to legitimate his activity and his role to make his accusation persuasive. Orrin Klapp's analysis (1949) of how people are made into fools also had its appropriate focus: the successful or unsuccessful strategies of the foolmaker, and of the person who either manages or fails to avoid that status and who manages or fails to reverse the passage once cast into it. To note one last example, Lloyd Warner's (1937) detailed description of an Australian tribe almost necessarily turned around a a discussion of sequential and collective passages, carefully regulated so that entire segments of the tribe were involved at particular times and places.

Analysis of a given status passage may be incomplete, however, if the social scientist focuses only on one, two or three relevant dimensions of the passage. It is also necessary that he trace the structural conditions under which passage is made, say, alone rather than collectively, or voluntarily rather than involuntarily. He must also research the consequences of these structural conditions for the various participants and the groups or institutions to which they belong—as well as their import for social interaction. A systematic analysis will also clarify the 'exceptions'—that is, the variable patterns of interaction and consequence that occur when a normally important dimension is absent or modified. We cannot expect that these tasks can be accomplished unless the analyst is aware that his analysis can usefully be conceived as pertaining to status passages. If not, then he can be expected to make only a very incomplete analysis of his materials, with regard to status passages. Were this kind of analysis conscientiously attempted, it would be detailed, woven densely and quite lengthy. Of course, it is possible to analyse one or two dimensions systematically within a single journal article, but fuller analysis would require much more space perhaps as many pages as in this book.

The major dimensions of a dying trajectory as a status passage are unquestionably the ones noted earlier, in opposition to Van Gennep's discussions. First, dying is almost always *unscheduled;* second, the sequence of steps is not *institutionally prescribed;* and third, the actions of the various participants are only *partly regulated.* It is also quite relevant that the transitional statuses of dying (though not necessarily death itself when it comes) are usually defined as *undesirable.* Among the other relevant but highly variable dimensions are: the *clarity* of signs that are available to the various participants; the amount of *control* that the participants (including the patient) have over aspects of his passage; whether the passage is *traversed simultaneously* by multiple patients or whether only the patient is dying; and which, if any, patients in a simultaneous passage are *aware* of particular aspects of that process.

References

Blumer, H., 1962. Society as symbolic Interaction. In A. Rose (ed.), *Human Behaviour and Social Processes.* Boston: Houghton Mifflin. Pp. 179-92.

Garfinkel, H., 1956. Conditions of successful degradation ceremonies. *American Journal of Sociology,* [61]: 420-24.

Glaser, B. G. and Strauss, A. L., 1965a. *Awareness of Dying.* Chicago: Aldine Publishing Co.

Glaser, B. G., and Strauss, A. L., 1965b. Temporal aspects of dying as a non-scheduled status passage. *American Journal of Sociology,* [71]: 48-59.

Glaser, B. G., and Strauss, A. L., 1967. *The Discovery of Grounded Theory: Strategies for Qualitative Research.* Chicago: Aldine Publishing Co.

Klapp, O., 1949. The fool as a social type. *American Journal of Sociology,* [55]: 159-60.

Roth, J., 1963. *Timetables.* Indianapolis: Bobbs-Merrill.

Simon, H., 1948. *Administrative Behaviour.* New York: Macmillan.

Strauss, A., (ed.), 1964. *George Herbert Mead on Social Psychology.* Chicago: University of Chicago Press.

Van Gennep, A., 1960. *Rites du Passage.* Translated by M. Vizedom & G. Caffee. Chicago: University of Chicago Press. The book was first published in 1908.

Warner, L., 1937. *A Black Civilization.* New York: Harper.

Derek R. Layder
Department of Sociology, University of Leicester

Notes on variations in middle class careers

This is an original article prepared especially for this reader. D.F.

Introduction

There has been a tendency in the mainstream literature of occupational sociology to limit the application of the concept of career to that sphere of the occupational structure which has traditionally been the preserve of the middle classes. Concomitant with this has been the tendency to assume that middle class careers are the same. The clearest statement of this tendency is by Watson: 'most middle class people enter into life careers of an almost identical pattern, whatever the nature of their work and the considerable variation in salaries' (Watson, as quoted in Bell, 1968). I suggest that this assumption stems from the location of middle class careers in bureaucratically organized settings, and that the bureaucratic setting is but one among a number of possible middle class career contexts. It is my opinion that any useful analysis of the general area of occupational careers must take cognizance of this contextual variability.[1]

The single most important source of variability in middle class careers is the organizational context within which such careers occur. There seem to be four analytically separate aspects of the organizational context which contribute to career variability: the type of social relationships between careerists; the nature and type of the work tasks; the clarity of status differentials;[2] and the system of appraisal.

Social relationships range from the highly formalized and relatively rigid relationships of superordination and subordination which are found in the

---

[1] My appreciation and analysis of the variability of middle class careers derives from the work of the Chicago school of sociologists who have emphasized both the commonality of career processes over a wide range of human activity and the variable properties of careers. A good example and summary of this approach is to be found in the selection from Glaser and Strauss which precedes this paper. The most important influences for me have been Becker (1970), Strauss (1959 esp. Ch. IV), Glaser and Strauss (1965), Roth (1963), Davis (1963) and Goffman (1961). I was introduced to this approach by David Field, who has also helped in the formulation of some of the ideas in this paper.

[2] The term 'status' is used to refer to 'social standing' or prestige within the occupation milieu. 'Status passage' refers to movement between statuses in the occupation.

larger scale bureaucracies, to the relatively amorphous and flexible relationships found in such occupations as acting. That is, at one end of the continuum the social order of the occupational context is highly institutionalized and crystallized in terms of an explicit structure of social relationships whilst at the other end it is relatively uninstitutionalized and uncrystallized and is co-ordinated by an implicit structure of social relationships. As one moves from the highly institutionalized end of the contextual continuum to the relatively non-institutional end, the career structures display less evenness and specificity in terms of their defining characteristics and such elements as the nature and type of success and social status become harder to assess and locate unambiguously.

The degree and nature of role and task specialization varies from clearly defined, limited and non-overlapping tasks and roles (bureaucracies) to diffuse, overlapping and easily interchangeable tasks and roles (acting). The extent and nature of such specialization is intimately connected to the types of occupational control which in turn limit and define the range of social locations in which the career can be worked out. Different kinds of occupational control systems also constrain the opportunity structure of the career, not only in terms of the number and nature of the statuses potentially available, but also in terms of the sequence of career movements and the extent of role versatility possible within the occupation. The clarity of status differentials also seems to be related to the type of control. Where the career takes place in contexts in which organizations have a large area of control over task performance, and where movement between statuses is institutionally defined and controlled, status differentials are likely to be clear and unambiguous. On the other hand where (as in acting) there is little or no organizational control and definition, statuses are likely to be unclear and ambiguous.

The final aspect to be considered here is the nature and type of appraisal. This refers to the mechanisms whereby careerists are selected (and rejected) for movement between the available statuses in the career structure. Appraisal criteria, and especially the variability of such criteria, are important elements in structuring the careerist's perspective on his present and future status for they affect his assessment of his position relative to others in the career, of how far he will go, of how long it will take, and of what behavioural changes he must make to facilitate his career aspirations. Appraisal systems range from highly organized systems with explicit specifiable criteria, as in bureaucracies, to more unorganized types with implicit and relatively diffuse criteria, where chance and accident play a more prominent role, as in acting.

The consequence of varying degrees of indeterminacy for the careerist will be the main consideration of the empirical discussion. The career structures considered here, (the 'bureaucratic', and the 'public audience' careers) were chosen because they fall at the extremes of the institutional/non-institutional axis.

The career in the bureaucratic context[3]

The formal structure of bureaucratic institutions has been well documented and so I do not propose to give an elaborate account of them here (see for example Hall, 1969: Chs. 5 & 6). The types of organizations characterized by such settings include civil service, banking and many 'branches' of industry. The relevant features of these organizations for the present discussion are the internal organizational control of the employee in terms of well-defined and clearly specified rules and the hierarchical ladder of success. Interpersonal relationships in these organizations take place against the background of a relatively fixed and inflexible structure of roles, positions and status expectations. The 'organizational chart' is an externalization and concretization of the inherent principles of hieratic order; an order in which every individual has defined status rights and obligations in relation to everybody else included in that order.

The formality of these highly institutionalized relationships testifies to the 'tightness' of the organizational structure of bureaucracy, which places limitations on the latitude of career movements and range of career patterns within the organization. This tendency for the bureaucratic structure to delimit career processes, is most clearly exemplified by the development and persistence of 'regularized status passages' through the organizational structure. That is, the emergence of career paths through the organization which, as a result of constant use, have become institutionalized modes of career ascent. These routes typically comprise step-by-step advancement through the greater part of the available set of hierarchical statuses. Career passage, however, is not simply or always comprised of vertical progression upwards through a bureaucratic hierarchy of increasingly higher statuses. 'Horizontal' movements, that is movements implying a change in function without a concomitant change of status, are also a normal part of bureaucratic careers. Whereas 'vertical' movements bring with them increments (or decrements) of responsibility and positional authority, 'horizontal' movements merely imply a change in work activity—although they may serve to give the careerist the 'breadth of experience' necessary for future promotion.[4]

Another aspect of the highly formal patterns of organization characterizing this type of structure is the synchronization of age with status. That is, the existence of a largely informal, but well known, system of expectations as to the statuses that careerists should reach at different ages: 'There is an exquisitely sensitive awareness of each grading within the organization in relation to age, as a sign of one's chances of moving to the top'. (Sofer, 1970: 274). One index of this age-status synchronization is the high level of awareness that careerists have of the progress of other careerists who entered the

[3] The main source for this section of the paper is Sofer (1970).
[4] They may also serve to 'cool out' unsuccessful careerists (Goffman, 1952; Goldner and Ritti, 1967).

organization at the same time as they did. The rate of progress by others (relative to himself) in this 'entry cohort' provides the careerist with a clear notion of his position and career progress.

Compared with the many other career contexts, the bureaucratic career provides the careerist with a plethora of visible and unambiguous signs of his progress. The highly developed age-status structure provides him with a clear set of reference points by which he can judge the pace of his progress. The existence of clearly defined organizational statuses and typical career routes between them provide him with a clear and stable set of references for gauging his direction of movement. This visibility and clarity result from the high degree of segregation and boundedness of bureaucratic roles and statuses and the associated fairly rigid system of functional specialization. Not only are career movements clear but to a large extent the sequencing of status changes is unalterable.[5] For example, it is very hard for the careerist to transfer from one internal status ladder to another—say from being a sales manager to an equivalent or higher position in the accounts department.

Typically entrants into the bureaucratic career do not possess any technical or professional qualifications, and the lack of such qualifications tends to make the careerist dependent on the employing organization to a degree not found in other types of middle class career. The skills developed by the careerist tend to be specific to the employing organization (particularly at the middle levels of the career) and hence inhibit mobility between industries and to a lesser extent between organizations in the same industry. The specialization of the work task tends to limit the learning environment of the individual and this becomes another element restricting the individual to a career within the context of one organization rather than between many organizations.

The mechanisms of appraisal and allocation of careerists within bureaucratic organizations reflect their underlying principle of rational coordination. The appraisal system is mainly embodied in formal personnel institutions and tends to comprise highly organized 'search systems' designed to identify, develop and promote talent from lower to higher statuses. Appraisal is likely to be continuous and the criteria employed to be public, explicit and codified. Although a certain amount of arbitrariness inevitably results from human elements, it is to a greater extent than in any other career context eradicated by institutional forms of ratification and the clearly defined regulations governing promotion. One important element of appraisal is the assessment of the job-relevant personal qualities of the careerist, for example, his judgement, reliability, or skill at negotiating. Thus, (as Ashton has pointed out in his paper in this book) the individual characteristics of the careerist become salient attributes with regard to his progress. It is clear, however, that the 'individuality' of the

---

[5] There are of course deviations from this model, as the phenomenon of 'skipping' hierarchical levels in promotion bears out, but here again norms promulgated by higher management develop as to what span of the hierarchy may be legitimately 'skipped' at any one time.

careerist is subordinate to and subserves the accomplishment of relatively standardized work tasks, which is in contradistinction to the other type of career discussed in this paper.

The careerist in the bureaucratic organization frequently becomes pre-occupied with trying to guess what kind of individual the organization requires to fill the position to which he is aspiring. In this sense the search for the appropriate self to present becomes a central feature of career striving. Thus, although in societal terms these careerists are 'individuated' by virtue of their 'responsible', functionally important and specialized roles, this individuation is clearly subordinate to and structured by organizational requirements. This is clearly reflected in the mechanisms of advancement. Statuses are assigned according to criteria which are relatively standardized, public and explicit and there is little room for innovation or elaboration of role behaviour. While statuses may provide a reliable source of imagery for the emergence of self concepts, they do so by providing the incumbent with a set of fairly well-defined characteristics upon which to base their identity. There are two aspects to this; the ideas of the kind of individual appropriate to the position, and the constraints placed upon the development of self-conceptions by the nature of the task involved.

The allocation of tasks in bureaucratic organizations is in terms of clearly defined and non-overlapping responsibilities. Typically bureaucracies cater for relatively stable administrative matters so that careerists are not usually implicated in the initiation of new activities, ideas or decisions. Rather, they are concerned with the implementation of 'tried and tested' solutions to familiar work problems. The type of skills required of the careerist are those connected with the manipulation of subordinates and superiors. This type of 'people management' is consonant with the hierarchic ordering of statuses and is to a large extent structured by it — the 'skilful' bureaucrat is one who can interpret, embellish and invoke rules of procedure and behavioural etiquette in appropriate situations. The vertical nature of hierarchic communication and control, stress the ability to receive, understand and transmit communications (orders) emanating from above. The careerist is not encouraged to elaborate on these communications (in terms of their context), and the only spontaneous elaboration he is allowed is with regard to the *manner* in which he transmits the communication. Paradoxically (and this is to be understood only in relation to other middle class careers) this leads to the conclusion that although the bureaucratic situation affords the careerist some expression of individuality, this expression is of a more or less predetermined kind because the smooth functioning of the organization is dependent on the 'playing down' of the verbalization and explication of differences and unique understandings.

Given the clear and relatively unambiguous character of the bureaucratic career, the careerist is likely to develop clear and stable conceptions of self. For most of his career an important element in such a self-conception will be the experiencing of the present as a preparation for the future. His future lies unambiguously before him in terms of a span of statuses which constitute the organizational hierarchy. Although the careerist does not know how far up the hierarchy he will progress he has a good idea of the kinds of success available to him. As he progresses it will become clearer to him how far he is likely to progress, and he will accordingly adjust his plans and perspectives on the future. Thus, the nature of the bureaucratic environment is such that it is conducive to the construction and elaboration of relatively stable self-concepts which incorporate fairly clear ideas of the long-term future. What Mannheim has called a 'life-plan' (Mannheim, 1940) emerges in a fairly well developed form at an early stage of the career.

The public audience career[6]

This type of career is situated at the non-institutional end of the contextual continuum and includes such activities as writing, music and acting. In contrast to the previously described careers, the public audience career is set in an environment which is not characterized by any explicit or formal structuring or control. It is therefore inappropriate to talk of status hierarchies in the same sense as in institutional careers. Although there undoubtedly are status differentials, the main characteristics of this type of career are the ambiguity of status and the reversibility and repeatability of the passage between high and low status. The operating context of the career is best seen as a relatively loose framework of relationships between the various categories of personnel implicated in the career. These relationships will have varying bases but the most pervasive and far reaching influence is that deriving from market considerations. This is because knowledge of, and access to the relevant sectors of the market by the careerist is decisive for his future career movement.

Since the environment of the public audience career cannot be controlled by any single employer or group of employers it follows that the career processes themselves are not subject to purposive control from above, as they are in the careers previously described. This is clearly shown by the fact that contracts are entered into for relatively short and specified periods of time, rather than being 'open-ended' as they are in other types of career. For example, musicians and actors typically work for many employers at different levels in the 'entertainment industry' during the course of their working lives. This situation whereby the careerist moves from one employer to the next after the completion of a job, means that the careerist has to be aware of job opportunities as they arise so that he can ensure some kind of continuity of his employment.[7] This potential information gap between the worker and his employment possibilities provides leeway for intermediaries such as theatrical agents to make 'service' careers in this sector. As the careers of the

6 This section is based mainly on my own research on actors.
7 This is especially true of actors and some types of musicians. (Becker, 1963. Chs. 5 & 6; Westby, 1959-60).

intermediary and his client are interdependent in terms of remuneration and prestige, then the intermediary can exert a great deal of influence (direct or indirect) over the careerist.

There is often a range of interdependencies with careerists making other careers in the public audience sector. These sets of interdependencies (and they may last from a few days to perhaps twenty years) are not planned and pre-arranged solely to accomplish some particular higher order objective, although a higher order objective, such as the production of a play, may be a by-product of such interdependencies. Rather, the interdependencies are entered into by individuals in order to facilitate or further their own long term career prospects (e.g. an actor choosing an agent and the agent accepting the actor as client). This volitional interdependence is in contradistinction to the situation of the careerist in a formal institutional structure who, as he passes through the stages of his career, becomes implicated (regardless of his personal wishes) into a series of organizationally determined interdependencies. In the case of the actor for example, the careers of critics, directors and theatre managers are all intertwined either with the fate of specific actors (e.g. a big-name star, who can make a mediocre production into a minor success by attracting a large audience) or with groups of actors (e.g. those putting on a particular play). In the light of these interdependencies, the environment of the public audience career can be characterized as forming a serial pattern of con-junctive socio-economic relationships.

The characterization of the environment of the public audience career as a series of conjunctive relationships serves to emphasize the extreme looseness and flexibility of its social order. Roles, statuses, and authority relations tend to defy rigorous definition. There is low boundedness between roles and hence there tends to be high interchangeability between them. For example, an actor may become a director for one play then revert to being an actor once more.[8] This highly indeterminate social order accommodates an extremely wide range of career patterns and indeed encourages such heterogeneity. As there are no clearly defined routes through the occupational milieu the careerist is forced to create his status in the milieu rather than move from one occupa-tionally defined status to another. There may be 'tried and tested' partial routes, e.g. the belief in the acting profession that before he can hope to make an impression in the larger theatre milieu of the West End of London the aspiring actor must work at least a season in a provincial repertory theatre in order to gain the necessary competence and experience in a large number and wide

[8] Horizontal career movements are quite frequent owing to the lack of boundedness between roles. Such movements are volitional in the public audience career and hence may signify different contingencies at different stages of a career. For example a young actor may undertake (if possible) a series of horizontal movements such as actor-dancer-variety artist-director to achieve a versatility of potential work functions, thereby in-creasing his employment opportunities. On the other hand an older, well-established actor may move into directing or theatre management, so as to prolong a distinguished career in the theatre.

range of acting roles. However, such experiences do not invariably lead to upward career mobility and hence cannot be taken as reliable indicators of career progress either by the careerist or by others.

The appraisal process and systems of selection in general are less elaborate, systematic and formalized in this type of career context than in the other types discussed. Appraisal is not with reference to the potential the careerist has for future 'promotion' but rather is in terms of situationally specific (non-cumulative) requirements. Status upgrading or downgrading is thus largely an unintended consequence of the appraisal process. Once selected, successful performance by the careerist may lead to an upgrading of his status and as a consequence his selection for better jobs, but this is not inevitable.[9] The criteria used in appraisal tend to be very diffuse although they tend to centre around several related aspects. The most important of these is the assessment of the individual's work abilities. However, because there are no absolute criteria, e.g. for judging good acting, an element of arbitrariness is injected into the judgement process and assessment choices will tend to reflect the idiosyncratic preferences of the appraisers, rather than systematic 'objective' criteria. Another aspect of appraisal relates to the type of personality that the careerists possess. These careerists are valued for their personal qualities (such as con-viviality and congeniality) in addition to their technical expertise. However, the 'individuality' of the careerist is valued for itself rather than in terms of consequences for his ability to manipulate others in order to achieve organiza-tionally defined goals. As there are no clearly defined guides for behaviour, as the status hierarchy lacks visibility, participants must rely on common standards of deference to ensure the smooth forwarding of the joint activity.

Relationships between appraisers and the careerist tend to be transitory owing to the nature of the work situation. Although appraisal is not in terms of future career movement it does, as I have indicated, have consequences for this. To a certain extent the people involved in appraising the careerist form a quasi-group and may be involved in inter-relationships of referral. Referral may also take place accidentally as an unintended consequence of other social activities internal to the occupation. The unclear processes of appraisal and referral are likely to generate uncertainties in the careerist. This is reinforced by the lack of an explicit status hierarchy by which the careerist can locate himself and by the loose organization of roles. At any point his personal identity may be called into question. As roles lack almost any form of prescrip-tion, the possibilities for elaboration of self-concepts are unbounded. Yet because there are no stable anchorage points for identity internal to the occupation (in the form of statuses) and also because work relationships tend

[9] At this point it is important to emphasize once again the reversibility and repeatability of status movement characteristic of this type of career. During the course of my research several actors told me that at one point they thought that they had 'made it' after starring in a successful play (or film) only to find that they could not get a job once the play had finished.

to be very intimate, self-concepts tend to be quite vulnerable and subject to the change and flux inherent in the social order. The fact that status mobility is potentially reversible and repeatable reinforces the precariousness of self-concepts. As the status passage is so indeterminate, the careerist does not know how successful he will ultimately be (i.e. what he will become) and, to a large extent, cannot place himself in relation to others in the context of the present. An added ambiguity is the lack of any age-status synchronization. This is partly because statuses are not rigorously defined, but mainly because success can literally come at any age. This can lead to some unlikely results. For example, a successful child actor, who is a relative failure in juvenile lead parts, but who develops late in life into a successful character actor.

There is one final aspect to be considered briefly—the consequences of the public audience career for the structuring of the careerist's perception of his future. As the careerist's future is never clearly apparent, he too is locked into a world of perceptual immediacy. He must be constantly on the look out for new opportunities or a 'break'. As Westby points out in relation to the symphony musician: 'The career . . . is not one of steady advancement through a series of finely graded positions with predictable promotions based mainly on presentation of credentials of service and tenure, but rather, one of watchfully awaiting the opportunity that may appear but once in a lifetime'. (Westby, 1959-60). However, the careerist in the public audience career is in a different situation to that of the working class careerist (See Ashton op. cit.) in that there is the potential for mobility beyond the context of the present, although movement upward through this social space is a less than certain proposition because increments in status depend not only on ability to perform the work function (even if this is exceptionally well done) but also on chance with regard to the kinds of work opportunities that come his way. It follows from this that until the careerist is in a position of power vis-a-vis his potential employers it is inappropriate to talk in terms of a 'life-plan'. Even then it would perhaps be more appropriate to speak of a lengthening of time perspectives on career futures. As far as the beginning and middle levels of the career are concerned the careerist is committed only to relatively short-term plans. These plans and frameworks within which the careerist views his future display a high level of flexibility which is partly enforced by the nature of the work situation, e.g. the necessity of high geographic mobility, and partly enforced by the structure of opportunity, i.e. the careerist has to perceive and take his chance as soon as they present themselves.

Conclusion

It has been argued that the context of the bureaucratic career constitutes a relatively closed system of statuses, rights, duties, and obligations which have a determining influence on the structure of the career. The structural constraints coupled with prior orientations and the orientations induced by the work situation typically combine to produce commitment to a career in the employing organization. The combination of skills restricted to the organization and the clarity and 'facticity' of the status hierarchy tends to produce commitment to a known specified future. The public audience career is characterized by an exceedingly ambiguous structuring of statuses, rights, duties and obligations and by potential repeatability and reversibility of status passage. The low boundedness between roles and the nature of the work situation enforce a 'cosmopolitanism' of outlook on the careerist, if only because there is no single employing 'organization' to which commitment and loyalty can be generated. They are committed to a career future which can hold no certain rewards for them and are locked into a world which is of an immanent, unfolding, and indeterminate nature. The discussion of these two careers suggests it is important to examine the wide range of contexts within which middle class careers are situated Such examination would serve to dissipate the myth of the uniformity among middle class careers, both at the structural and experiential levels.

References

Becker, H. S., 1970. *Sociological Work: Method and substance.* Chicago: Aldine.
Becker, H. S., 1963. *Outsiders.* New York: Free Press.
Bell, C., 1968. *Middle Class Families.* London: Routledge & Kegan Paul.
Davis, F., 1963. *Passage Through Crisis.* Indianapolis: Bobbs-Merrill.
Glaser, B. G. and Strauss, A. L. 1965. *Awareness of Dying.* Chicago: Aldine.
Goffman, E., 1952. 'On cooling the mark out', *Psychiatry,* [15], 451-63.
Goffman, E., 1961. *Asylums.* New York: Doubleday.
Goldner, F. H., and Ritti, R. K. 1967, *Professionalisation as Career Immobility.* Am J. Sociology, Vol. 72, 489-502.
Hall, R. H., 1969. *Occupations and the Social Structure.* Englewood Cliffs, N.J.: Prentice-Hall.
Mannheim, K., 1940. *Man and Society in an Age of Reconstruction.* London: Routledge & Kegan Paul.
Merton, R. K., 1961. 'The bureaucratic personality', in A. Etzioni (ed.), *Complex Organizations: A Sociological Reader.* New York: Holt.
Roth, J., 1963. *Timetables.* Indianapolis, Bobbs-Merrill.
Sofer, C., 1970. *Men in Mid-Career.* Cambridge: University Press.
Strauss, A. L., 1959. *Mirrors and Masks.* Glencoe, Ill: Free Press.
Westby, D. L., 1959-60. 'The career experiences of the symphony musician', *Social Forces.* [38], 223-30.

David N. Ashton
Department of Sociology, University of Leicester

Careers and commitment: The movement from school to work

This is an original article prepared especially for this reader. D.F.

Introduction

While considerable attention has been focused on establishing the 'factors' that influence occupational choice, relatively little attention has been given to how these factors operate to influence the *process* of choice. Similarly, the question why, having made their choice, young people accept their position in the occupational structure has rarely been raised. It is suggested in this paper that the answer to both these problems lies in the acquisition of different frames of reference and self-conceptions by different groups in society. These frames of reference function to establish certain orders of relevance and types of reward which can only be realized in specific types of occupation. In this way they play a crucial part in determining the type of occupation young people eventually follow.

The work of Bernstein and others suggests that groups located at different positions in the social structure experience the world in significantly different ways.[1] The patterns of behaviour which they habitually take part in shape the way in which they experience and act towards the world. This patterning of experience I refer to as a frame of reference. The transmission of frames of reference starts within the family, but the differences that can be observed in both the style and the content of what is transmitted are seen as a product of the position which the family occupies within the overall class structure. The differences cover a range of areas, of which the most crucial seem to be style of life, type of communication, and the nature of social control.

Let us look at the two 'polar types' which emerge from a consideration of the work of Bernstein and others. The first is that found among the lower working classes. Here, by virtue of their common occupational position, strong communal bonds tend to develop. Work offers little variety, for the individual is presented with a clearly delineated role which provides for a limited range of activity within which there is little discretion or choice in following the

---

[1] What follows is basically a simplification of the model presented by Bernstein (Bernstein, 1972). See also D. Henderson (1970), M. Deutsch (1967), J. Goldthorpe *et al* (1969), J. Ford *et al* (1967), R. D. Hess and V. Shipman (1965). Edited versions of the last two items are included in this reader).

commands of superordinates, The individual's experience of work will be similar in most respects to that of other members of this category. Most of the individual's activities take place within the confines of shared experiences and are therefore predictable. Because everybody has similar experiences the meanings regulating activities do not have to be made explicit and as most activities take place with essentially the same audiences, roles need not be, and are not, clearly segregated; hence role relationships tend to be diffuse and inclusive.

As a consequence of this the use of language is geared toward the expression of the communal rather than the individual and is not used to explicate the underlying principles or bases of action (as it is in the second type). The main identities of these individuals are predominantly based on their ascribed status, especially their age and sex. As work and community life do not provide them with many experiences that will enable them to differentiate themselves uniquely from others, their conceptions of self tend to remain largely unelaborated.

In this type of community the child is brought up in 'positional families' (Bernstein, op. cit.) where it is expected to obey instructions by virtue of its ascribed status as a child. This strict status segregation coupled with rigid allocation of responsibility means that the child's early socialization is focused on the contents of situations (he relates to others on the basis of what he is, son, brother, etc.) rather than on underlying principles. The child is not provided with a wide range of experiences, neither are they of the type where principles become apparent. The range of discretion given to the child is limited; it is taught to recognize and accept its position in relation to others and is not encouraged to question the bases of such relationships. It is taught to take over and respond to the requirements of roles, i.e. to role take, but not to role make.[2] The impact of this on the child, is that he is socialized into a world of the immediate present, in which action is determined by the visible and the obvious, rather than by consideration of underlying principles or long term consequences. In short the child learns to see the world in terms of the here and now. The conception of self which emerges from this type of experience would seem to be rather unelaborated and to include the idea of oneself as subordinate to others by virtue of the individual's inferior status position— an inferiority which continues in both school and work.

[2] This is the distinction made by Turner: 'Roles "exist" and vary in degrees of concreteness and consistency, while the individual confidently frames his behavior as if they had unequivocal existence and clarity. The result is that in attempting from time to time to make aspects of the role explicit he is creating and modifying roles as well as merely bringing them to light; the process is not only role taking but *role making*'. (Turner, 1962, p. 22.) What I focus on throughout this paper is the 'varying degrees of concreteness and consistency' to which Turner refers, in the belief that it is this aspect which both allows and encourages the creative role making aspect of role behavior. My argument here is similar to that spelt out by Ford *et al* in their discussion of role-distance. (Ford *et al, op. cit.*)

The second type contrasts in a number of important ways and is found particularly among the professional and managerial middle classes. Their work provides them with membership of occupational groups within which they are called upon to exercise high levels of discretion and control in the execution of tasks. Community bonds are relatively weak, as the types of relationship entered into tend to be wider and less bound by the physical proximity of the interactants. Thus they tend to be involved in a number of discrete and non-overlapping groups, and their relationships tend to be more specifically defined in terms of rights and obligations within these groups. Because of the relative lack of shared experiences with others over a wide range of activities the underlying orders of meaning tend to be specified fairly clearly. That is, assumptions and principles are explicated.

This type of 'openness' and explication of underlying factors is carried over into the family. The child is brought up in 'person-oriented' families. Here there is a wider range of discretion allowed to the child, and it has a greater range of alternative actions open to it. Further, it is more often responded to in terms of its unique social, affective and cognitive characteristics than in terms of simply their ascribed positions of brother, son, etc. In this type of family the child is encouraged to *make* his role rather than passively learn what is expected of him, for it is allowed to participate in the decision-making process. Bernstein has characterized these families as having 'open' systems of communication, and it is this openness of communication between family members which is crucial. It is in the arguments with parents, and the elaboration of reasons underlying actions and decisions by parents in response to questions that 'the basis of the social' is made explicit and the child learns how to make his place in the social world. Because the child is presented with this continual explication of the reasons and principles underlying the social actions he partakes in, and because he is likely to partake in a greater range of activities than is the lower class child, his conceptions of self are likely to be more elaborated. In the middle class, even in childhood, there are more possible bases of identity upon which to develop ideas of oneself as efficacious and competent than in the lower classes.

For the majority (but not all) of young people their concepts of self and ways of thinking about the world are validated and stabilized in the course of their interaction with teachers and others during their school career. Having repeatedly made choices within terms of their frames of reference they predictably choose occupations that will result in its further reinforcement or development. Their experience of work thus provides additional confirmation of their orientation to the world. For having made their choices, they become members of occupational groupings, and enter into relations with others at work, that are similar to those experienced by their parents. Through the mechanisms involved in the processes of commitment (Becker, 1960) and involvement they then become locked into a future in their 'chosen' career.

School experience and occupational choice

We now turn to consider the interaction of frames of reference, school experience, and occupational choice in three typical configurations: the 'careerless', the working class career, and the middle class career.

The careerless

The largest single group of young people that enter this occupational channel are those from lower working class families.[3] On entering the lower streams, aspects of the frame of reference transmitted within the family are stabilized and reinforced by the child's experience of others within the school. This is particularly with regard to their orientation to the concrete and the here and now, and their image of themselves as destined for semi-skilled and unskilled work. The use of restricted codes by these young people, in schools that operate predominantly with elaborated codes, generates communication problems between pupil and teacher. This situation is aggravated by the social barriers stemming from the different life experiences of teacher and pupil, which are greater in this channel than in any other.

These barriers are further intensified by the formal organization of the school, which rigidly separates those children destined for some form of educational certification from those who are denied the chance. From the teachers' perspective the allocation of young people to the lower streams is a result of their limited ability. A further set of beliefs frequently held by teachers describes the character of these children as 'louts', 'dunces', 'layabouts'. Evidence from recent research in this field suggests that such beliefs are held not only by teachers and others in positions of authority, but also by pupils in higher positions. These derogatory images are communicated to the children in lower streams who learn to see themselves as 'failures'.

For these young people the process of commitment to semi-skilled and unskilled work thus starts in the early stages of their movement through the school. Their allocation to positions in the lower streams effectively denies them the opportunity to develop their cognitive and manipulative skills beyond a minimum level. In so doing it denies them the opportunity of obtaining any form of educational certification. This commits them to a future in semi-skilled work by denying them the opportunity of developing the requisite skills and obtaining the qualifications necessary for entry into other types of occupation. On moving through the third and fourth forms these young

---

[3] The evidence on which this and the following two sections of the paper are based is derived from Hargreaves (1967); Douglas (1964); Ford (1969); Carter (1962), and King (1969); supplemented by some of the findings of research conducted in the Department of Sociology, University of Leicester, under the direction of N. Elias. This was based on a sample of young workers who left school in 1960 and 1962 and were interviewed after having been at work for between one and three years. I should like here to acknowledge my debt to Norbert Elias. A more detailed exposition of the evidence presented in this and the following section can be found in Ashton (1973).

people face a situation that reinforces their concern with the here and now. Pupils in higher streams face the problem of mastering academic subjects as a means of obtaining future academic qualifications but for these young people there are no such future rewards to be obtained from mastering academic subjects. The problems they face in the absence of intrinsic interest in the subjects, are those of obtaining some sort of reward or satisfaction in the here and now—problems that are frequently solved in the classroom through 'rulebreaking', and 'messing about'. This rejection of education, and hence of the possibility of entering those occupations that require educational certification, constitutes a process that further commits them to semi-skilled work.

In moving through the final stages of their school life, their attitude to school becomes one of increasing hostility. The pupils having no incentive to learn, the task for the teachers becomes primarily focused on the problem of maintaining control. As the school offers no future rewards to these pupils and little support for their identity, then the teachers cannot utilize, as they do for the young people in higher positions, the threat of withdrawing these supports as a sanction. Increasingly they resort to the use of physical force. For the young people, the experience of this arbitrary use of physical force and their maintenance in positions of childlike dependency provides a background against which work of a routine and fragmented nature can be experienced as providing freedom and independence. Faced with a situation in which there are few incentives for further learning and being in a position in which they are regarded as inferior by others, the main areas of support and reassurance they have as to their own identity is that provided by the peer group whose values and norms offer them support in their counter-rejection of the dominant values transmitted within the school.

At the end of their school life, when it comes to making a decision about their 'choice' of job, these young people are already committed to semi-skilled and unskilled work by their educational experience. Moreover, given their self-image as academically inferior, their concern with obtaining rewards in the here and now, and their desire to leave school as soon as possible, jobs of this type have certain attractions. Some may have thoughts about the possibilities of an apprenticeship (but dismiss it either because of the poor immediate rewards, such as its low income, or because it is considered to be beyond their reach), but for the majority, their 'choices' both at this stage and after two or three years' experience of such work, indicates that they are positively attracted to certain aspects of semi-skilled and unskilled jobs. From the point of view of the young workers both entering and changing jobs within this channel, the kind of requirements that work is expected to satisfy and the kinds of rewards sought, are usually those that can be obtained in the here and now. It is the rewards associated with 'working with machines', 'meeting people', working inside or outside, or obtaining the highest possible income, that are important to them, and hence are used as a basis for discriminating between different jobs.

The working class career

The majority of young people in this channel came from upper working class and lower middle class families. That is families within which the type of communication and control systems utilized are likely to contain elements of both the 'polar types' outlined in the Introduction. Consequently their frame of reference is unlikely to be confined to the 'concrete' and the 'here and now'. In addition they may also have acquired an image of themselves as capable of 'getting on' in life These aspects of their frame of reference are likely to be reinforced and stabilized by their experience of school.

During their passage through school, these pupils enter into a relationship with the teachers that is different from that of the pupils in the lower streams. They are likely to have acquired values and standards of conduct that exhibit a higher degree of congruence with those of the teachers. Moreover, having acquired both 'restricted' and 'elaborated' codes they find it easier to operate within the school. Both of these factors are likely to facilitate the child's integration into the school, enabling him to experience school life as one of personal development. This positive orientation of the child to the school and its teachers is reinforced by the formal organization of the school with the rigid separation of these children into the higher or middle streams where they are systematically treated as superior to those in the lower streams. They are seen as innately more intelligent, capable of benefitting from their education and frequently the best resources of the school are mobilized to ensure that they do succeed.

Once again, the process of commitment to their future type of work begins to operate from the early stages of their school life. Through the process of allocation, the pupils are denied access to those educational positions that provide the opportunity of acquiring advanced and intermediate forms of certification that would ensure access to occupations that provide the chance of making a middle class career. They are already committed to working class occupations. Yet, although they are in positions that provide the possibility of acquiring elementary certification, this does not necessarily commit them to entering those occupations that provide for a working class career. They could, if they so wished, enter careerless occupations. What primarily functions to commit them to occupations that provide for a working class career is the acquisition of a specific type of self-image and orientation to work.

As regards their self-image, the process of allocation serves, as it does for those in the lower streams, to symbolize the pupils' 'inferiority' and 'failure' in relation to those who enter higher streams or grammar schools. However, while they see themselves as academically inferior to some and hence not capable of effectively performing the tasks required of those who enter occupations that provide for a middle class career, their position within the school does symbolize their 'superiority' in relation to those in the lower streams. Unlike those in the lower channel, the process of allocation and the set of beliefs that legitimate it provide them with support for the development of their identity. They are thought of by their teachers as intellectually superior to those in the lower streams, as 'good material' capable of further developing their skills. This is supported by the fact that their position within the school provides them with the opportunity of developing their cognitive and manipulative skills. Thus they become committed to enter occupations that provide for a working class career, for these are the only type of working class occupations that enable them to 'get on', to 'make something of themselves'. 'Careerless occupations' that do not provide these chances are seen as 'dead end jobs', and as inferior and unsuitable.

In addition to acquiring this type of self-image their experience of school may also lead them to acquire a different type of orientation to work than is found among the careerless. Not only do they obtain certain immediate rewards from the prestige associated with their position in the school and from the sense of personal achievement derived from it but they are also offered the chance of greater future rewards. The problems they face at school are not primarily those of relieving boredom, but those entailed in mastering academic and practical subjects in order that they may obtain the greater future rewards associated with educational certification and the chance of entering an occupation that provides a working class career. Throughout their school life they are systematically offered and pointed toward the promise of a greater reward in the short-term future.

In contrast to the pupils in the lower streams, school life is experienced as rewarding. The integration and involvement of the pupils in the higher streams in their school, and their acceptance of the values transmitted within it, mean that these pupils are infrequently exposed to the use of physical force. Thus, although many complain of the child-like dependency of their positions in school they do not exhibit such an intense desire to get out of school as those who enter careerless occupations. In their last year, school never takes on the function of a custodial institution as it does for those in the lower streams. Rather, it is marked by a gradual realization that school has little more to offer that is relevant to their future. However, unlike those in careerless occcupations, the end of their school life does not necessarily mark the end of their formal education, since their education and training often continue during the course of their apprenticeship.

On making the transition from school to work, these young people are already committed to skilled work. From their point of view, professional and managerial jobs are beyond their reach while semi-skilled and unskilled jobs are beneath them. What is of crucial importance to them is that their job should enable them to develop their skills further and in so doing secure the short term future rewards that they think are to be derived from 'having a trade in your hands'. What attracts some are the higher earnings that they can expect from their trade in the future, for others the security their trade offers, or the superior status of skilled work. What they regard as crucial is that their jobs should provide these opportunities and rewards for the sake of which they are willing to accept a low initial income.

Having chosen this type of occupation, the young people are still faced with the problem of choosing a specific trade. This problem is frequently resolved by reference to the immediate rewards and satisfactions they derive from the activities involved. Like those who enter careerless occupations, these young workers seek immediate rewards from their work *but* only within the context of occupations that provide greater rewards in the short term future.

The middle class career

Most of those who enter these occupations have parents in the same occupational channel, that is, they come from a background similar to that outlined in the second of our 'polar types'. These children are likely to have acquired an image of themselves as capable of making a middle class career, and to be aware of the relationship between this and successful school performance. For these young people their experience of school serves not only to validate the frame of reference acquired within the family, it also serves to confirm the values and standards of conduct of the home. There is likely to be a 'good fit' between the culture of the home and that of the school, particularly in the case of second generation grammar school pupils.

The allocation of these young people to positions within the higher educational channel functions to commit them to middle class careers in a number of ways. By ensuring that the vast majority of them will obtain educational certification at an intermediate or advanced level, it provides them with access to these occupations. In addition the time and energy invested in obtaining these qualifications can only secure the highest returns for the young people through their entry into this type of occupation. However, of equal importance is their acquistion of a specific type of self-image. For the allocation of young people to selective schools and the higher streams within the comprehensive schools is surrounded by a set of beliefs widely held by teachers and others that these pupils are 'the cream of their age group' intellectually superior to others and the material from which the future leaders of the country will be drawn. Such beliefs provide the pupils with an image of themselves as inherently superior to pupils in other educational channels. For a child from a middle class family, the process of allocation may merely provide additional confirmation of a self-image he acquired from his parents. For a child from certain types of working class family however, this process is likely to bring about a transformation of his self-image, as both he and his parents become aware of the new range of occupations that are open to him.[4]

[4]Bernstein and Brandis (1970, 117-118) briefly touch on the possibility that the school may by its favourable evaluation of a child and the transmission of this evaluation to the working class mother, alter the mother's attitudes and actions so as to discriminate in favour of the 'bright' child.

In the pupils' passage through the school, this image of themselves as possessing superior abilities is reinforced. They move through positions in which the greatest emphasis is placed on the development of their cognitive skills and for which they are offered the highest rewards available in secondary education. They are provided with the most highly qualified teachers. Teachers that not only expect them to perform well, but who also believe that they should enter 'interesting' and 'worthwhile' occupations. Through their interactions with teachers and others in the course of this movement the pupils learn to see themselves as bright and possessing special abilities. Many believe themselves to be generally successful, others to be 'good at science or maths' and others 'good at figures'. Most of them learn to see themselves as capable of developing their cognitive skills to a relatively high level. In so doing they learn to see manual occupations, which are believed to make minimal demands on these skills, as below them and not worthy of their consideration.

A further way in which these pupils are committed to entering occupations that provide the chance of making a middle class career is through their acquisition of a specific orientation to work. Throughout their scholastic career the emphasis placed upon the successful performance of their tasks is primarily in the light of the long term rewards associated with successful educational performance and entry into a 'good career' and only secondarily in terms of the immediate satisfaction or rewards to be obtained from them. For these pupils then the present is experienced as a preparation for the future. Unlike most of those who enter careerless occupations, successful school performance is not only relevant for the future performance of occupational tasks, but essential for entry into the kind of occupations for which they believe themselves destined.

In contrast to young people in the lowest educational channel for whom many of the values transmitted through the school are irrelevant, for these pupils the situation is different. Not only do parents and teachers stress similar values but the beliefs and values they do stress are important in ensuring their success in their future occupation. For example the value placed on loyalty to the organization and the importance of personal advancement are both transmitted within the school and are important in ensuring the success of young people who become involved in the competitive struggle for advancement that is characteristic of occupations that provide the chances for making a middle class career. For these young people their experience of this struggle for advancement at school and their acceptance of these values functions to commit them to and prepare them for such occupations.

These pupils—particularly those from middle class families—are relatively highly integrated into the school. Their experience of school is rewarding, but after having gained their qualifications, school had little more to offer, although like many apprentices, the end of their school life does not mark the end of their formal education.

On moving into work, the choices they make have already been determined by their frame of reference. Like those in occupations that provide for a working class career, they also use the immediate rewards and satisfactions that they derive from the activities involved as a means of discriminating between occupations within their channel. Where they differ from those in occupations that provide for a working class career, is in the importance they attach to obtaining progressively higher rewards in the long term. They *only* consider working outside or working with figures in those occupations that *also* provided the possibility of obtaining progressively higher levels of reward for the greater part of their occupational life.

The work situation

Once having entered into the work situation, the young workers become 'locked into' their occupations through processes of commitment and involvement. At the lower levels of the occupational hierarchy the process of commitment is primarily responsible for 'locking' the young workers into their occupation, while at the higher levels the process of involvement is of primary importance. What follows is an attempt to establish the way in which some of the mechanisms associated with these two processes operate, particularly in the initial stages of careers.

The careerless

In addition to the commitments made at school, once they have entered work a further set of commitments are made. As they are engaged on routine and repetitive work, few demands are made on their cognitive and manipulative abilities, and they are unable to develop the complex skills necessary for other occupations. Their lack of such skills, and the age restrictions on entry to apprenticeships means that after one or two years it becomes impossible to transfer to occupations in other channels. Concomitantly their experience of work reinforces their image of themselves as inferior as they come to realize that they are committed to a future in low status careerless occupations and to accept the definition of themselves as unsuited to other occupations.

However while they are committed to the occupational channel there are relatively few commitments made to specific jobs within it. There is no lengthy training period during which they could invest time and energy in acquiring specialized skills that could tie them to their job. Employers are not unduly concerned if the worker moves between jobs, for the minimal skill level ensures that replacements can easily be found. Further, even if these young workers continue in one job for any period of time there is little possibility of higher rewards in the future. As at school, these young workers find that the only rewards they can expect are those to be derived from the 'here and now'. In the absence of any future rewards associated with promotion, relatively transient factors such as income, the kind of activity involved in the job, the friendships formed at work, become all important as foci of commitment and

Table 1. Elements involved in commitment to and involvement in work.

Occupational channel	Factors in choice	Nature of skills	Commitment	Job outcomes	Involvement
Careerless	Immediate rewards	Easily learnt	To occupational channel	Known and fixed. Job identity irrelevant	Low throughout
Working Class Career	Short term prospects and immediate rewards	Object centred. Long training required. Not transferable	To specific occupation in channel	Known short term rewards. Job identity becomes an important part of self conceptions	Initially high to moderate. May decrease later in career
Middle Class Career	Long term prospects and immediate rewards	Person centred. Long training required. Not initially transferable but may become so later	To specific occupation or profession	Known short term rewards, but indeterminate long term rewards. Success in job becomes increasingly important part of self conceptions	Initially moderate to high. Increases with success in career

the state of the labour market tends to become a major determinant of their 'job stability'.

The absence of any opportunities for advancement and the routine character of the tasks they have to perform result in these young people experiencing very little involvement in their work. The execution of their tasks tends to be controlled in some detail by the employing organization, either through the type of technology employed or through the commands of the supervisor. They are permitted little discretion over the way in which they work, and little opportunity to develop any skills in which they can take pride. Work presents them with very few if any problems in which they can develop interest and is not an area of activity in which they can develop the feelings of competence or self esteem on which involvement largely depends. Their jobs do not provide —as they *do* for young people in other occupational channels—the opportunity for making rather than taking their roles and hence their work provides little basis for the elaboration of their self-conceptions. The roles they learn to take and the activities associated with them are not only clearly delineated and circumscribed by the employing organization but they are also very similar. Hence they enter into similar role relationships with each other and collectively experience similar relationships with their supervisors. Work does not provide them with membership of organized occupational groups on the basis of which they can differeniate themselves. Neither does work provide the possibility of making a career on the basis of which 'present' and 'future' self can be differentiated. For them there is no way whereby their future at work can be differentiated from the present. No matter how hard they work or how conscientious they are, such behaviour cannot bring about any significant change in their present or future situation at work. Thus unlike the young workers in other occupational channels the majority of these young workers do not see themselves as 'making a career' or see work as a means of self-advancement.

The working class career

Like the careerless, these young workers are committed to their occupational channel, by their level of educational achievement and by the frame of reference acquired in their movement through the school. Whereas the careerless become locked into the occupational channel, these young workers on entering work become locked into a specific trade within the channel. The complex nature of the tasks they are eventually expected to execute requires a lengthy period of training during which the apprentice is expected to master certain theoretical and practical skills. As employers invest some of their resources in training the apprentice a formal commitment may be required through the signing of indentures. Less formal commitments are made as the young workers invest time and energy in learning the skills of their trade, for as they succeed in mastering these skills they progressively unfit themselves for other occupations within their channel.

As at school, they are working for short-term future rewards, but if they are to secure them they must remain within their 'chosen' trade. If they leave not only will they fall behind others in the struggle for advancement but because of the age restrictions on entry and the reluctance of employers to take 'unreliable' workers they may find it difficult to obtain entry into another occupation within this channel.

Not only are these young workers more firmly locked into their occupations than the careerless, but the character of their involvement is different. Even in the later days at school these young workers are concerned to make a career, and choose those occupations that will enable them to achieve a relatively high level of competence through their work. This initial level of involvement is reinforced through their experience of work which confirms the conceptions of self acquired at school. The performance of their tasks is such that the employers cannot control the execution of them in any detail, and they are allowed a greater degree of discretion in the performance of their tasks than the careerless. They can take pride in the mastery of their skills and the fairly autonomous exercise of them and thereby develop a high level of involvement in their work. Thus work provides the basis for the development and elaboration of positive self-evaluations and associated self-conceptions which may become central and organizing elements in their behaviour outside the work situation.

Their work also provides the opportunity for them to differentiate between their 'present' and 'future' self for they can expect to move through a series of between two and four positions in the course of their occupational career. However, despite the degree of autonomy and discretion these young workers may exercise this only takes place within the limits of clearly defined work roles. Further, their position at work is very similar to that of other members of their trade, and indeed to that of members of other trades. Thus work does not provide for the same degree of elaboration of self-conceptions which is provided for the middle class careerists by their work experiences.

The middle class career

For young people who enter this occupational channel (professions, banks, civil service, management) many of the mechanisms that operate to commit the apprentice to his trade also operate: they also become committed to a specific occupation, and they are faced with a lengthy period of training during which they are expected to master relatively complex theoretical and practical skills. Both at work and in their further education they are investing time and energy in acquiring skills that are not transferable in the initial stages of their career. Therefore if they are to maintain their position in the struggle for advancement they must remain in their occupation for to move into another occupation would mean that they would fall behind their fellows and have to start all over again from the bottom of the career ladder. The more time and energy they invest in acquiring their occupational skills, the more committed they are to continuing within their occupation if they are to obtain the future rewards they seek. They are also likely to be committed through certain generalized cultural expectations. For example, employers will not expect them to change jobs frequently as this is regarded as indicative of undesirable personality traits such as untrustworthiness. This attitude is frequently shared by the workers, many of whom are aware that if they are to succeed at work then they must remain in their 'chosen' occupation for the majority of their working lives.

While the commitments made in the initial stages of their career are similar to those made by young workers who embark on a working class career, the character of their involvement is different. The initial choice of an occupation will not necessarily entail such a high degree of involvement as in the case of the working class careerist since it is likely to be guided mainly in terms of the possibility of long-term success. However, during the course of their careers they are likely to experience higher levels of involvement than the working class careerist. One of the main elements in generating this higher level of involvement is the continuous development of feelings of competence through the mastery of a range of skills throughout the course of their career. While the apprentice may acquire pride in his mastery of his skills, once these skills are learnt he may well utilize them for the rest of his working life. The entrant to a bank by contrast faces a very different situation. He can expect to learn new skills at each of the many steps on the career ladder, as he moves up he may be constantly involved in learning new skills and mastering new problems; skills not only in the manipulation of job materials but also in the manipulation of people. Moreover as he makes progress in his career the tasks on which he embarks may provide for progressively greater levels of autonomy and discretion in their execution, reinforcing the feelings of competence and efficacy on which the process of involvement depends. Finally, unlike the apprentice, the bank employee may also become responsible for the work of others, the successful manipulation of whom may provide further areas in which involvement may be intensified.

In generating high levels of involvement these occupations also provide the basis for a greater elaboration of self-conceptions than can be found among the other young workers we have considered. These elaborations are likely to reinforce the self-conceptions acquired at school. As we have seen these young people have learnt during the course of their school career to measure their personal success through their work performance. However, unlike the majority of those making a working class career who know with a fairly high degree of certainty that they will achieve their ambition, these young workers are far less certain of achieving their goal. This uncertainty is connected with the fact that the roles they have to learn are not as clearly defined as they are for the skilled worker. The internal differentiation of roles within the occupation and the constant movement of personnel through them mean that there are relatively few areas where shared experiences can be built up. The principles regulating behaviour in the various role relationships entered into must therefore be made explicit. Because of the variety of these relationships the world of work becomes multi-faceted and provides a variety of areas where self-conceptions may be elaborated. An important element in this elaboration is that if they are to manage their relationships with others adequately and achieve their career ambitions they must learn to present a different self to the members of the different status groupings they come in contact with. Further, not only do these careers generate high levels of involvement they also demand it, for the successful playing of their role demands their immersion in it to an extent not required of the skilled worker. In order to maximize their chances of success they have to be prepared to subordinate their other interests to their work. They have to search for cues that will indicate the kind of behaviour and skills expected of them by those in higher positions and regulate their behaviour accordingly. They will have to organize their work and leisure activities so that they 'meet the right people' and they must be prepared to show interest in their work even at the expense of domestic responsibilities. If promotion is offered they may have to break away from neighbourhood and friendship groups due to the geographical mobility entailed. In short, in order to obtain membership of the higher status groups and so obtain the kind of rewards they seek, their occupational identity has often to take precedence over other identities such as husband or friend and often becomes the central and organizing element of their self-conceptions.

Conclusion

I have attempted to show the linkages in the three analytically separate areas of home, school and work, the experiences of which form a coherent whole for most young people. It is suggested that this coherence stems from the perpetuation of frames of reference and associated self-conceptions initially acquired within the family and reinforced during the passage through school and work. These frames of reference and self-conceptions are crucial mechanisms of commitment which serve to channel individuals into different types of educational experience and thence into different types of occupation. Once an individual has entered a particular occupational channel it becomes difficult to switch to jobs outside it. For the majority of young people the frame of reference acquired within the family of orientation and confirmed by their experiences at school and work is carried over and utilized in their family of procreation. At one extreme are the unskilled workers who at work have a very limited range of discretion in the performance of their tasks and are subject to imperative modes of control. When they establish their own families they are likely to use such modes of control, and to allow their children only limited discretion for as they have not been exposed to other forms of interaction these are the only terms within which they know how to operate. In comparison with the careerless the skilled workers have a greater degree of autonomy at work, but only within a clearly delineated framework of rules that define their role in the work situation. In their families they are likely to allow their children some discretion within clearly defined limits, and to emphasize the learning of rules rather than learning the manipulation of rules for it is within this framework they have had to operate. Finally, there are the middle class workers whose work is characterized by open systems of communication, relatively high levels of autonomy, and inter-personal forms of control. These are also the predominant patterns of communication and control which they experienced at home and school and which they in turn will use in their family of procreation.[5]

References

Ashton, D. N., 1973. 'The transition from school to work: Notes on the development of different frames of references among young male workers', *Sociological Review.*

Becker, H. S., 1960. 'Notes on the Concept of Commitment', *American Journal of Sociology,* [66] 32-40

Bernstein, B., 1972. 'A Socio-Linguistic Approach to Socialization: with some reference to educability'. B. Bernstein, *Class, Codes and Control,* London: Routledge and Kegan Paul, pp. 143-69.

Bernstein, B., and Brandis W., 1970, 'Social Class Differences in Communication and Control' in W. Brandis and D. Henderson, *Social Class, Language and Communication,* London: Routledge and Kegan Paul, pp. 93-123.

Carter, M. P., 1962. *Home, School and Work,* Oxford: Pergamon.

Douglas, J. W. B., 1964. *The Home and the School,* London: MacGibbon and Kee.

Deutsch, M., 1967. *The Disadvantaged Child,* New York: Basic Books.

Ford, J., 1969. *Social Class and the Comprehensive School,* London: Routledge and Kegan Paul.

Ford, J., *et al.,* 1967. 'Functional Autonomy, Role Distance and Social Class', *British Journal of Sociology,* [18] 370-81.

Goldthorpe, J., *et al.,* 1969. *The Affluent Worker in the Class Structure,* Cambridge: Cambridge University Press.

Hargreaves, D. H., 1967. *Social Relations in a Secondary School,* London: Routledge and Kegan Paul.

Henderson, D., 1970. 'Contextual Specificity, Discretion and Cognitive Socialization with special reference to Language,' *Sociology,* [4] 311-338.

Hess, R. D. and Shipman, V., 1965. 'Early experiences and the Socialization of Cognitive Modes in Children', *Child Development,* [36] 869-886.

King, R., 1969, *Values and Involvement in a Grammar School,* London: Routledge and Kegan Paul.

Turner, R., 1962. 'Role-Taking: Process Versus Conformity', A. M. Rose (ed.), *Human Behaviour and Social Processes,* London: Routledge and Kegan Paul. Pp. 20-40.

[5] Since this article was written I have been working on a more comprehensive analysis of the transition from school to work in collaboration with David Field. This is to include consideration of what happens to young people who experience discontinuity from school to work, the part played by intermediaries (e.g. career advisors), and the slightly different career paths of young women. This is to be published in 1975: David N. Ashton and David Field, *Young Workers.* London, Arrow Books.